DATE DUE			

Newsgathering

NEWSGATHERING

by

Daniel R. Williamson

COMMUNICATION ARTS BOOKS

HASTINGS HOUSE, PUBLISHERS

New York 10016

LIBRARY OF CONGRESS CATALOGING IN PUBLICATION DATA

Williamson, Daniel Raymond, 1943-
  Newsgathering.

  Includes index.
  1. Reporters and reporting   I. Title.
PN9781.W64   808′.066′07019   78-21242
ISBN 0-8038-5068-9
ISBN 0-8038-5969-7 pbk.

Published simultaneously in Canada by
Copp Clark, Ltd., Toronto

Designed by Al Lichtenberg
Printed in the United States of America

CONTENTS

PREFACE

Reporting for a daily newspaper isn't a job, or even a profession. Instead, it is an often quixotic quest for an item of truth, which entails a reward of fleeting satisfaction that is far more important to the dedicated journalist than the paycheck he receives.

The methodology of reporting, of acquiring the closest facsimile of an item of truth that can be obtained, is as practical and down to earth as the reporter's role is idealistic. The fundamentals of good reporting stem from common sense, not theory. The successful practitioner uses these methods as the merest core of his skill, embellishing them with experience and personal style, and constantly adapting them to the ever-changing professional environment in which he operates.

In *Newsgathering*, I have attempted to offer the basic techniques of reporting in a realistic context through the use of examples of their application that are based on actual reporting experiences. The objective is to illustrate the purpose and value of the techniques discussed so that the reader can fully appreciate the advantage of acquiring them.

Throughout the text, the highly individualistic approaches to reporting are emphasized by the provision of alternative reporting tactics used to cover a given news event. With the exception of the most basic fundamentals, such great latitude in reporting styles is permitted that reporters can legitimately acquire the same story through strikingly different styles of approach.

In examining the manuscript, I find that I'm indebted to many people who made this project possible. Arnold Rosenfeld, editor of *The Dayton Daily News*, generously offered valuable material, as did his great investigative reporter, Gene Goltz, who is now on *The Cincinnati Post*. Russell Neale of Hastings House provided patient encouragement, as did my wife, Diane. Attorney William Wentz offered wise professional counsel on material concerning libel.

In tracing the evolution of the book, I find that I am especially indebted to two individuals: Professor Charles Scarritt, of the University of Alabama (now retired), who instilled in me—and in hundreds of other journalists—a deep love for reporting; and to Dr. William Hartman, former chairman of the Department of Journalism at the University of Northern Colorado, who instilled a love for teaching. To these two friends and mentors, I dedicate *Newsgathering*.

| PART | FUNDAMENTALS |
| ONE | OF REPORTING |

To be an effective newspaper reporter, it is first essential to learn the fundamental methods and tools of the trade. The first chapters are designed to provide these fundamentals within the context of a proper perspective for their use. Each element discussed has been proven to be effective in actual reporting situations. Examples used to illustrate are based on actual cases encountered by reporters.

1 | Introduction

Describe a newspaper reporter. Picture him in vivid detail in your mind, dwelling on his physical appearance, his mannerisms, his personality, and his professional environment. What is he like? How does he project himself as he talks with news sources?

The images that are derived from these and other similar questions will weave together to form one individual's impression of the nature of that strange creature: the newspaper reporter. Chances are, the reporter most often imagined is a male, although the profession has long been enhanced by many first-rate women reporters.

Other characteristics are often those projected in motion pictures or television. He may be a bit seedy, and cantankerous, such as the monster-chasing newshound in the *Night Stalker* television series a few years ago. Perhaps he is bright, fashionable, and valorous, like Robert Redford's role as Bob Woodward in *All the President's Men*. For midnight movie-watchers, the image may be of a 1930s-variety reporter: obnoxious, callous, unscrupulous, wearing a battered hat with a press card struck in the band, reaching for a bottle of booze in his desk drawer as he types a story with two fingers (one when he is taking a swig).

Still others may form their images from watching televised news events in which dozens of reporters hound an unfortunate newsmaker at a press conference or outside of a courtroom. Reporters obviously travel in packs, overwhelming their prey by sheer numbers.

With the exception of the Redford role, the more common portrayals tend to be anything but flattering to reporters. Collectively, reporters serve as the nation's image-makers, determining whether the public will view a politician as a benevolent statesman, a cigar-chewing political machine boss, or a hapless, inept blunderer. It is, then, ironic that reporters, as a professional group, are victimized by a nasty, distorted public image.

Few modern reporters even come close to fitting professional stereotypes. At the risk of creating still another stereotype, let's take a look at a fictitious "average reporter" on a medium-sized metropolitan daily newspaper:

At the age of thirty, he has obtained the respected niche as city hall reporter. After receiving a bachelor's degree in Journalism from a state university, he served a two-year military commitment, then worked for three years on a small daily newspaper to gain experience. After learning the basics of the trade, he became competent enough to catch the eye of an editor at the larger newspaper, who hired him four years ago. He was first assigned to the police beat where, for two years, he covered the full assortment of crimes, disasters, and squabbles within the police force. By consistently beating competing newsmen with his coverage and by improving his writing skills steadily, he won a promotion to the position of education beat reporter. He skillfully covered the many emotional issues confronting the school board, the teachers' association, and local colleges, until he was shifted to a general assignment position. In that capacity, he performed investigative reporting, wrote countless feature stories, and competently filled in wherever needed to cover whatever type of story came along. When the veteran city hall reporter retired a year ago, he inherited that prized news beat, which includes coverage of the full range of city government activities, city council meetings, and city politics.

In personality, dress, and professional techniques, he doesn't in the least resemble movie stereotypes. He wears a stylish sports coat and tie, both of which spend a reasonable amount of time at the local drycleaner's. He doesn't even own a hat, much less one with a press card in the hatband.

In dealing with news sources, he is friendly and polite. On his beat, he is well respected as an aggressive but scrupulous and accurate newsman. He has carefully built a reputation for honesty and objectivity so that, on a given issue, proponents of all viewpoints will candidly talk with him. He is extremely conscious of personal and professional ethics, and he refuses to bend them.

Away from work, he is an average, suburban husband and father, who enjoys spending his off-time fishing with his children, gardening, or watching televised sports. He drinks very moderately, smokes a pack of cigarettes a day, and attends church regularly with his family.

If this image is somewhat dull and commonplace, then keep in mind that the reporter participates in enough excitement in a week of hectic coverage to sate anyone. The dull, regular guy who is mowing his lawn on a Saturday afterooon may be cowering behind a police cruiser the next day, dodging bullets. Also keep in mind that this version of a common reporter is by no means universal. Newsrooms certainly have their share of people with drinking problems, social problems, and personalities that would be right at home in Attila-the-Hun's horde.

Reporters, then, are simply human beings who, together, share the common ground of a job. The ability to perform that job—not the ability to conform to an image—is the essential requirement. That human being may just as well be a single woman as a married man, or, perhaps, a grandmother. He or she may be black, white, Hispanic, or Oriental. The only important characteristic is the ability to obtain and write news in a professional manner.

Perhaps a more interesting question is: Why would anyone want to be a reporter? The pay is generally low, hours are long, pressure is constant and intense, and physical risk frequently exists.

Frequently, reporters make the rueful observation that "you have to be nuts to stay in this business." They are only half-joking.

Perhaps the best answer to the question is that reporting is one of the most glamorous, exciting, and ego-inflating professions. Let's look at some of the attractions:

1. A reporter soon knows everyone who is anyone on a first-name basis. He has coffee with the chief of police, lunch with the mayor, and dinner with the president of the city's major industrial company. He has ready access to top politicians and celebrities. Governors, senators, sports stars, and executives regard him as a friend or as a deadly enemy. He is respected, liked, or feared by the newsmakers. He is someone special, as long as he carries a press card.

2. A reporter is in-the-know. His curiosity is constantly aroused and, after he digs around, it is usually sated. The state of being in-the-know transcends that information that is disseminated to the public. He knows the story behind the event. He knows that a prominent councilman is having an affair, that the police chief is feuding with the fire chief, that a company president is a closet racist. He knows the *real* reason behind the city council's refusal to adopt a strong bill for gun control. He is also very knowledgeable of police procedures, political organization, and labor negotiations. In his own mind, he may be convinced that a bureaucrat is dishonest or that a policeman is brutal. Much of what he knows may remain unprinted because it cannot be proven, or because it is not in itself newsworthy—for now. Yet, he enjoys the purely human satisfaction of simply knowing.

3. The job is exciting. A police reporter quickly becomes acquainted with the interesting "street people"—muggers, prostitutes, pimps, pushers, and all-around hoodlums—who become his sources. He joins policemen in the risky excitement of shootouts, drug raids, high-speed chases, and riots. He is on the scene at fires, bank robberies, and homicides. The city hall reporter is on hand when the mayor dramatically announces his resignation due to health, or for a

wild council meeting in which police officers demonstrate for higher pay by tossing their badges on the mayor's table.

4. The job is challenging. The reporter may match wits against a shrewd and corrupt public official who is speculating in land acquisition while manipulating favorable zoning changes for his properties. He may go "undercover" to investigate illegal hiring practices by a private security guard firm. He may spend weeks piecing together a disturbing picture of gambling activities in the city, or seeking evidence to expose powerful slumlords. Even coverage of a routine crime may be superbly challenging as the reporter fights a pressing deadline while prying loose information from police sources.

5. The job is a rewarding means of public service. Most reporters are very conscious of their responsibility to the public. A reporter serves as a watchdog for the public, constantly alert for actions or situations that are contrary to public interest. A reporter may write a major exposé on corruption or abuse of power in high places. He may skillfully draw attention to poverty in the city, drugs in high schools, racism on the police force, or governmental incompetence. In the wake of the exposure, corrections are frequently made. While reporters rarely see themselves as knights in shining armor, they take immense satisfaction from the knowledge that, through their efforts, constructive changes have been made.

While these benefits are rewarding, the price for them is high. The negative aspects of a career in reporting are:

1. It requires a great deal of work. Reporters rarely punch time clocks. A police reporter may arrive at the police station at 7 a.m., plunge into a multitude of stories that will require his full concentration through the noon deadline, then, after a hurried lunch, rush to a series of interviews for an in-depth look at a police problem. A late-afternoon crime or disaster may break just as his scheduled working day ends, forcing him to stay until 6 p.m. or so. Later in the evening, he may be called in to cover a major police raid or a fire, or to meet with an informant. The city hall reporter may arrive for work at 8 a.m. and stagger home at midnight after a city council meeting. The work is mentally and physically exhausting.

2. An element of physical risk is constantly present on many beats. Few veteran police reporters miss the opportunity to join police on a major drug raid, even though the danger of gunplay is high. A reporter who covers a riot can fully expect to dodge flying bricks and inhale tear gas. An investigative reporter is often threatened by his quarry.

3. Intense pressure is ever present. The age-old enemy, time, is perhaps the most insidious of all pressures, ticking away toward deadline, forcing the reporter to expend all of his wiles and energies to get a story in time. Pressure of competition is also considerable, as a

reporter is expected to consistently uncover stories before his rivals sniff them out. Another pressure is the lingering threat of libel, which hangs over even the most innocuous story, waiting to pounce on the smallest error. Still another pressure comes from the city editor, who constantly presses the reporter for more stories, for new ideas, for better writing

4. Low pay prevails on all but the most elite newspapers. The rule of thumb is that the smaller the newspaper, the lower the pay. Despite the investment in a college education, a reporter may make less money than a factory employee in the same city. In recent years, pay scales have improved, but, as an indication of pay trends, a reporter with several years of experience on a medium-sized metropolitan newspaper made about $250 to $300 a week in 1975. Starting pay for a college graduate on a small daily often ranged between $100 and $150 a week, while major metropolitan newspapers paid $300 to $400 a week for a veteran reporter's services. Salary scales are not widely advertised, so these figures are only a rough approximation based on contacts with reporters in these categories. Pay varies considerably between different areas of the nation, and among individual newspapers. The individual reporter's pay also varies with experience and competence.

By comparison, a $300 a week salary for a competent, veteran reporter on a metropolitan daily was, in 1975, roughly equivalent to that of a mid-level federal employee, and only slightly more than a veteran policeman or fireman. An alternative career in public relations would probably be more lucrative.

The attitude of many newspaper executives toward reporters' pay is less than generous. With the high interest in journalism careers among college students, competition for top jobs on good newspapers is fierce. The editors, with a thick stack of applications constantly on hand, are in a "buyer's market" for talent. Also, editors are well aware that reporters aren't in the business to make lots of money. Once, when approached for a pay raise by an up-and-coming young reporter, a city editor chuckled nastily and said, "I don't have to give my reporters a pay raise. A by-line does just as well." Unhappily, he was right.

Qualifications for Reporting

To compete successfully for good reporting jobs, a journalist today must acquire an impressive résumé of education, experience, and strong references. As a minimum, he must have a college degree, preferably in journalism, with a few years experience on a small newspaper. Recommendations from supervisors, college faculty, and influential journalists are sorely needed.

Perhaps the best way to examine needed qualifications for newspaper reporting is through the eyes of an editor who determines hiring. Arnold Rosenfeld, editor of *The Dayton* (Ohio) *Daily News* offers his views:

> You can give all the tests, and look at all of the credentials in the world, but nothing will ever replace good motivation and desire as useful tools of reporting. It is very difficult as a prospective employer to identify those elements once you have decided that a person is at least a competent professional. Anybody who wants to report, or write, or edit, wants to do that just about more than anything in the world. We look for that kind of person—a person additionally of good sense, maturity, and balanced judgment.
>
> I remember, a long time ago, interviewing a job candidate who had, on the face of it, better credentials than I do. Somewhere along the line she asked me how heavy her work load would be and, at that moment, lost out on the job. I am willing to guess that the work load of anyone who is awfully good is going to be very heavy. That is the kind of signal you try to pick up. You don't want to exploit anyone, but you are looking for what kind of commitment people have to writing and editing. We also watch out for storm signals involving people with deep ideological commitments, who tend to look at almost any news story from any one of a number of highly specialized viewpoints. For instance, if a person is likely to look at any story from the perspective of radical ecology, I am afraid I will have a real problem with that person's work somewhere down the line.

Rosenfeld then offered some practical pointers for young journalists who are job-hunting:

1. Calculate the market. It would be nice to have your first job at the *New York Times* writing thoughtful columns, or at the *Washington Post* understudying Woodward and Bernstein in bringing down governments. Realistically, try the *Troy Daily News*.

2. If you are interested in a job, show up in person or at least, if you can't afford a cross-country tour, show up at the high-priority papers—the papers you'd really like to work at, or at which you have the best chance of getting a job. Don't be a "file" if you can help it.

3. Know something about the place. Do the editor you are visiting and yourself the favor of having read his paper and knowing something about it. Know for instance, if it's an a.m. or p.m., what its circulation area is, and if it has a Sunday edition. Know something about what it's doing. Look at it critically. He may ask you what you think of the paper, and he is not necessarily expecting or requiring a flattering answer—just an intelligent one.

4. Be interested in the job you're applying for. Don't tell him

you are interested in the paper only as a stopping-off place for something better. Don't ask him how long you will be expected to do the job you're applying for before being promoted to something better. Nobody wants a reporter who is dissatisfied with the job at hand at the same time he is hired.

5. Don't ask about pension plans, vacation, insurance, and job security clauses in the contract. Quite frankly, the editor will expect you to be terribly interested in the job at hand. You are beginning a job in journalism, and at your age he won't be expecting you to be fascinated with the prospect of comfortable retirement. In any case, you'll be told all that later.

6. If you are good, your work load will be heavy because you will receive the best assignments. Every good writer-communicator wants to do that more than just about anything else. Making sure that you have a pleasant time at home with your family will be viewed by most editors as having secondary priority.

7. Bring with you as many examples of your actual work as you can produce. Résumés are interesting, but they are really not all that useful.

8. Explore the possibilities of free-lancing or obtaining low-paying correspondency as an opening wedge. It will have a number of beneficial effects if you can arrange it. It will show you are ambitious. It will bring you into a working relationship with your editor. It will allow him to get visible evidence of your worth. It will give you experience. It will give you clippings to show someone else.

9. If someone shows only minor interest, offer to free-lance a story for him, and ask him for an assignment. It may help.

10. Be enthusiastic about the job and about its possibilities. The thing that you will be judged on mostly is your attitude.

11. Don't be shy. It's time to talk reasonably about your attributes, and what you feel you can bring to the job that uniquely qualifies you for it.

If Rosenfeld's advice on finding a job proves helpful, then his equally candid admonishments to young journalists who enter the chaotic world of the newsroom should be heeded. Bear in mind that Rosenfeld's perspective is from the management side of the table, but, of course, it's the management that passes judgment on the fate of the budding career of any new journalist. He says:

"What follows is not an attempt to turn any serious and committed person into a management-oriented automaton who keeps his head down and does what he is told unquestioningly. But, rather, it is an attempt to propose a code of mutual good faith with a warranty expiring upon continued or gross violation." He then enumerates:

1. Don't yell until you're hurt. Don't begin by accusing anyone of

sins you've seen committed elsewhere or only heard or read about. It doesn't make a lot of sense to be disillusioned in advance. A lot of editors are not very bright and pretty craven. On the other hand, a fair number of them have gotten where they are because they have earned it. They are fully equipped with skill and commitment, and they won't enjoy being treated from the beginning as if they were not. By the way, disagreeing with you is not an objective measure of competence.

2. Don't think your high journalistic principles are unique until you find out otherwise. Although it may look that way to you, most editors were not born in their chairs one day in a puff of smoke. Most care deeply about what appears in their papers. Every beginning reporter to some extent re-invents the journalistic alphabet. Try not to be too naive about it.

3. Be skeptical about everything you are told, whether it's from management or your friends on the staff. Be as professional in your relations with the office as you are in your craft. Get both sides. You owe it to yourself as a journalist.

4. Judge by your own experience. It's the only objective information you really have on management performance. Everything else, whether it comes to you from management or staff, is tainted.

5. A newsroom is primarily structured to produce news. It does not exist primarily as an instrument of its own interior process. News is not an industrial by-product. Clashes of opinion and will are part of the creative process, and the newspaper business would be the poorer without them. News performance cannot necessarily be gauged by newsroom morale, although it is a useful measuring standard. What counts is in the paper. When someone tells you that newsroom morale has never been lower, he is often saying his has never been lower. There is, however, some of the element of the self-fulfilling prophecy in this.

6. Time most often does mean quality, but not always. You can produce quality material—and in quantity—if you are willing to learn how to do it. Nobody likes to be pressed hard to do good, accurate work. But you can do it. In any case, try to learn what the real limits of conventional performance are before you accuse an editor of attempting to get low-quality work out of you on a deadline.

7. Understand how your newsroom is structured. Follow the chain of command even if it is only marginally apparent. Try to work out your problems with your immediate superior before complaining to his. You can't complain about the need for everyone to communicate if you are unwilling to communicate rationally yourself. Do the boss the favor of letting him know what's on your mind. If he's any good, he'll want to know.

8. Your ideas about stories are only ideas until you have facts to

support them. All journalists operate within the limits of some kind of conspiracy theory of the world. Your ideas about the potential of a story are only the beginning, not the end or proof. The only thing that you can get into the paper is what you can prove, and what has been fairly submitted for reaction. Disagreement with your ideas is not necessarily objective evidence of management cowardice. Refusal to print objective facts may be.

9. No editor will find you credible as a journalistic theoretician until you have mastered the basic skills of the craft. It may be wrong, but no city editor is really going to listen to you on cosmic issues if you can't get a name or address correct. Learn to do it. It makes you a credible witness.

10. Work hard. No editor is likely to advance your career if you seem more concerned with your free time than with the job he wants you to do. Consider no job too humble for your talents.

11. Be realistic about your paper's capacity to produce. Editors frequently labor under limitations they're not happy about either.

12. Be aware of your own ideological conflicts of interests, and lean against them. Conflicts of interest extend beyond an editor's alleged relationship with his local business community. They also extend to what you think of as axiomatic and obviously for the common good. Put yourself under the same ideological microscope that you use on others.

13. Understand your community. Understand how your paper is attempting to communicate with it. A paper exists to be read by people, not primarily to provide fulfilling careers for writers and editors. Many journalists lead elitist, isolated lives and don't realize it. Have some pity on the reader. Write for the reader, not for the person you admire three desks down.

14. Proceed in good faith until you have good reason to act otherwise.

15. If all else fails, quit. Resignation is as useful a tool in journalism as it might have been in the Nixon administration.

Rosenfeld's remarks effectively underline the sober, businesslike nature of newspaper journalism. While reporters and editors (including Rosenfeld) may be well endowed with a sense of humor, this trait rarely carries over to a discussion about the profession. A newsroom is not a podium from which a young reporter can blithely expound a viewpoint. It isn't a stage, where the journalist can *play* the role of the fearless reporter—the lead role, of course, with editors playing supporting parts. It is a place of business—very serious business—where dedicated men and women work extremely hard to carry out the critical function of keeping the public informed.

Anyone who is seriously interested in a successful career in journalism must, then, prepare for the job and not for the mere acquisition of the image of being a reporter.

HISTORICAL PERSPECTIVE

Such demanding qualifications and ethics for newspaper reporters have evolved only in recent years. Remember, the profession of journalism is relatively new. While the birthdate of the profession is highly arguable, a case can be made to the effect that professional journalism did not truly evolve until well into the nineteenth century.

Certainly, Colonial American newspapers lacked professional standards. Frequently, the printer merely wrote his own material from word-of-mouth reports that reached his ears. Ethics of accuracy, objectively, fairness, and even the most basic sense of public decency were often missing. During the American Revolution, Loyalist and Patriot newspapers slanted their accounts of the war shamelessly, often adding rumor or out-and-out falsehood to further editorial views.

After the Revolution, the newspapers quickly aligned themselves with the emerging political parties. The partisan newspapers were scandal sheets of the lowest order, maliciously attacking leaders of the opposing party.

When the "Penny Newspapers" came into widespread vogue during the 1830s, providing daily news at a price that the general public could afford, competition for solid news became fierce, forcing publishers to hire assistants who could deftly find and write news. By the time of the Mexican-American War in 1846, American journalism had produced a number of truly professional reporters who performed well in providing quick and fairly accurate accounts of the conflict.

As great editors—such as Benjamin Day, James Gordon Bennett, and Horace Greeley—emerged, reporting became more and more aggressive and effective. The American Civil War ushered in a new era of journalism, because electronics, in the form of the telegraph, allowed correspondents to file their accounts with great speed. By the end of the war, the prototype of modern news stories had evolved: a lead and the inverted pyramid. The telegraph wire had contributed greatly to this development. Since the military restricted the time available to reporters in using the wire, a correspondent, after waiting hours to file a story, often watched in agony as the telegraph operator abruptly stopped tapping out his story as a top-priority military message came in. So, reporters arranged their material so that information was rendered in descending order of importance. If only half the story was sent, then it was the most important half. As a side note, many scholars attribute the traditional "30" at the end of a story to a procedural sign-off used by many telegraph operators.

In the late nineteenth century, a dark age dawned for journalism as powerful editors, led by Joseph Pulitzer and William Randolph Hearst, engaged in ruthless circulation wars that gave birth to "Yellow Journalism." News columns reeked with gore, scandal, and the artful play on emotions called "sensationalism." As the relations between the United States and Spain deteriorated, Hearst and Pulitzer took turns outdoing each other in fanning public fervor for war, contributing considerably to the eventual outbreak.

The taint of the era of "Yellow Journalism" still lingers over modern journalism, although the occasional abuses of today's newspapers hardly hold a candle to the turn-of-the-century variety.

As the circulation wars abated, professional standards of integrity began to emerge, while job qualifications were quickly upgraded. The legendary, hard-nosed city editors emerged to quickly oust careless or incompetent reporters, and to exert constant pressure on those who were good enough to stay.

College-trained journalists, once the object of newsroom contempt as being over-educated and under-experienced, became increasingly accepted as the twentieth century progressed. And, after World War II, a college degree became more and more essential. Today, many reporters have advanced college degrees.

The off-shoot of this educational upgrading and the jelling of professional standards is that American journalism is entering a new era of high professional quality, founded on a strong sense of ethics, fueled by a high sense of idealism toward public service, and led by a new breed of well-educated, aggressive news reporters who will be influenced by the high journalistic performance in the Watergate scandal for many years to come.

SUMMARY

In chapters that follow, more specific information about the nature of reporting will be abundantly provided, but, for now, let's concentrate on a general image of that central character of this text: the reporter.

Today's reporter is, in one sense, a public servant who is employed by a privately owned business. In most cases, the reporter is an idealist, who passes up higher-paying, easier jobs in return for the fame, adventure, personal satisfaction, or public service that is inherent in the job.

A reporter must possess the ability to endure great pressures: rigid deadlines, shrewd adversaries, tough competition, long work days, and a constant sense of extreme vulnerability to grave consequences from small human errors.

Reporting, then, requires a serious and steadfast commitment on the part of its practitioners.

EXERCISES

1. Write a full description of the character, and physical description of the image of a reporter that you had before reading this chapter. How does he interact with news sources? How does that image differ from the image of a modern reporter as given in the text? Where did you learn the characteristics of your reporter-image?

2. Which advantages of reporting most appeal to you? Why? Which disadvantages are most negative to you? Why?

3. Does the image of a modern reporter appeal to you? (Discuss)

2 | Newsroom Organization

A half hour before deadline, a casual observer in a newsroom would doubt that the forthcoming edition of the daily newspaper would be published at all—much less published on time.

Chaos is an inadequate description. Dozens of reporters frantically orchestrate stories on clattering typewriters, telephones ring incessantly, harsh, urgent voices bellow across the open room, and newspersons sporadically lurch from their desks and dash to place still one more story in the city editor's overflowing in-basket. To top it off, the building quivers with the deep, powerful hum of the presses spewing out an earlier edition.

A professional cliché is that the publication of any edition of a daily newspaper is a miracle. Most reporters accept it as fact. The process requires scores of people who work under overbearing deadlines, performing many dissimilar functions that somehow culminate in the thud of a newspaper landing on a subscriber's front porch.

The newsroom is the center of that massive, sometimes frenzied effort. It is the place where the business's commodity—information— is processed and packaged for home delivery.

The disorganized, bedlam-like appearance of the newsroom is deceptive. Each function is carefully, firmly directed to achieve maximum efficiency in the framework of a highly systematic organization, in which each individual is responsible for—and answerable for— the smooth and completely professional performance of a task.

The system is built on the premise that each individual is a professional who can be trusted to perform the assigned job, and complete that work under the conditions of deadlines and accuracy. Reporters are to gather all significant news, write their stories, edit them to ensure accuracy, and submit them to the city desk on or before deadline. The city editor and his assistant city editors are expected to quickly scan each story to determine professional acceptability, correct any minor errors that eluded the reporter, and pass the stories on to the news editor. The news editor is to make accurate decisions on whether to include the stories and, if so, the general treatment of the stories. Copy desk editors must quickly process the stories by trimming them to an assigned length, writing headlines, correcting any errors that slipped through the reporter and city desk, and placing the stories in the dummy that will determine just how the newspaper will appear. Persistent failure in the performance of any of these functions may quickly lead to dismissal.

To properly envision the organization and the flow of work in the newsroom, let's look at an organizational chart, and a physical layout of a typical newsroom for a daily newspaper.

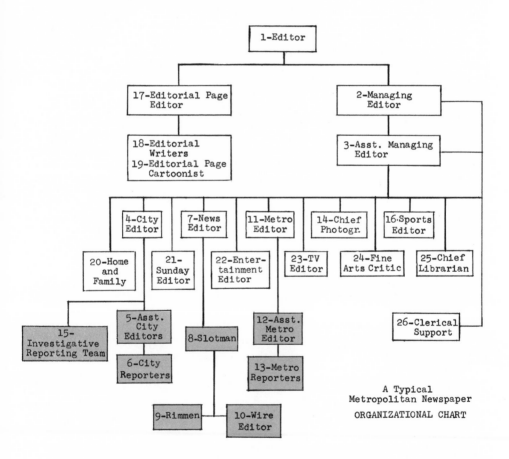

A Typical
Metropolitan Newspaper
ORGANIZATIONAL CHART

Shaded areas indicate "Chain of Command" over a city-side reporter and his domain.

Let's check the "lineup" to examine the functions of each of the professionals who are involved in the process of gathering, assembling, and packaging information:

1. The *Editor,* sometimes called editor-in-chief, is directly responsible for the total performance of the system. While small-town editors often roll up their sleeves and perform day-to-day work alongside their staffs, editors of larger newspapers function primarily as managers and decision-makers. The editor is the agent of the publisher. He enforces all of the publisher's editorial policies, and establishes guidelines for those policies. The editor oversees each function, and has the final word on any significant change in procedure. He may overrule editorial writers about a proposed editorial stand. He can order the managing editor to reorganize his staff. At times, he may decide whether to run a particular news story if legal, ethical or sometimes, political problems might be involved.

Peculiarities of editors can sometimes be kinky. An editor may grumble that sentences are getting too long, so an edict to the effect that no sentence shall exceed twenty words is posted on the bulletin board. He may dislike a certain word, such as "presently," and declare it taboo. Such dictates quickly become law. The editor is *the* boss.

2. The *Managing Editor* is the operational chief of the newsgathering and editing system. Besides enforcing the editor's edicts, the managing editor directly supervises the day-to-day functions of each part of that system. He may step in to dictate procedural changes, or personnel changes to improve the performance of a given function. He can direct a special undertaking, such as the investigation of police corruption or local slumlords. He closely watches the performance of each editor and newsperson, prodding them to even better performance.

From the reporter's point of view, the managing editor holds a special awesome power: that of hiring, firing, promoting, or offering pay raises—with the editor's approval.

3. The *Assistant Managing Editor* often serves as the managing editor's troubleshooter. He may inherit an array of administrative odd jobs, such as approving expense accounts and other such paper work, as well as the function of roving enforcer (sometimes "hatchetman"). He may have a special expertise that complements that of the managing editor. For example, the managing editor may have an extensive reporting background, but little copy desk experience, while the assistant managing editor may have had years of copy desk background. In the managing editor's absence, the assistant managing editor is in charge.

4. The *City Editor* is the center of the newsgathering operation. He supervises all reporters assigned to city beats, makes or approves assignments, checks the work of each reporter to ascertain its pro-

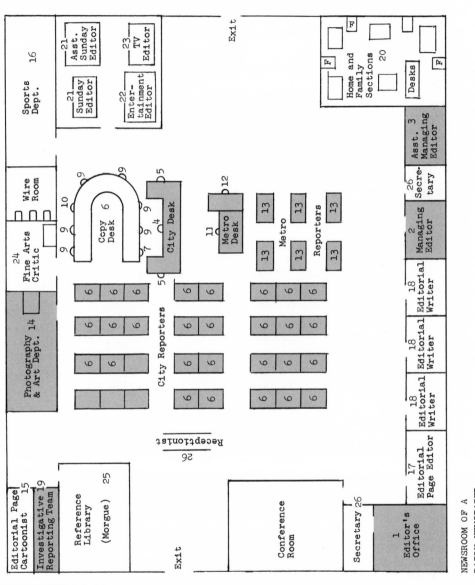

NEWSROOM OF A
DAILY NEWSPAPER

fessional quality, and determines the functional role each reporter fills —subject to the managing editor's approval.

By journalistic traditon, the city editor has the image of an ogre, a heartless, slave-driving taskmaster who lashes hapless reporters to the limits of their capabilities. In fact, many city editors live up to this image out of necessity. It is their job to prod reporters into the best possible performance, and to direct their efforts so that day-to-day coverage of city news is complete. The pressures of the job are enormous.

At times, the city editor functions as a battlefield general. During a riot, he may carefully position reporters in several critical spots to obtain news, and direct the movements and functions of each newsperson. At other times, he must act as a shield between vengeful officials who are angered by an unfavorable (but true) story and the reporter who wrote the account. He must weed out the relatively small number of legitimate news tips that flood in over the telephone or in the mail from the great volume of self-serving public relations announcements and "nut calls," then divide the legitimate assignments among reporters.

The "nut calls" are a special source of irritation. With a deadline only minutes away, the last thing a city editor needs is for a drunken citizen to call to report a flying saucer hovering outside his window, or for an irate person to call to report that the garbagemen didn't pick up her trash.

5. *Assistant City Editors* relieve the city editor of some of this pressure. They work more closely with individual reporters to offer calm guidance. Sometimes the assistant city editors will divide newsbeat specialties among themselves, so that each is responsible for reporters' performances in a given area. As the deadline approaches, assistant city editors assist the city editor in reading incoming copy and assessing its professional quality. Like the city editor, they may return the story to a reporter if they judge that additional information is needed, or if the story is poorly written.

6. *City Reporters* are mostly divided among beats—special areas of news coverage—such as police beat, city hall beat, education beat, and so on. Some are designated general assignment reporters, who must be capable of covering any beat if the regular reporter is indisposed. Other general assignment reporters may be assigned to a mishmash of coverage, ranging from luncheon speakers to small political rallies.

Whatever the specialty, a reporter's job is to provide complete coverage of any newsworthy development on his beat by gathering all relevant information that's obtainable, writing the information in a clear, professional manner, and editing his own copy before submitting it to the city desk.

Naturally, several conditions exist that govern this performance. The information must be as complete as possible, with every significant question about the event answered or at least asked. It must be verifiably accurate in all respects, written with a clarity that not only relays information effectively, but also in a manner that reasonably precludes misinterpretation. The information must also reach the city desk within rigid time limits.

Most of all, the reporter must satisfy his city editor, not only by his performance on each story submitted, but in his overall coverage of the beat specialty.

7. The *News Editor* supervises the copy desk operation, which edits all copy—both local and wire—submitted for inclusion in the issue. The copy desk must also decide whether the story will be carried and, if so, where it will be placed and how much of it will be printed. The copy desk also provides headlines for all stories and chops the stories to fit available space.

The news editor often personally decides whether to print a given story and the approximate "play" the story will receive. He may issue instructions to bury a given story on an inside page or to run it on page one.

8. The *Slotman* physically composes the layout on each page and determines the exact placement of stories. After receiving a story and instructions from the news editor, the slotman finds an appropriate place on a page dummy, then scribbles instructions for story length and headline size at the top of the story. When the story has been edited and cut, and its headline written, the slotman approves or rejects that work before forwarding it to the composing room where it will be set in type.

9. The *Rimmen* edit each story to check for accuracy, clarity, and any possible legal questions that may have eluded other editors. They trim stories to designated length, write headlines, and pass the stories back to the slotman.

10. The *Wire Editor* is normally a senior rimman who is given the special responsibility of selecting wire service news items and, with the approval of the news editor and slotman, of processing the copy and writing headlines. At times, the wire editor (sometimes called telegraph editor) will weave together stories from both major wire services to give readers the most complete package of information.

11. The *Metro Editor* is responsible for coverage of news in outlying areas of the newspaper's circulation pattern. In addition to a staff of reporters, the metro editor may also rely on part-time or full-time correspondents (stringers) in each town, and news bureaus in each county seat. Some newspapers with state-wide circulation may have a state editor to cover far-flung counties well away from the metropolitan

area. The metro editor's responsibilities are similar to those of the city editor, except that they are applied to coverage beyond city limits.

12. The *Assistant Metro Editor* essentially functions the same as an assistant city editor.

13. *Metro Reporters* are the gypsies of the newsroom—they may be roaming outlying areas for days, using the telephone to relay stories. A metro reporter functions as a general assignment reporter in covering just about anything that comes down the pike in his geographic area. He is normally given a certain slice of territory to cover. Working with correspondents in that area, he covers meetings, police actions, town disputes, and other newsworthy events.

14. The *Chief Photographer* is in charge of the visual coverage of news and features. While smaller newspapers require reporters to double as photographers, larger operations hire professional photographers to accompany news reporters. It's not uncommon for a metropolitan newspaper reporter to be completely inept with a camera—and it doesn't matter, since that's the photographer's job.

The chief photographer dispatches photographers upon the request of reporters or editors. Most modern newspapers use radio-equipped cars for photographers. If the police reporter requests a photographer to join him at the scene of a crime, the chief photographer can use the radio to direct one of his cameramen to the scene. A police radio may also be a fixture in the photo department, so that the chief photographer may direct photo coverage of an incident before the city desk requests it.

Some newspapers also add a staff of artists to the chief photographer's domain, for special illustrations.

15. *Investigative Reporting Teams* have become popular assignments on many newspapers in this day of professional glamour for such journalists. The team is normally headed by a veteran investigator, perhaps supplemented by aggressive young reporters. The investigative team may spend months in research before printing a word about a given subject. They may quietly zero in on a huge gambling operation, city hall corruption, or unethical business practices, working long hours into the night. While the calling is certainly rewarding, it also entails such demanding, often risky, work that many reporters choose to pass up the specialty.

16. The *Sports Editor* has his own, special kingdom. Operating directly under the managing editor, the sports editor is simply given a designated number of pages to fill on a given day. And he fills those pages with specialized news designed to state the particular appetites of local sports fans.

17. The *Editorial Page Editor* is, organizationally, on equal footing with the managing editor—although his domain is much smaller. The editorial page editor supervises a staff of editorial writers and the

editorial page cartoonist in composing opinionated material for the editorial page, selecting a fair variety of syndicated political columnists, and processing letters to the editor. Unless overruled by the editor, the editorial page editor dictates editorial stands taken by the newspaper.

18. *Editorial Writers* are the resident thinkers of the newspaper staff. Each writer normally has an area of expertise, from which he can expound at length on the virtues and advantages of the newspaper's viewpoint on a given issue—and the terrible consequences inherent in opting for the opposing view. Most editorial writers have had experience as reporters—a good antidote to the ivory tower syndrome. Much of the editorial writer's time is spent in research, both in reading and in talking with people on both sides of an issue. Editorial writers normally submit their proposed editorials at least one day in advance of publication, so that the editorial page editor can determine whether the stand is in keeping with newspaper policy.

19. The *Editorial Page Cartoonist*—an often-zany, creative creature —can frequently convey a message in a much more effective fashion than the most brilliantly written editorial. While most newspapers require that the cartoonist's viewpoint conform to editorial policy, a few bold newspapers turn the cartoonist lose—with outrageously refreshing results.

20. The *Home and Family Editor*, who is usually a woman, heads the specialized news operation that was traditionally called the Women's Page—before the age of Women's Lib. She supervises coverage of society news, fashion trends, engagements and weddings, cooking tips, and other such items that supposedly interest housewives. Today, there appears to be a trend toward more in-dept reporting in this area, to cover such serious concerns as abortions, rape, legal rights of single women, sex discrimination, and other such problems.

21. The *Sunday Editor* publishes the special Sunday supplement, usually a magazine, inserted in the week's fattest newspaper. He may also edit other special sections.

22. The *Entertainment Editor* reviews movies and other popular entertainment, and writes critical reviews of restaurants.

23. The *TV Editor* edits the page containing the daily television schedule and program synopses, edits the weekend TV guide that lists upcoming programs for the week, and often writes a daily column reviewing TV shows and offering background on celebrities.

24. The *Fine Arts Critic* reviews plays, books, and renditions of classical music and opera.

25. The *Chief Librarian* is in charge of the reference library— better known as the morgue. (Note: reporters are advised to refrain from calling the reference library the "morgue" in the presence of the chief librarian.) The chief librarian supervises a staff that clips each

story from the newspaper and files it in an appropriate envelope, by subject and by names of people mentioned in the story. The reference library is a critical resource for any reporter. Precious background material on any issue, individual, or subject of news value can usually be found there, along with an assortment of standard references, such as encyclopedias, almanacs, legal references, out-of-town telephone directories, and past newspaper issues dating back many years.

26. *Clerical* support is needed in any newsroom. Secretaries are normally assigned to the editor and managing editor to handle a large volume of correspondence. Many city editors also have a clerical assistant to help answer the constantly ringing telephones and sort paper work. Most metropolitan newspapers also have a receptionist to direct visitors to the reporters and to screen out pests who try to descend on reporters who are busy fighting deadlines.

As you can see, the newsroom organization is carefully, precisely arranged to accommodate every task that must be performed in processing news. The parts are all there, carefully primed and adjusted to work with optimum efficiency. A detailed account of the performance of that organization under deadline pressures will be found in the following chapter. For now, let's take a much closer look at that part of the organization that is concerned with the acquisition of news within a city.

The city desk operation—city editor and assistant city editors—directs coverage of all news that occurs within the city. The city desk retains the overall picture of events transpiring within city limits, and dispatches reporters to cover those occurrences.

Before the first news event happens, the odds are that a reporter has already inherited responsibility for covering it by virtue of his newsbeat assignment. Most reporters are assigned general areas of expertise—fields of coverage called newsbeats—in which they are held accountable for reporting any items of news interest that may transpire.

The reasons for using a beat system are logical:

1. To try to cover everything that happened in a large city without such organization would result in a debacle. The beat system provides a routine starting point for the entire system of newsgathering.

2. A beat reporter should be fully aware of all continuing news developments on his beat. Thus, a city hall reporter knows the background behind a political maneuver even before it occurs. A police reporter knows exactly why and how narcotics detectives are staging a crackdown on heroin. An education reporter is familiar with the factional in-fighting on the school board that resulted in a given action that became news. Through such familiarity, much time and effort is saved in covering events.

3. The beat reporter is well versed in the routine manner of procedures by officials on his beat. A veteran police reporter can discern an interesting crime offense report from a score of routine ones within seconds. A city hall reporter can perceive a subtle parliamentary ploy that the mayor may use to outmaneuver opposition during a city council meeting. The education reporter can easily follow the intricacies involved in contract negotiations between the school board and the teachers' assocation.

4. Beat reporters establish personal relationships with key officials who provide background information, news leaks, and story tips. Without such relationships, really deep and penetrating coverage would be impossible.

Ideally, each event that occurs within the city would naturally fall into the domain of a beat reporter. Think of city news in terms of being a circle that is neatly sliced into newsbeats. Each news item that occurs would fall into that circle, and onto a newsbeat. Each reporter would be held responsible for any such tidbit that lands on his beat.

In practice, it isn't nearly so simple. Major news stories are nortoriously uncooperative in accommodating the beat system.

Let's say that heated contract negotiations are underway between city hall and the Fraternal Order of Police—the official bargaining unit that represents city policemen. The coverage, then, sprawls across the "line" between the police and city hall beats, thus creating an overlap.

Although some inter-newsroom competition is bound to happen under such circumstances, the city editor carefully coordinates coverage by both reporters. The city hall reporter approaches the negotiations by mining his lode of city hall sources to find out what's going on behind closed doors in negotiations. His sources may disclose the city hall objectives in the negotiations, and the disagreements—from a city hall point of view. The police beat reporter attacks from the other side, using his police and Fraternal Order of Police contacts to discover police bargaining objectives, and negotiation drawbacks from their viewpoint. If one reporter discovers an interesting revelation on his beat, or perhaps obtains a bitter accusation against those on the other side of the table, then the other reporter is quickly informed of the development so that he can obtain the other viewpoint. Within the limits of human nature, this overlapping, coordinated approach—often with dual by-lines—provides the public with a truly balanced, informed picture of the intricacies and the real issues behind the story.

While some major stories sprawl across the line separating two or more beats, a few events seem to walk a tightrope, falling in no established newsbeat. If, for example, a presidential candidate comes to town to speak from the courthouse steps, the question of coverage responsibility quickly arises. No medium-sized metropolitan daily newspaper can afford to establish a permanent beat for a presidential campaign visit. It's a one-shot major news story. Several beats may be involved in a supportive manner, with the police reporter putting together an interesting story on security arrangements, the city hall reporter delving into local political reaction, the education reporter covering the candidate's brief visit to a local school, and the county reporter writing a feature story on the reaction of county courthouse employees to the invasion of the candidate into their domain. Yet, the prime assignment of covering the speech simply doesn't fit into the structure.

So, the city editor resorts to his top troubleshooter, a veteran general assignment reporter, who has over the years covered several news beats. The general assignment newsman is competent to cover any breaking story, including a presidential candidate's campaign speech.

The system, then, is complete. A carefully constructed pattern of newsbeats is designed to catch recurring types of news. And, beneath that beat pattern is a safety net of general assignment reporters, who tackle any substantial items that sift through the pre-established areas of responsibility.

The Beats

In the organizational scheme given earlier in the chapter, city reporters were lumped together under an inclusive heading. A closer look at a typical beat operation provides insight to the general types of news that occur frequently, the major sources of information, and the overall coverage operation:

City Hall Beat. This prestigious and coveted newsbeat involves the total coverage of city government, including actions by city council, by the city manager (or full-time mayor, or administrator), bureaucracy within city hall, city politics, and the actions and functions of city agencies, such as Model Cities, urban renewal, and such.

Police Beat. Often a starting assignment for a young reporter, the beat includes all crime coverage, civil disturbances, accidents, unnatural deaths, and institutional coverage of police and fire departments (including such matters as union activities and policy changes). It is by far the most physically demanding news beat, and among the more difficult to cover.

Courts Beat. The courts reporter provides news of major criminal and civil trials and legal actions. He must quickly acquire a broad knowledge of legal terms and proceedings, and fully understand the conduct of each stage of a civil or criminal trial.

County Beat. If the city is also county seat, a reporter is assigned to cover the county courthouse, much the same as the city hall reporter covers his domain.

Education Beat. This reporter is responsible for coverage of news and items of interest that occur within the city school system, and at colleges, universities, and other educational institutions in the area. He attends meetings of the school board and board of trustees, and establishes contacts with various student government bodies and teachers' associations.

Medical Beat. A reporter is responsible for coverage of local hospitals, mental institutions, clinics, nursing homes, and actions by associations of physicians, psychiatrists (or psychologists), and dentists. This beat often involves investigative reporting into the operation of such institutions, particularly in light of the regularity with which scandals occur in the administration of such facilities.

Military Beat. Coverage of activities at large, local military installations is a must because of the economic impact of such bases on the city. This reporter, who normally has a broad knowledge of military procedures, would cover such events as, say, a new Air Force weapon system developed by base personnel, major layoffs at the base, or the assignment of a new base commander.

Labor Beat. In an industrial city, the reporter must cover scores of separate unions by establishing a working contact with union officials. He is, of course, particularly busy during contract negotiations at major industrial plants in the area.

Business Beat. Although this reporter, unfortunately, commonly acts more as a public relations person for the Chamber of Commerce, his job is to provide objective coverage of business news and private enterprise development in the city. If a large new department store is planned, he covers that news. If the president of the city's largest firm retires, he does the story. He may carry the title of business editor, laying out and editing the business news pages.

Consumer Beat. In recent years, many newspapers have assigned reporters to cover news and situations of interest to consumers. Often, such news persons write regular columns on consumer tips, and engage in investigative reporting into frauds or misleading practices by merchants.

Religion Beat. This reporter provides fair and objective coverage of the activities of churches and synagogues in the city. Many newspapers carry a weekly religion page or insert to package this information. While the emphasis on coverage of religious activities varies greatly among newspapers, such information receives substantial reader attention.

General Assignment Beat. Several reporters are assigned to this category. Generally, they are either experienced, highly competent veterans, or new reporters who are learning their trade through on-the-job training. The veteran general assignment reporters, as noted earlier, can and do cover just about anything that comes along. They can also easily fill in for a beat reporter who is ill, absent, or burdened with a special assignment.

The new reporters are given a scavenger's diet of secondary news, such as coverage of speeches at clubs and organizational luncheons, obituary writing, daily weather news, and the rewriting of copy submitted by semiliterate stringers and publicity releases.

Obituary Writer. On large metropolitan dailies, the obituary writer is an artist in his own right, providing well-written stories on the deaths of national and international figures. On smaller newspapers, however, the obituary writer is simply a technician who writes death notices in a formula-style—and he can do it in his sleep. The obituary writer's main concerns are accuracy and the updating of notices from edition to edition.

State Capital Beat. Although it would seem that this beat belongs in the metro or state editor's domain, this reporter is frequently placed under the city editor's thumb, on the grounds that much of his coverage is directly related to events affecting city government. Although the reporter covers activities by the governor's office and the state legislature, his primary responsibility is to cover the performance of legislators from the local area, and news of special interest to local readers. In essence, he supplements wire service coverage by providing local angles.

Washington Correspondent. Like the state capital reporter, this newsperson works under the city editor to provide coverage of items of local interest, but on a federal level. Obviously, the labyrinth of Washington, D.C., is far too much for one reporter to cover comprehensively, so the correspondent carefully focuses on items of narrow interest, leaving the major national news items to be covered by the Washington press corps.

Obviously, the beat system that is outlined here is only one of many variations. Other newspapers may not have a military beat or a consumer beat, substituting, instead, an ecology beat or an agriculture beat. The alignment may also be different. The police beat may be divided into police beat and fire beat, or combined with courts beat to become a conglomerate justice beat. City hall beat responsibilities of local political coverage may be lopped off and assigned to a political beat reporter. The numbers of specialties also tend to increase or decrease directly with the size of the newspaper staff—for obvious reasons. A small daily cannot afford the luxury of a labor beat, while New York and Washington newspapers may maintain narrow-interest, specialty beats.

Some of these common beats will be discussed in detail in later chapters.

SUMMARY

The total effect of the newsgathering system on a metropolitan newspaper is much like that of a gigantic rake that moves through the city each day to collect news. Each reporter serves as a tooth in that rake, and each is clearly responsible for the area over which he passes.

Yet, like most analogies, this one is imperfect. The newsgathering system, while highly organized and carefully designed, is also flexible and reactive. Where the organization is limited, human resourcefulness takes over. A city editor can quickly adjust the "teeth"—the reporting asignments—to fit a given unusual situation. The reporters, themselves, are free to pick up major news items that occur on other beats or between beats, with the city editor's permission. The managing editor can direct that the "rake" should be redesigned at any time, or that certain "teeth" should be replaced or reassigned. And the editor can send down a thunderous decree that will turn the rake into a lawnmower.

EXERCISES

1. You are city editor of a metropolitan daily newspaper. Using the beat structure given in this chapter, choose the appropriate beats for the following assignments, and explain why you made that selection:
   a. A major fire destroys a chemical plant in the city.
   b. The mayor announces the layoff of forty policemen in a budget cut.
   c. A racial fight erupts in the corridors of a high school.
   d. City health inspectors find serious violations in a hospital kitchen.
   e. A hotel chain announces plans for a $40 million hotel downtown.
   f. A local furniture store owner is accused of fraudulent merchandising.
   g. A minor gubernatorial candidate gives a speech at a shopping center.
   h. A riot occurs when non-union laborers try to cross a picket line of striking union members at a plant.
   i. A shootout occurs in the county courthouse between two clerks.
2. List, in order, the supervisors who are *directly* over the city reporter, and explain how their responsibilities affect the reporter.
3. Devise a beat system for your student newspaper, which could accommodate all major sources of campus news. Discuss, in detail, how your system would function.

3 | Deadlines

The clock is an appropriate symbol for newspaper deadlines, not only in the sense that it is the ultimate determinant of whether a given story can even be considered for a given day's final edition, but also in the sense that it is analogous to the entire newsgathering process.

When the minute hand finally reaches the designated time of deadline for the edition, it doesn't stop or even pause. It immediately continues, signaling the beginning of a new cycle toward a new deadline twenty-four hours away.

In the same way, the newsgathering operation doesn't grind to a halt at deadline. As soon as the last story has cleared his in-basket, the city editor begins prowling the newsroom to ask reporters for their assessments of possible stories for the next day.

In fact, many stories may be in the works for several days or even weeks before they are printed. An investigative reporting team may spend months on a story. A police reporter may have begun his research into a story on city narcotics traffic two weeks earlier. A city hall reporter, who has just turned in an excellent page-one account of a lively city council meeting, may rush to a luncheon interview with the mayor to gather information about still another story in the works.

There's a misconception held by many people that reporters only work half a day, then head for the nearest tavern as soon as deadline passes. In fact, the tedious, demanding phase of fact-finding is just beginning for most reporters. Freed from immediate deadline pressures, they can concentrate on investigative stories, in-depth stories, features, and other long-range pieces, or begin preparations for stories on news developments that they see emerging on their beats.

As soon as the last story for the day has been passed to the copy desk, the city editor may push back his chair, sigh deeply, then grab the clipboard that holds a list of stories expected for the next day's editions. While most breaking hard-news stories cannot be anticipated or planned for in advance, the city editor invariably has a solid supply of in-depth or interpretative stories, features, investigative exposés, and running series already in hand or on tap. Also, his clipboard list can anticipate such planned news events as speeches, public meetings, and scheduled trials. Most of these stories have already been assigned to general assignment reporters, or to appropriate beat reporters.

After studying the upcoming list, the city editor rises to make his rounds, stopping at the desk of each city reporter. A typical exchange goes like this:

City Editor: "What do you have coming for tomorrow?"

City Hall Reporter: "Well, let's see. You know that we have a morning city council meeting. It should be interesting. I expect to see a bitter fight between conservatives and liberals over the proposed handgun registration ordinance. Also, there's a rumor floating around that the city manager plans to spring a new, streamlined city hall organization sometime soon. I think I can turn up something by tomorrow. The other thing, of course, is the naming of the new police chief. That decision should be coming very soon. I'm betting on the assistant chief, but I can't substantiate it yet."

City Editor: "I'll put you down for the meeting and for the organization story. Joe is working on the police chief story from police beat, but if you can shake something loose on city hall, go ahead."

City Hall Reporter: "I can't promise a story on organization; it's just a rumor. It may not pan out."

City Editor: "How widespread is the rumor?"

City Hall Reporter: "I picked it up from four different sources, including one on city council."

City Editor: "If it's that strong, it's worth a story, even if it isn't valid. If the thing checks out, I want it tomorrow. If the city manager spikes it, I want that story instead. A strong rumor is news as far as I'm concerned. Your job is to find out whether it's true."

The city editor arbitrarily lists the organization rumor, then walks away from the exasperated reporter, who is deeply regretting mentioning the story in the first place. The city editor is satisfied that he has sufficiently prodded the newsman into aggressive coverage.

After each reporter has received the proper dose of pressure, encouragement, or praise—depending on what the city editor perceives that he needs at the moment—the newsroom empties as reporters go to lunch. In most occupations, lunch time is a period of relaxation in the midst of a busy day. But, for many reporters, lunch time is a continuation of the day's work.

The city hall reporter has a luncheon interview with the mayor, during which he presses questions about the proposed new organization —probably giving both the reporter and the official indigestion.

The police reporter informally dines with two polcemen, who grumble about the sad state of affairs in the department, the acting police chief's incompetence, and the disgraceful performance of local judges in not sentencing criminals to long prison terms. From these gripes, the reporter picks up tidbits of story leads and information that may be useful later. Also, by being a good, apparently sympathetic listener, the police reporter establishes a better relationship with his sources.

After lunch, beat reporters visit their prime news sources to try to pick up story tips and general information. To a casual observer, many such contacts appear to be nothing more than time-wasting chats among friends that cover such diverse topics as the local baseball team's chances of being in the World Series, old war stories, or the latest popular joke. Yet, under careful maneuvering by the reporter, the conversation drifts into a discussion of interesting events and developments within that organization.

If a reporter picks up a strong tip, he cautiously pursues the topic, trying not to create a stir that could alert competing reporters. He may stick with safe sources, those who provide information only to him, and not to his competitors as well.

Frequently, the beat reporter may be researching a feature story or interpretative story as he makes his rounds. By focusing attention on such "soft" topics, he may pick up valuable tips on other subjects while performing the task. Moreover, if competitors learn of the interviews, the "soft" story provides excellent camouflage for the more current and explosive story that the reporter is obtaining simultaneously.

General assignment reporters divide their time between covering assorted speches and meetings that aren't accommodated by the beat system and in researching features and in-depth stories.

The total effect of the afternoon "off-cycle" coverage by reporters is like that of prospectors sifting for gold in a stream, picking up small nuggets of news, while searching for that great mother lode. The process is often tedious and laborious, but frequently productive.

Returning to the newsroom late in the afternoon, reporters inform the city editor of new developments and stories that they have picked up. They write the stories that can be processed without further research and updating, polish feature stories and in-depth stories that are scheduled for the next day, and research clippings and other references in the "morgue" for background information. As they complete stories, they file them in the city editor's in-basket so that the stories can be edited and processed before the morning flood of copy begins. Such non-pressured writing is a special joy to reporters who can take the time to extend their best writing efforts—something that they can't always do under deadline pressures.

At quitting time, a few reporters wearily linger. Perhaps the city council meeting is tonight instead of tomorrow morning. The city hall reporter must stay to cover the event. The police beat reporter may have been tipped about a major narcotics raid later in the evening. A general assignment reporter may have inherited the chore of covering a political party's fund-raising $100-a-plate dinner. Others are engrossed in trying to understand a complex planning document, or in piecing together bits of information that, somehow, may fit into a major exposé.

As the evening progresses, reporters with night assignments drift to the appropriate locations. Many newspapers have a night editor, an owlish soul who keeps watch over the city, with one ear cocked for major disasters as reported over police radio, the other pressed against a telephone receiver as he types stories dictated by correspondents and other reporters who are on far-flung assignments. Other newspapers have replaced this lonely job with a recording device that keeps dictated stories overnight for early morning typing by a clerk.

As reporters complete their night assignments, they trudge back into the newsroom to write the stories and file them in the city desk in-basket before going home.

By 6:30 or 7 A.M., the city editor or one of his assistants is already at his desk, wading through the pile of overnight stories. The copy desk slowly stirs as rimmen begin moving the copy on hand, getting it out of the way before the pace picks up.

The police reporter is the first arrival from the city reporting staff, usually staggering in around 7 A.M. On the previous evening, the reporter had covered the narcotics raid, which wasn't completed until after midnight. After hastily skimming the morning newspaper for stories that originated on his beat, clipping those that require a follow-up, and checking with the city desk for reports of major overnight police activities, he walks to police headquarters to begin his hectic task of coverage.

By 8 A.M., other beat reporters arrive, read the morning newspaper, and, after the unnerving experience of seeing page-one stories in the competing publication that they missed, they head for their beats.

This newspaper prints three editions each day, thus reporters face three separate deadlines:

1. A 10 A.M. deadline for the "Home" edition, which is delivered to far outlying areas of circulation. Because of distance, the edition must be printed early so that trucks can deliver copies in time for the targeted home delivery hour, which may be 4 P.M.

2. An 11 A.M. deadline for the "Final *" edition, which goes to

the outlying suburbs. Reporters refer to the edition as the "star" to differentiate it from the *real* final edition, which isn't marked with an asterisk.

3. A noon deadline for the "Final" edition (no asterisk), which is circulated within the city and in nearby suburbs.

If the edition names appear to be somewhat devious, the deception is deliberate. Each reader wants the most current edition delivered to his doorstep. To satisfy this desire, each edition is given a name that implies that it is the last, most complete packaging of the day's news. Many metropolitan newspapers resort to this practice, perhaps varying the names, or using a different coding.

With the home edition copy deadline at 10 A.M., activity in the newsroom begins to build by 8:30 A.M. The police reporter calls in to dictate several crime stories, based on overnight police actions. He also alerts the city editor to other stories that he has discovered, which should be ready by final deadline. The city editor looks around the newsroom, spots a reporter who isn't working on a deadline story, and transfers the call to him. Seconds later, the reporter in the newsroom has the telephone receiver jammed between chin and shoulder, as he types out the story from the police reporter.

As other reporters call in, the process is repeated, and copy begins to fill the city desk in-basket. Every few minutes, the telephone rings as still another reporter checks in with a story.

The metro desk, which must gather and assemble news of special interest to readers in the far-flung areas where the *Home* edition goes, is especially busy, with a steady stream of calls from correspondents and reporters.

By 9:15 A.M., photographers begin rushing in with film of events that will run in the early edition. Because of the extra time needed to develop and process the photos, the photo deadline is half an hour earlier than the copy deadline.

The copy desk is operating at full-tilt, with the news editor nervously shuffling between city editor, wire editor, metro editor, and slotman, to assess and place the stories that are coming in from diverse sources. The assistant managing editor joins a hurried conference between news editor and wire editor as they discuss conflicting accounts of the same story carried by the two major wire services. Moments later, he rushes to the composing room to assess a mechanical problem that threatens to delay production.

As the clock ticks toward 10 A.M., noise levels reach a crescendo, with clattering typewriters, ringing telephones, and terse shouts across the room. Then, as the home edition deadline passes, the sounds abate as activity ebbs momentarily before building again for the second deadline.

The city editor, managing editor, assistant managing editor, assistant city editors, and the news editor meet briefly to discuss the story lineup for the final edition. By 10 A.M., the city editor is aware of almost all of the stories that his reporters will produce that day. In the brief conference, major stories are evaluated and ranked, and any problems or sensitive aspects affecting a given story are hashed over.

Meanwhile, reporters continue to pry and dig to find and cover still other stories, or complete major articles that they are preparing for deadline. A new wave of phone calls occurs as reporters offer updated versions of initial stories for the "star" final edition, or altogether new stories.

For example, if a bank robbery occurs at 9 A.M., the police reporter is hard pressed to provide even sketchy, basic information for the home edition. An hour later, after pressing police and FBI sources for additional information, the police reporter calls in a far more comprehensive account. With this new depth of information, he completely revises his story and dictates it to the same reporter who typed the initial version. The reporter in the newsroom, meanwhile, had checked clippings to discover that the bank had been robbed previously only six months ago. He had also called bank officials who were not accessible to the reporter at the scene of the robbery to obtain still other information. As he types the fresh account dictated by the police reporter, the newsroom reporter weaves in this additional information. Still another updated version will be submitted for the final edition.

At 11 P.M., the final copy for the star edition reaches the copy desk, as the building quivers with the deep-throated hum of presses that are already spewing out home edition newspapers. Within minutes, copies of the edition reach the newsroom, to be quickly snatched up by reporters and editors. The brief moment of relative calm after the star edition deadline passes is punctuated by groans and curses as reporters and editors find typographical errors in stories. The copy desk quickly makes corrections in stories scheduled to continue into the final edition. The first edition, then, serves as a trial run, a dress rehearsal for the final edition. Sometimes, major embarrasments are discovered and corrected.

In one such case, a managing editor was disturbed when he heard uproarious laughter in the newsroom. He hurriedly walked to a knot of reporters who were snickering about a line in the lead story. A typographical error had changed an innocuous word into a gutter profanity. The managing editor wasted little time in lodging a colorful complaint with the composing room supervisor—and directing a quick correction. Final edition readers missed this startling "blooper."

Before final deadline arrives, let's pause to take a careful look at the cogs in the system for processing stories:

Reporter: Gathers information about a given story, writes the story, carefully edits it to ensure accuracy and professional quality, then puts it in the city desk in-basket.

City Desk: The city editor or an assistant city editor reads the story to ascertain its value and professional quality, correcting any obvious errors that may have slipped by the reporter. He may summon the reporter to question him about the material, or return it to him for further work if the story is poorly written, inaccurate, or if vital information has been omitted. Once satisfied, the city editor or assistant city editor passes the story to the in-basket of the copy desk. If the story is especially significant, or if the copy desk has been alerted to expect it, he tersely tells the news editor about the story and offers his evaluation.

News Editor: Assesses significant stories to determine their value, and decides generally what position they are to receive in the newspaper. He passes on the stories to the slotman, with instructions ranging from "put it on page one" to "bury it deep inside."

Slotman: Dummies in the story, as directed by the news editor, and determines its exact length and the size of the headline that will be used for it, then passes it on to a rimman.

Rimman: Carefully edits the story—he's the last safeguard in the system to catch inaccuracies—and cuts it to fit available space. He then writes the headline, and gives the story back to the slotman.

Slotman: Checks to see that the headline is appropriate and the editing is adequate, then codes the story for the designated edition and placement. The story is then sent to the composing room.

In the normal course of events, the managing editor and editor are excluded from the sequence of copy flow. Yet, under special circumstances, both may become major factors in determining how —or if—a story is to appear in print.

Because of the complex political nature of city hall, the city hall reporter may frequently encounter stories that gingerly toe the fine line between fact and interpretation that often meanders through a treacherous gray area, fraught with ethical and legal traps.

When such a story breaks during the deadline cycle, quick and authoritative decision-making must occur—often in the offices of top management. For example, the city hall reporter may have uncovered a story that, in effect, accuses the chief city planner of engaging in a conflict of interest.

The city editor's eyebrows rise as he scans the story, which alleges that the chief city planner secretly holds a real estate sales license that specifies that he is affiliated with one of the city's larger real estate firms. The firm is frequently involved in zoning change requests, which must be approved by the city plan board. The chief city planner serves as a non-voting advisor to the board, with considerable sway over the board's actions. The firm has enjoyed a very high rate of success in having its applications approved.

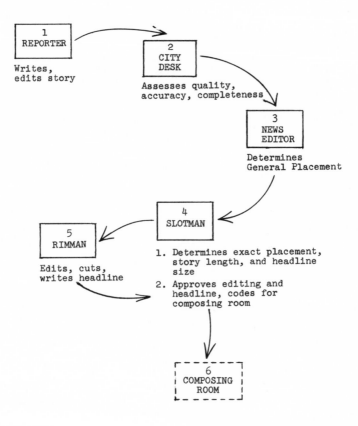

The story also includes a denial of wrongdoing from the official, although he admits holding the license. "I plan to retire in a few months, so I obtained the license for use after retirement," he says. "Although the firm kindly allowed me to use its name on the application for the license, there were no strings. It hasn't influenced my work in the least."

However, the city hall reporter found that the license had been issued two years before, and that the chief planner had made several recommendations for approval of zoning change requests made by the firm, over the objections of his staff. The reporter also cites "persistent rumor" that the chief city planner had made financial investments in land parcels that had later increased greatly in value after being re-zoned for industrial use.

City Editor: "It's a great story, but some of the details disturb me. Have you actually seen a copy of the application for the sales license?"

City Hall Reporter (grinning triumphantly): "Not only have I seen it, but I have a copy of it right here!"

City Editor: "Well, why didn't you say so in the story? We need to bolster credibility. Give it to the photo department, we'll run a reproduction of it alongside the story." (He pauses to insert a phrase in the copy that tells readers that the newspaper possesses a copy of the application.) "Now, the story says that the firm has been involved in several zoning change actions. Do you know how many?"

City Hall Reporter: "Dozens of them. It's impossible to come up with an exact figure before deadline because I would have to wade through records."

City Editor: "How many do you personally know about? I want fact, not supposition."

City Hall Reporter: "I have attended several plan board meet-ings at which such requests were made by the firm. I can back up the term 'several'."

City Editor: "Okay. Now, about his impending retirement. Had he announced his retirement earlier? Was the city council aware of this intention?"

City Hall Reporter: "I didn't ask, but I see what you're driving at. If this is the first indication of his retirement plans, then the fact that he made that announcement when confronted by a con-flict of interest charge puts everything in a different perspective. I'll check it out with the mayor and give you an insert in a few minutes."

City Editor: "Be careful with it. Don't draw a conclusion; just give the information and let the reader decide. Now, did you con-tact the real estate firm?"

City Hall Reporter: "I haven't been able to reach the firm's president for comment. I mentioned that toward the end of the story."

City Editor: "Oh, okay. Now, can you substantiate the allega-tion that he made recommendations over the objections of his staff? I'd like to see specific cases cited."

City Hall Reporter: "So would I, but if I cite them, he could possibly figure out my sources' names. The objections were made in closed-door meetings, with only three staffers attending. One of them told me about it, and another confirmed it. The third would head straight for the chief planner if I asked, thus pointing the finger at the other two. I know of four, possibly five instances."

City Editor: "Okay, now tell me about the rumor of his land investments."

City Hall Reporter: "That's been floating around for some time. I can't locate any records to confirm them because he's probably using a dummy corporation. One member of his staff told me he was certain that the rumor is true."

City Editor: "I think you're going out on a limb. Check out the retirement angle and get back with me."

As the city hall reporter makes his phone calls, the city editor takes the story to the managing editor and explains the problems.

The managing editor weighs the information, then tells the city editor, "The rumor about his land investments is simply too vague and tenuous. The story is very solid and explosive without that segment. If the official can knock down the charge, then he can severely undermine our credibility on the rest of the story. It's not worth the risk, so drop it.

"I'm a little nervous about the allegation that he made recommendations favorable to the firm over his staff's objections. I can understand the need to protect sources, but we could be vulnerable here. I'll let you know the decision in a few minutes."

The managing editor then advises the editor about the story and asks for policy guidance.

The editor smiles appreciatively at the reporter's aggressive work. "That's very good reporting. I agree with you that the rumor portion should be dropped. Tell him (the reporter) to dig into it later. I want to know how that checks out. As for the problem of protecting sources, I'll back the reporter. He's much closer to the situation, and he knows just how far he can go without blowing his sources. I doubt if we're all that vulnerable on this point, anyway. If the planner howls and denies it, then we'll come back with the particulars. It makes a good bear trap."

The managing editor discloses the decision to the city editor, who, in turn, tells the reporter. Only, as these things usually work out, the editor's casual comments about a desire to see further investigation into the planner's land investments were subjected to some interpretation by the time they reached the reporter.

"The boss liked your story," the city editor says. "Now, he wants to see a follow-up on the land investments angle. He wants it tomorrow."

SUMMARY

Deadlines, and the system used to publish a newspaper under them, provide a vivid example of the high-pressured working atmosphere in a metropolitan daily's newsroom. In the example of the city hall reporter's exposé, countless decisions had to be made—and made correctly—at every stage of the process of acquiring, writing, and preparing the story for print. In gathering information, the reporter weighed each alternative source of information and each tidbit of fact received, then made a decision as to where it seemed to lead and whether it was significant enough to warrant further research. In writing the story, the reporter used only a small portion of the material he had gathered. Time and again, he consciously decided whether to include a fact, or to omit it as being irrelevant, unsubstantiated, or redundant. He also exercised judgment in determining exact phrasing of each segment of the story, knowing that precise and well-measured wording was essential in such a sensitive, controversial story. Further decision-making by the editors and copy desk personnel followed, in due course, as is illustrated in the example and in the routine copy flow system.

The point is that decisiveness under pressure is a basic requirement of any newsperson on a daily newspaper. That requirement adds immensely to the burden of responsibility that each newsroom employee must bear.

EXERCISES

1. Using the example of the city hall reporter's exposé about the chief planner's conflict of interest, show, step by step, how the story will be processed through the copy desk system, after the city editor passes it on to the next person in the "chain."

2. Name the positions responsible for these actions in the newsroom:

   a. Finding and correcting a misspelled word.
   b. Writing the headline.
   c. Determining whether the story is complete, accurate, and of adequate professional quality.
   d. Deciding whether the story is to be printed.
   e. Deciding generally how the story is "played" (prominence).
   f. Acting as the final arbitrator of policy decisions.
   g. Determining exact story length and headline size.
   h. Cutting the story to fit allotted space.
   i. Approving the headline and sending the story to the composing room.

3. Explain your reasons for selecting the positions you named in question 2, discussing the role that each position plays in each action.

4

News, and
Where to Find It

The ability to perceive, to recognize, news when it occurs is obviously an important attribute for any reporter, even though most major events that are covered by the newspaper are so blantantly newsy that a small child could recognize their value to the readers of a newspaper.

It takes little training or talent to declare as news such events as a presidential election, the outbreak of World War III, or a million dollar bank robbery. Yet, many vitally significant news stories are far less apparent, often hidden behind events of secondary importance, or so brazenly obvious that no one notices them.

Perhaps the point is well illustrated in an age-old story about a young reporter and his city editor, just before the turn of the century.

The young reporter's performance had been less than adequate, and the city editor was pondering whether to fire him immediately, when the wire editor excitedly approached, waving a copy of a story.

"There's been a terrible flood at River City; hundreds of people are missing, and the whole city is destroyed," the wire editor said.

The city editor was dismayed to note that the young reporter was the only newsman available for this big assignment. With considerable misgivings, he sent the reporter to cover the flood in the city fifty miles away. He thoughtfully provided the green journalist with added incentive by telling him it was his last chance to prove his ability.

Arriving at the scene, the reporter wasted no time in assessing the situation and capturing the devastation with great imagery. He wired back a story that began:

GOD IS WEEPING ON A HILLSIDE OVERLOOKING THE WRATHFUL FURY OF THE RAGING FLOODWATERS THAT DEVASTATED RIVER CITY . . .

After receiving the story, the city editor immediately wired back instructions for a different approach:

FORGET FLOOD. INTERVIEW GOD. TRY TO GET PIX.

Now, that's a city editor with a true sense of news perspective. As a postscript, the fate of the young reporter failed to survive the generation to generation recounting of the anecdote among reporters. Perhaps he became a great novelist after an abortive newspaper career.

Perhaps the young reporter could have benefited from a definition of news. A good definition is:

> News is a current event or situation that is of interest or significance to a substantial part of the readership.

The key to really understanding news lies in putting it in the perspective of the readers, the audience that the reporter serves. Let's use that key to examine each part of the definition:

1. *Current.* A standard professional cliché is that yesterday's news-is only good for wrapping fish or lining bird cages. The value of the commodity that is packaged in that roll of newsprint—news—evaporates like a shallow puddle of water on a sunny summer day.

News simply doesn't keep. A story of such importance as President Richard Nixon's resignation in the Watergate scandal quickly faded in value, replaced by the ascent of Mr. Ford to the White House. This, in turn, was soon replaced by President Ford's pardon of Mr. Nixon for whatever transgression he may have committed while in office. Each story dominated page one for a day or so, slid to inside pages as follow-up events occurred, then drifted into the never-never land of public memory as time passed.

The flow of news is such that regardless of how important a story may be, it is quickly pushed into history by still other important events.

Currency, then, is a major determinant. In a metropolitan area, a page-one story in the morning newspaper normally moves inside the afternoon newspaper, unless important new developments are uncovered, then disappears from the pages completely as fresh, important twists taper out.

This does not mean that a reporter on an afternoon newspaper can ignore any story carried by the morning competition. An important story can dominate news for several days, as long as new disclosures are forthcoming, and as long as public interest in the matter is strong.

2. *Event.* Most news stories occur as an event that happens at a given time and place. A crime is an event, in that the specific occurrence of the act can be pinpointed. An announcement, a meeting or campaign rally, a disaster, or an election is also an event.

A distinguishing characteristic of a story about an event is that it invariably carries some reference to the time and place of occurrence. Currency is all important, as newspersons struggle to inform readers of the particulars of the event before its importance diminishes.

3. *Situation.* A situation doesn't necessarily occur, it simply *exists.* Perhaps a public official has been accepting bribes for several months. When that situation is uncovered and disclosed in the newspaper, the situation becomes news. If a political figure is found to hold several dilapidated houses in the city slum, using his official powers to ward off city building inspectors who seek to have safety and health violations repaired to protect tenants, then that situation becomes news as soon as it is reported.

News that is based on an existing situation is characterized by the strange trait that it doesn't become news until it is disclosed to the public—the act of exposing it creates the news. While news stories based on situations are rarer than those based on events, they tend to be more important and more satisfying to the enterprising reporter than coverage of events that are there for any newsperson to cover.

At times, news of a situation can create news of events. Turning again to the Watergate scandal, the dogged exploration of the vast web of wrongdoing uncovered great news stories based on a situation. These, in turn, sparked a series of momentous events that became great news stories. Yet, the journalistic investigation was initially launched by a "third-rate burglary" of Democratic National Headquarters—news of an event.

4. *Interest.* Reader interest in the event or situation is a vital factor, in that newspaper stories are aimed at these customers. The effect of reader interest is especially evident in the treatment of crime news. The act of homicide is the same, whether by knife, gun, or hands. Yet, editors may determine that one homicide rates much greater play than another that occurred on the same night, because of potential reader interest.

To illustrate, let's take two hypothetical murders and evaluate them for reader interest:

Case A: A twenty-one-year-old man was killed in a barroom brawl as he argued with a friend about a gambling bet. The argument grew more heated until his friend whipped out a cheap handgun and shot the victim twice. The suspect immediately gave the gun to the bartender, and waited for police to come and arrest him.

Case B: A ninety-year-old man was killed in a barroom brawl as he argued with a ninety-one-year-old friend about the weather. The argument climaxed when the assailant broke his walking cane over the victim's head, killing him. The suspect remained at the scene to surrender to police.

Any self-respecting news editor could see that Case B offers much more appeal to reader interest because of the bizarre nature of the murder weapon and because of the advanced ages of both victim and suspect. Which story would appeal more to your interest? Good news editors are often blessed with a child-like fascination for such interesting quirks that enables them to perceive items of reader interest with a fresh excitement, even after decades of exposure to a huge volume of news. Such a blessing is also vital to reporters, who must be able to recognize, to discern those qualities that separate the routine from the truly interesting items.

5. *Significance.* Some important news items are extremely low on the reader-interest scale, yet vitally important to the well-being of the citizens. A story on a complicated, subtle change in zoning policy may be about as popular with readers as a dose of bitter medicine. Yet the impact is important enough to warrant prime positioning of the story in the newspaper.

Imagine, if you will, a headline that proclaims:

CITY COUNCIL PONDERS
ZONING POLICY CHANGES

To assume that the reader is aware of the meaning of "zoning policy changes" may be overly optimistic, in the first place. But, even if the reader perceives the drift of the headline, chances are that he won't delve into the story that follows.

Why should the reader wade through a story about such dull and complicated matters? Because a change in zoning policy—city rules that govern how land can be used—may affect almost every property owner in town. Moreover, the headline implies that city council has not yet reached a decision on changes, thus the citizen still has time to express his opinions and desires to proper officials, once he familiarizes himself with the issues by reading the story.

Sadly, all too few citizens exercise this right and responsibility of being informed and of expressing informed opinions. Yet, in assessing the value of such news items, reporters and editors are obliged to make such stories available, not only on the basis of news value, but as part of the public service function inherent in the profession of journalism.

It should be noted that many major news stories are both interesting and significant. Stories about results of a city election, a confrontation between parents and school officials, a sudden increase in crime, or a speech by a major political candidate contain both values.

6. *Substantial part of the readership.* A given news item must have interest or significance to many readers to justify its inclusion in the newspaper. The newspaper is a mass medium, designed to convey information to a very broad and varied audience. The narrower the

segment of that audience to which an item appeals, the less news value it has.

For example, a story on city election results offers interest and significance to all readers who live in the city. A story about a new pattern of one-way streets affects and interests the large number of citizens who drive in the downtown area. An item about a proposed new center for performing arts would stir excitement among readers who enjoy music and live theatre. The selection of a new executive secretary of the chamber of commerce would appeal to the business community. A new labor contract at a city industrial plant would interest readers who are directly or indirectly affected by the provisions. And a story about the untimely demise of Mrs. MacDonald's cat would greatly interest Mrs. MacDonald, her family, and possibly the next door neighbor. Needless to say, the cat's obituary would hardly be considered newsworthy.

Even when armed with a solid understanding of the nature of news, a reporter often faces the problem of encountering too much of it. By any definition, the commission of a felonious crime is news, yet, the police reporter in any large city encounters scores of felony reports each day. Obviously, it is impossible for one person to write a separate news story on each crime. It is, moreovor, impossible for the newspaper to provide space for such comprehensive crime coverage, particularly when considering that each newsbeat, to different degrees, faces a similar overabundance of news items. A newspaper is not a bulletin board for news items. It is, instead, a means of presenting the small fraction of all available news items that are deemed most interesting and important.

Obviously, someone must exercise careful judgment in selecting items for coverage and inclusion. Much of that responsibility falls on the reporter, who must quickly decide whether to pursue or neglect a given item. The wisdom of his decisions quickly become apparent when competing newspaper and electronics media reporters' selections are published. If the reporter persists in discarding items that receive major emphasis in other media, then his days of employment may be numbered.

So, how does a reporter acquire this wondrous ability to accurately select news items for a substantial part of his readership?

Fortunately, most significant news is obvious to anyone with reasonable intelligence. Even a novice police reporter would conclude that a triple homicide at city hall is worth pursuing. The most inept city hall reporter would decide to write a story about the mayor's resignation. And even an imbecile would give a military takeover of the city by Ugandan troops a few modest lines of copy. Yet, many good news items become stories only because one reporter was more perceptive than his colleagues. A "routine" burglary may become page-one news when one alert reporter notices that the address of the victimized home is that of the police chief. A zoning change on a small parcel of land from single-family residential to commercial may be overlooked by a dozen reporters before one newsperson delves a bit further to find that a major new department store will be built on the land. A routine obituary notice may blossom into national news when someone notices that the deceased was once a powerful national labor leader who had retired years ago to live quietly in the city.

It is this kind of perception and alertness that separates the true professional from his run-of-the-mill competitors.

While much of this ability to perceive news is derived from such virtues as talent, experience, and intelligence, the rudiments of news selection can be examined logically and methodically, using general guidelines for determining news value. Here are key elements to be used in evaluating news:

ELEMENTS OF NEWS

Timeliness: As discussed in the definition of news, the value of any item of information decreases rapidly after initial publication. Without major news developments, a story that ran on page one of the morning newspaper would receive only minor play in the afternoon newspaper. Essentially, the target audience for the story has been reduced to those readers who did not see or hear reports of the item in other news media.

Proximity. The distance between the reader and the effects of the event or situation is inversely related to reader interest. A major fire that guts a local industrial plant is page-one news. If the fire occurred in a nearby city, the story is considerably less important. If the fire occurred in a faraway city, it becomes a small filler on page 40. If the fire occurred in Outer Mongolia, it isn't of value to the local newspaper.

Sometimes, the effects of a story are so far-reaching that the physical distance factor is diminished. A story from the state capital, a hundred miles away, concerning a bill to raise state income taxes is major news because its impact is felt by local citizens. Yet, a similar action by legislators in a neighboring state is ignored because readers aren't affected.

Prominence: Although it may seem undemocratic, some people are simply more newsworthy than others. The degree of prominence of those involved in an event or situation directly influences the value of the news.

If Barbara Davidson, a journalism student at State University, encounters a stubborn tree while rushing down a ski trail, breaking three tree limbs and a leg, the painful event wouldn't raise a single eyebrow among local reporters. But if Barbara Davidson, Mayor of Denver, encountered the same tree with the same unhappy results, the accident would be news.

Any ordinary citizen can receive newspaper coverage by involvement in an extraordinary event, such as a grisly crime. Yet, very prominent people can receive heavy news coverage for even minor, everyday mishaps or misdeeds. This is especially true when normally minor occurrences affect the public performance of a public figure. If the mayor suffers a broken leg from a skiing accident, and if that injury impedes the official's ability to perform her public duty for several days, it's news.

Oddity. Unusual, bizarre, or humorous twists to otherwise routine news events may greatly enhance news value. A typical holdup of an all-night carry-out store may escalate in value when the reporter notes that the two gunmen who pulled the robbery did so in the nude. The birth of twins at the local hospital is common enough, but the arrival of quintuplets is news.

Oddity is often a subtle trait, requiring alertness on the part of a reporter. A dull school board meeting may provide a choice item for a perceptive reporter who knows a good story angle when he sees it.

Perhaps a board member dozes during part of the proceedings, only to be jarred into consciousness by the sound of his name.

"Mr. Peters, how do you vote?" the chairman asks impatiently.

Peters desperately seeks a means of knowing how to cast his vote, without admitting his embarrassing lapse into slumber. He turns to the board member sitting beside him and asks, "How did you vote?"

His colleague grins at his discomfort and says, "I voted yes."

"Then, I vote no," the napping official proclaims with relief.

The befuddled performance didn't go unnoticed by one reporter who perceived what had happened. The two board members had bitterly feuded with each other for years. The sleepy, inane "no" vote gave him a means of conveying this significant enmity to his readers, using the sharp edge of humor. The issue that was the subject of the embattled vote was whether to approve the minutes of proceedings from the previous meeting.

Impact. The broad effect of a news item is an essential ingredient in judging its value. The impact can be generally ascertained by measuring a given news item against this question:

How greatly does it affect people who read the newspaper?

If the police reporter is aware of a general dissatisfaction among policemen about a small pay raise offered by the city, he may decide to forego writing a story until more tangible reactions develop. Grumpy policemen who continue to perform their work are not necessarily newsworthy. Except for the families of policemen, who must put up with gloomy husbands and fathers, the citizenry as a whole feels little impact from the dissatisfaction.

But if the reporter discerns an alarming drop in police performance because of this dissatisfaction, the unhappy policemen become news. If they escalate their dissatisfaction by taking job actions, such as a work slowdown or an outbreak of the "blue flu"—mass absenteeism on a given day—then the situation becomes an enormously important news story because everyone in the city is affected or potentially affected by the deterioration of police protection.

Numbers. The number of people involved in a given news event, or the number of related occurrences affects the value of the story.

A report of a vandal throwing a rock at a car and shattering the windshield isn't especially newsworthy. But when a hundred vandals go on a destructive spree, smashing forty car windows, then the incident becomes a full-scale riot.

Similarly, if two cars engage in a fender-bender on the freeway, it's not worth news space. But if thirty cars pile up in a massive accident, it is.

The news value of numbers reflects that part of the definition of news that concerns the range of effect of the item. A two-car pileup affects only the victims, their families, and the other motorists who are inconvenienced by the mishap. A thirty-car chain collision would affect a great number of people who were involved or inconvenienced by the mishap. Numbers also reflect an oddity. A two-car collision is common, but a massive multi-car crunch is unusual.

Sometimes, the numbers value can be attained by finding a common thread with which to tie together separate events. A single holdup of a store for a relatively small amount of money is common in a large city. In fact, a dozen such robberies during a given night is not unusual. Yet, if the reporter notes that the same pair of thugs staged all twelve robberies, then he has a major news story about the hardworking holdup men.

Emotion. Some news items have a strong appeal to human emotion, which greatly increases their value. A story that appeals to the readers' fear, sympathy, anger, desire, or other emotions will stimulate considerable interest. The readers, after all, are human beings who can be aroused by stories that indicate a threat to their safety or well-being, appeal to their baser instincts or egos, or evoke feelings of sorrow or pity.

Crime stories often carry potential emotional appeal. If a crazed sniper or mad bomber is running loose, most readers may feel a genuine fear. A story about a massive crackdown on prostitution, especially one that contains spicy details, can draw out baser desires. As for anger, more than one lynching has occurred over the years when a newspaper detailed alleged outrages by some hapless prisoner.

The latter example should serve to underline an important point: Stories that involve extremely emotional stimuli should be handled with responsible restraint so that the public isn't prodded into unwise actions or a collectively unreasonable state of mind. To illustrate, a police reporter was riding around with an officer one night, collecting material for a feature story, when the officer was dispatched to investigate a burglary complaint. An elderly woman tearfully greeted the policeman and explained that her tool shed had been broken into. The woman was afraid and nearly hysterical. After gently questioning the woman, then chatting with neighbors, the policeman found that the "burglars" were neighborhood boys who had entered the shed to retrieve a baseball that had bounced inside through the open door.

After telling the children to politely ask the woman for permission to retrieve the ball in the future, the policeman calmed her by relaying an apology from the children.

"I'm just scared to death with all this crime around here," the woman explained. "It's just not safe to walk the streets."

After leaving the house, the policeman said, "This has to be the safest neighborhood in the city. A felony around here is unheard of, but people read the stories you write about the city's high crime rate, and they get scared. They don't understand that the problem isn't in good neighborhood, it's a case of poor people robbing other poor people. But crime stories have created a general fear in the whole city."

Although the problem of reporting crime news in a manner that doesn't lend itself to such misunderstandings is complex—perhaps without an acceptable solution—a reporter cannot include a catch-all disclaimer in each story to the effect that some neighborhoods are perfectly safe; the incident served as a reminder to the reporter to handle emotional stories with care.

Caution should not be misinterpreted to mean that emotion-stirring aspects of news stories should be ignored or downplayed to the point of distortion. If a grisly crime occurs that may evoke emotions of anger or fear, then the reporter is obliged to report the incident completely and accurately. Yet, if a story obviously contains implications that can be misleading or inflammatory, the reporter must exercise special care to maintain a clear perspective for readers.

Consequence. Frequently, a news item may appear to be of minor or narrow effect, yet, upon closer examination, the item's news value may be much more significant because of indirect consequences.

During a city election, for example, the arrest of the mayor's nephew on a charge of selling narcotics could have a great impact on the mayor's chance for re-election. The same story, without the election circumstance, would receive relatively minor play.

This type of scenario is very common: A set of circumstances or a prior chain of events may create a tinderbox effect, to be ignited by a normally minor news item. Long-standing injustices and grievances in an urban ghetto may explode or accelerate to a level of dangerous tensions, sparked by a routine police action that would normally have gone unnoticed.

The consequence factor often requires interpretative reporting. If the city hall reporter perceives that a certain legislative action is a maneuver that portends legislation of great consequence, he must somehow convey that consequence in his news story, even though, in itself, the action is seemingly minor.

For example, a zoning-change request may seek to designate an old residential area for commercial development. By itself, the action is logical and beneficial, since the neighborhood has, in recent years, deteriorated badly. Yet, an alert reporter notes an oddity: the neighborhood is a tiny pocket of black residents in a predominantly white section of the city; and it is the city's oldest black neighborhood. Residents oppose the rezoning because they hope to maintain the cultural neighborhood identity that has been passed down among several families from generation to generation. The reporter also learns that the residents' attempts to secure loans and urban renewal funds for property improvements have been systematically thwarted by planners who see their homes as obstacles to logical progress. The consequence of the rezoning action suddenly pushes the story into prominence.

Perhaps the best measure of consequence lies in a reporter's imaginative extension of probable effects of a given news item through the question, "I wonder what will happen if . . ."

Eyewitness. Invariably, the value of any news story increases when a reporter is physically present at the event. This is partly because of the professional advantage of having a trained observer on hand to recognize the human drama and to capture the flavor of the event, thus making the story more vivid and complete. Of equal importance, such eyewitness accounts of news events provide boosts to the professional image of the newspaper. Readers perceive, and are impressed by, the aggressive, competent, first-hand reporting. A routine drug raid becomes page-one news when the police reporter provides a vivid, exclusive account of how it happened, from the time the front door was open until the suspects were carted away.

Obviously, many news events or situations involve many or even all of these criteria for news selection. The lead story of city election coverage would, to at least some degree, contain most elements.

A logical mind may attempt to formularize the news value criteria to arrive at a flawless, inflexible method for judging the newsworthiness of any given story. Yet the attempt is bound to fail for lack of comprehensive, tangible components.

How can degree of prominence be established? Can impact be recorded on some journalistic seismograph? Would anything as volatile as human emotion lend itself to convenient, objective measurement? The answer is that such notions are absurd. Human subjective judgment is the only practical means of assessing the gravity of a given news item. A reporter must exercise that judgment, based on experience, knowledge, and sometimes intuition, as he seeks to assess whether one news item is of greater interest and/or significance to his readers than another.

The elements of news, as listed previously, are meant only to serve as a general listing of factors that must be considered when a reporter exercises this news judgment.

To take a realistic look at the news judgment process, let's examine the problem of a police reporter as he looks over his listing of prospective stories and tries to rank them according to news value priority so that he can allot his limited time properly.

News items include:

1. A $5,000 house burglary, in which the criminal climbed into the living room window at the home of Julian P. Jackson, the city prosecutor, and ransacked the house. The Jacksons came home early from a party and walked in on the armed burglar, who quickly bound and gagged them as he completed his work. Neither victim was harmed.

2. The shooting death of a sixty-one-year-old watchman at a warehouse, in another burglary. The watchman was shot in the back. Nothing was removed from the warehouse, as the burglars apparently fled after the shooting.

3. A narcotics raid that netted heroin with a street value of $200,000. Three suspected drug dealers were arrested.

4. The robbery detectives claim to have arrested six members of a gang of robbers who have allegedly committed more than eighty holdups within the past year.

5. A fatal automobile accident, in which a drunken driver lost control of his car and smashed into a bridge abutment during rush hour, causing a mile-long traffic jam on the freeway.

6. The announcement of a controversial new police firearms policy that would prohibit the officers' use of their revolvers, except when they or innocent citizens are directly threatened by an armed suspect. Policemen have reacted bitterly since the early morning announcement, arguing that the new policy may endanger officers by causing them to hesitate in drawing their weapons at a critical moment.

In establishing his priorities, the police reporter has no time to pull out a handy checklist of news values to rank the stories. Instead, he uses his experience and knowledge to assess the slate.

Here is his priority list:

1. *Firearms policy.* The impact of the action potentially affects every citizen in the city, since police performance is affected. The

possible consequences in the form of damage to police morale and, in turn, police protection can be severe and lasting.

2. *House burglary.* Although homicide normally rates far greater importance than burglary, this burglary involved a prominent victim, an unusual quirk (victims encountered the burglar in the act), and a strong emotional appeal to readers. The horror of encountering an armed burglar in the sanctity of your own home is frightening. Moreover, it evokes a lingering fear of house burglars that many people share.

3. *The homicide.* Murder evokes a strong emotion of fear, especially when murderers are still at large. This fear is heightened, in this case, because the watchman was mercilessly shot in the back.

4. *Narcotics raid.* This major drug "bust" receives the nod over the robbery detectives' arrests because the consequence in abating drug traffic in the city is considerable, and because drug problems arouse emotions among many parents. Also, drug addiction is a major, underlying cause of much crime, as desperate addicts seek money to support $60-a-day drug habits. Oddity is also present in the form of the unusually large amount of drugs recovered.

5. *The robbery arrests.* While citizens may feel a bit less threatened by the removal of the thugs from the streets, and the consequence of perhaps slightly abating the robbery rate may exist, the reporter's experience leads him to deflate the importance of the story. He knows that zealous detectives often "clear the books" by convincing cooperative criminals to admit to crimes that they didn't commit in exchange for charging them with only one or two of the crimes. This improves their crime clearance rate considerably.

6. *The fatal automobile accident.* While the death of the intoxicated driver, and the frustrations of inconvenienced motorists, is newsworthy, the accident had no lasting consequence (except to the driver). Its news value appeal lies in some emotional identification—most drivers share a reasonable fear of fatal accidents—and the number of people temporarily affected.

In each of the news items, proximity and timeliness existed to different extents, and shared some oddity, emotion, and impact.

SUMMARY

While the reporter in this example did not consciously use the guidelines to analyze news value, a close examination discloses their presence in his decisions.

Each day, on each newsbeat assignment, a reporter makes several such decisions, assuming the burdensome responsibility of determining just which items will be offered to inform the newspaper's readers.

The listing of story choices that the police reporter faced in the example is merely the collection of "finalists," stories that survived his earlier process of screening and decision-making. The five stories were the choice items from a stack of a hundred separate offense reports, a dozen departmental press releases, and a morning press conference that touched on several police policy items.

The choices and the criteria in assessing news value also vary considerably with the size of the city. A family quarrel that ends in a homicide may have little news value in New York City. But a similar incident in Greeley, Colorado, is possibly page-one news.

A reporter, then, must not only be able to recognize news, but to accurately assess the interests of readers in his own city, and the significance of a given item in the context of that community.

EXERCISES

1. Clip each news story on page one of your local newspaper, then determine why each is considered news. Identify the elements of news contained in each story.

2. Rank the following news item examples according to overall news value. Explain your logic in the placement of each story:

   a. City Councilman Roger McClellan is hospitalized following a mild heart attack. A hospital spokesman said McClellan is in "fair" condition, and is expected to recover. He will, however, require extended rest to recuperate.

   b. A three-alarm fire burns down the Colonial Hotel, the city's oldest landmark. The fire, which investigators attribute to arson, injured six firemen, but none of them required hospitalization.

   c. A ten-year-old girl was arrested by a policeman who saw her trying to crawl into the window of a house at midnight. The girl admits to a dozen other burglaries in her neighborhood. Her father is a prominent physician.

   d. City Hall reporter discovered that City Council had secretly agreed to have a tax increase referendum placed on the ballot, despite public assurances that taxes would be lowered.

   e. The teachers' association issues an ultimatum to the school board, threatening to authorize a strike if the board does not agree to contract-negotiation demands.

5 | Ethics and Libel

The reporters squirmed impatiently as the newspaper's attorney briefed the staff on the fundamentals of libel in an annual lecture that the company considered a prudent preventive measure—and which the veteran reporters considered a bore. After all, most of the journalists were experienced professionals who considered themselves well versed on libel.

Almost as an afterthought, the attorney said, "Of course, you all know that a quotation is not really a defense against libel, if the remark is malicious and false."

Suddenly, several reporters sat bolt upright in their chairs.

"You don't mean direct quotes, do you?" a ten-year veteran asked hopefully. "You mean paraphrases, right?"

"Wrong," the attorney said. "If you accurately and directly quote a remark that is false and malicious, and if you fail to take reasonable measures to ascertain its validity, then you may, under certain circumstances, face a solid libel suit."

In the moment of stunned silence that followed, reporters frantically tried to recall quotations that they had used in that day's edition, which had passed the final deadline an hour earlier.

"But, we aren't making the statement, we're simply repeating what someone else said," another reporter suggested desperately.

"Then you will have company," the attorney replied. "While you are being sued for libel, the originator of the remark can be sued for slander."

The point of this exchange is that libel laws are far too serious and complicated to be taken lightly. Although the journalists all possessed an extensive knowledge of libel, they had unknowingly flirted with legal suits for many years.

While freedom of the press is among this nation's constitutional cornerstones, it by no means provides journalists with an invitation to infringe on the rights of other citizens. Two major forms of restraint exist to govern the conduct of the press: legal restraints, such as libel and statutes protecting individual privacy; and ethical restraints that govern the profession to ensure that the great responsibilities of the press to the public aren't somehow lost in the heat of competition.

Perhaps every reporter should occasionally remind himself that the press card is not a license. A reporter has no special privileges that aren't granted to any other American citizen. He cannot trespass on private property if the owner demands that he leave, even if every policeman in town is present. He cannot use newspaper space to maliciously inflict vengeance on his worst enemy without facing possible legal action. He cannot indulge in personal prejudices by writing ethnic jibes against, say, red-haired Americans, without risking professional repercussions from his editors and colleagues who adhere to the ethics of the profession.

INVASION OF PRIVACY

Although laws differ from state to state, a reporter must be aware of the distinction between individuals who are public figures and those who are not. The legal ramifications entailed in the commission of an error can be severe.

In general, a reporter should not prepare a story that:

1. Concerns the lawful actions of a citizen who does not seek the public spotlight or hold a position of public trust unless those action constitute legitimate news.

For example, a reporter may not safely write a story about:

(a) A neighbor's poor taste in choosing the color of his house paint.

(b) A plumber's flirtation with a waitress.

(c) The horsethief great grandfather of his worst enemy.

The reporter *can* write stories about:

(a) The neighbor's house-paint horror, if it violates city ordinances and instigates a neighborhood brawl.

(b) The plumber's flirtation, if it escalates to rape, or if it fuels a marital dispute that ends in violence.

(c) A horsethief who is, incidentally, the reporter's worst enemy.

(d) An automobile accident involving the neighbor, the plumber, the waitress, and/or the worst enemy. A news event supersedes privacy rights.

2. Concerns the non-public aspects of the life of a public figure. This is often a matter of delicate judgment, since the lives of sports

stars, public officials, and celebrities often lack clear definition between public and private areas.

A reporter should exercise extreme caution in reporting such events as:

(a) A sexual affair conducted by a professional football player, a celebrity, or even a public official, unless that event somehow affects that person's projected public image or public performance. The most publicized of such events involved participants who were political figures, and whose escapades raised serious questions about the performance of their public duties. A liaison between a minor city official and a co-worker may have no effect on the performance of public duties.

(b) A personal embarrassment outside the domain of public life. A family problem, such as poor grades attained by the mayor's son at school, hardly qualifies as legitimate news.

Yet, a reporter may safely write a story about:

(a) A public (or private) figure who is arrested for soliciting a prostitute, for violating other laws in his or her conduct, or whose involvement could influence public performance.

(b) A public figure whose personal embarrassment may affect public performance, or stems from a violation of the law. If the mayor's son is arrested for burglary, it's news. If the mayor's outlandish table manners offend a visiting foreign dignitary, then his job effectiveness is affected.

Please note that in each case cited, the truth of the allegation is not in question. Even if absolutely correct and provable, an allegation that constitutes invasion of privacy is still subject to legal consequences. If the allegation is false or unproven, then the legal consequences may escalate to libel.

LIBEL

The ultimate repercussion that looms over the head of each reporter, each time he hands a story to his city editor, is libel. Besides obvious legal and financial penalties entailed, the loss of a libel suit that arises from a reporter's story may forever damage his professional reputation and undermine his career.

The mere threat of libel blunts the aggresiveness of some reporters, and muffles the voice of less courageous newspapers. Any crime story carries with it the constant peril of libel, thus making the police beat the most vunerable of all reporting jobs. An exposé of any wrongdoing or incompetence has libel potential. In fact, any reporter who conscientiously seeks to meet his "watchdog" responsibilities to the public must constantly tread through a minefield of potential libel.

In recent years, the alarming increase in the number and costs of successful libel suits against newspapers has added to the professional apprehension. Yet, even so, most libel suits are successfully defended by newspapers. Here's why:

1. Many suits are groundless from the onset. Often, the plaintiff simply uses the suit to strike out in anger at the newspaper, even though chances of winning are nil. A public figure who is harshly criticized or severely damaged by an article or editorial may file suit in an attempt to discredit the unfavorable publicity—even when he knows that he is wrong. Other suits are filed by citizens who simply don't understand libel, sometimes even after attorneys advise against it.

2. Reasonable professional conduct by newspapers removes much of the threat of a libel loss. If a newspaper makes a reasonable attempt to ascertain validity of material, prints a correction as soon as the error is evident, and errs without malice, chances of a libel judgment against the publication are greatly reduced. Such high professional standards have become increasingly important, in view of recent trends. Recent damage awards have been a staggering departure from older cases, especially with a United States Supreme Court ruling that invites state courts to award damages for such "speculative" damages as mental anguish.

3. Newspapers often obtain top legal counsel to review potentially libelous material before publication and to provide top-quality defense when a suit is filed. Few individuals can afford equally superb attorneys.

4. Most journalists do have a solid understanding of libel fundamentals, especially those in high-risk specialities. They avoid libel from the beginning.

5. By practicing the basics of competent reporting, a reporter's chances of committing libel are slim. Any item of information should be routinely verified—especially if the item is potentially damaging.

6. Ironically, many individuals who have solid grounds for a libel suit never file one. As noted, the police beat is the riskiest area because innocent citizens can easily be misidentified as suspects. Yet, time and again, editors have unruffled the feathers of such irate victims by apologizing and quickly providing a retraction. To many, a legal action simply isn't worth the hassle.

7. Many cases are settled out of court, with the newspaper paying a sum in exchange for the dropping of the suit. This practice leaves the newspaper's reputation untarnished by a libel loss, and provides the victim with a money settlement without a long court battle. While the settlement may be far less than the victim initially sought, it may still be a very high price to pay for an innocent mistake. Recently, settlements have been getting larger, since news media face the bleak prospect of trying libel cases before unsympathetic jurors. While a

settlement for $10,000 or $20,000 seems small in comparison with, say, a $100,000 judgment initially sought, most reporters consider it a very stiff price to pay for a momentary lapse of judgment.

With this perspective of libel, a reporter is clearly obliged to do everything in his power to avoid such potentially costly errors. Despite such dangers, however, a reporters should not overreact to the threat to the point that he no longer performs his "watchdog" responsibility for the public. With a clear understanding of the nature of libel, and with a rigid adherence to the basics of professional conduct, a journalist may aggressively seek to expose wrongdoing.

While libel is far too complex to be comprehensively examined in the space of one brief chapter, the material below serves to outline the basic principles of libel that a reporter should know for daily use.

Definition: Libel is the publication of false and malicious material that depicts an individual, a business or organization, or a limited and identifiable segment of the citizenship in a derogatory manner that holds the aggrieved party up to public ridicule, a contempt, or hatred, and detracts from that party's reputation within the community.

While the definition is lengthy, the essentials are:

1. *Publication.* Libel cannot be committed without the act of publication. Material must be printed or broadcast to constitute libel. Since the American press is not subject to prior censorship, no action can be taken until the damage has been inflicted. However, conversations that convey the defamatory material are subject to legal action for slander.

2. *False and/or malicious.* This allegation *normally* must be false, and it *normally* must be published with either intent to damage—even though the falsehood is known—or with reckless or negligent disregard, without a reasonable effort to ascertain accuracy. However, in rare cases, the act of malice, alone, can constitute libel—even if the material is true. State laws vary somewhat in this area.

3. *Depicts an individual,* a business, an organization, or a highly limited, identifiable group *in a derogatory manner.*

   (a.) Depicts does not translate into "states." It may be in the form of a direct allegation, innuendo, or a direct or indirect quotation.

   (b.) An individual, a group of individuals, or an organizational entity can be libeled.

   (c.) Derogatory manner. The material must be unfavorable.

4. *Detracts from reputation.* The standing of the aggrieved party in the community is damaged by the material. A business must establish that a financial loss was incurred. Until recently, the injured party had to establish that his or her reputation had been damaged

in the community. However, the latest trends are for large judgments to be awarded, even with little evidence of impairment of reputation. Instead, awards are made for "actual injury."

Types of Libel

Essentially, libel occurs in three forms:

1. *Libel per se*. The accusation is clearly stated, and the accused is directly identified.

Example: Mayor Jones accepts bribes from real estate operators.

2. *Libel per quod*. The accusation and/or identity of the defaced party is clouded in innuendo, yet the identity of the party and the allegation can be discerned by some readers. A variation: If material leads readers to identify the *wrong* party with the alleged misdeed, libel may exist.

Example: The city's top elected official spends evenings at The Joy Club on Route 1. In this case, the mayor is the implied protagonist. If The Joy Club is a notorious house of ill repute just outside of town, and if many town people know it, then the mayor has been indirectly accused of improper conduct. If the allegation is false, the mayor may be able to collect libel damages.

3. *Indirect libel*. A direct quotation or paraphrase containing the elements of libel constitutes indirect libel. The victim may sue the source of the quotation for slander, as well as the newspaper for libel —unless the reporter made a reasonable attempt to verify the charge.

Defenses Against Libel

Although libel can occur in even the briefest mental lapse by a reporter, the newspaper may avoid losing a libel suit, even over an error involving a clear instance of libel. A glance at the basic defenses against libel shows why:

1. *Provable Truth*. Although truth is not an absolute defense in most states, it is by far the most effective. Only in extremely rare instances can a newspaper suffer a judgment against it for accurate material. However, the newspaper must be able to legally establish that material is true.

2. *Privilege*. Some informational sources offers immunity from livel, even if the information is false. Two types of privilege exist:

(a.) *Unconditional Privilege*. By law, reporters may report information from a few specific sources with immunity from libel, even if the reporter knows that the material is false and malicious. Proceedings on the floor of the United States Congress are *Unconditionally Privileged*.

(b.) *Conditional Privilege*. Most public records and meetings, official statements by governmental entities, and court proceedings offer conditional privilege: Material can be safely used as long as the reporter isn't aware of an error or falsehood. For example: A reporter quotes a witness who testifies in a trial that a police officer has accepted bribes. If the testimony is later proven false, the officer cannot successfully sue the newspaper, unless he can establish that the reporter knew that the allegation was false but maliciously printed as truth to settle an old personal grudge.

3. *Fair Comment and Criticism.* While hopefully restricted from news pages—except when quoted—the printing of an opinion that criticizes the public performance of a public figure is defendable. An editorial can safely accuse the city manager of incompetence, a critic may happily "pan" a new play, or a sports writer may criticize the quarterback's game performance. This is guaranteed as a form of freedom of speech. However, this defense does not apply to the non-public aspects of the life of a public official. The mayor may be accused of incompetence, but not of alcoholism (unless it can be proven). The quarterback can be criticized for shoddy passing, but his personal conduct off the field is not in the realm of fair comment and criticism, unless it directly affects the public aspects of his life.

4. *Absence of malice or negligence.* Even if material is false, the newspapers can either avoid or greatly abate a libel judgment by establishing that the reporter made every reasonable effort to ascertain the truth, and that the material was carried without the malicious intent of harming the victim.

Example: The reporter cross-checks a damaging item of information with three different sources, then reasonably concludes that it is correct. Before printing the item, he confronts the accused and offers him the opportunity to rebut or disprove the allegation. Instead, he is thrown out of the office. A later libel suit would have little chance of success—even if the allegation was provably false.

5. *Retraction.* By far the weakest defense, retraction serves only as a mitigating circumstance that may influence the jury to award a smaller judgment against the newspaper. A retraction is a correction and public apology for a libelous item. Many states have statutes setting forth specific requirements for retractions.

Avoiding Libel

In most instances, the incidence of a libel suit is coupled with a breach in basic ethics or professional reporting practices. Human errors do occur, yet the risk is minimized by the adherence to:

1. *Accuracy.* A reasonable attempt must be made to ascertain accuracy in each story, regardless of how seemingly minor it may be.

2. *Fairness.* Whenever derogatory information is uncovered, the

reporter should make every effort to contact the "other side," so that denials can be included with the allegation or the allegation can be disproven before reaching print. If circumstances make it impossible to contact the subject of the allegation, then the reporter should include a line in the story to that effect, then contact the subject as soon as possible for a follow-up story that would offer the counterview.

ETHICS OF REPORTING

Although cursed with a professional image that misleads many citizens to conclude that a reporter will do anything short of murder to obtain a juicy story, journalism has evolved ethical standards that are religiously followed by most practitioners. While transgressions of ethical conduct are rarely illegal, most reporters adhere to them because:

1. Professional survival is at stake. A reporter's ability to gather information depends greatly on the willingness of news sources to trust him. If a reporter acquires a reputation for dishonesty or questionable ethics, then he may be unable to compete.

2. Most reporters are dedicated professionals who hold their responsibilities in idealistic reverence.

3. Peer pressure against an unethical reporter can be enormous. Most human beings seek the respect and friendship of their co-workers. Professional ostracism often occurs against those lacking in professional conduct.

Journalistic ethics are deeply rooted in a desire to protect the credibility of the publication. Major restraints include:

Objectivity.

A reporter is expected to present a complete, unbiased account of any news item that he covers, without the insertion of personal opinion or prejudices. Major features of objectivity include:

1. *Impartiality.* If a story involves controversy—either directly or implicitly, then the reporter is obliged to offer all viewpoints, with reasonably equal balance. This is far more difficult than it may seem, since reporters often have strong opinions.

2. *Absence of conflict of interest.* Involvement with causes or organization can make a reporter vulnerable to suspicion of partiality. If, for example, a reporter is active in an environmentalist organization, his stories about industries that pollute may be suspect. If he is a member of a political organization, then his political coverage may be influenced. Many reporters decline to join any organization, and care-

fully avoid even the appearance of association with any cause that may become news.

3. *Opportunity of denial.* A subtle threat to objectivity is that of forgoing the step of offering an individual the opportunity to deny or refute an allegation against him. At times, deadline pressures make it impossible to confront the accused, but a reporter is obliged to give even the most villainous fiend a chance to rebut a damaging allegation against him, especially in an exposé. Besides ethical considerations, this step constitutes a major safeguard against libel.

4. *Avoidance of cronyism.* Beat reporters are especially susceptible to this breach of ethics, becoming personally involved with news sources. A police reporter may be tempted to become "one of the guys," an unofficial member of the police force—and an unofficial public relations person. If personal relationships influence news coverage, then cronyism exists.

5. *Avoidance of vengeance.* The flip side of cronyism is vengeance, when a reporter declares a personal vendetta against a particular official. If personal enmity becomes an obsession to "get" a particular individual by unfavorable coverage, objectivity is endangered. This does not mean that a reporter should ignore wrongs committed by an individual who happens to be his worst enemy. Instead, it means that he must not allow personal feelings to influence his reporting.

Honesty

Journalistic lore is filled with age-old tales of reporters who gleefully engaged in fabrication of stories, and other assorted sins. Yet, even when the odds are against being caught, the risk of professional disaster is such that, morality aside, dishonesty is an unwise practice.

1. *Report truth, not fiction.* A mind that can fabricate a brilliant but fictitious event for the enthrallment of readers can be put to better use in reporting actual events. While wholesale fabrication is rare, a few unscrupulous reporters continue to embellish ("enliven") an actual event. A common variation is the "phantom witness," who offers a vivid account, laced with opinionated observations. The reporter has interviewed himself. Another close relative of the phantom witness is the "stage manager," who happily directs or alters the event to make it a better story. An extreme example is the reporter who urges the suicidal woman to jump from the ledge so that he can have his story.

2. *Keep commitments.* If a reporter verbally agrees to accept information on an "off the record" basis, then he cannot ethically break that commitment. The same is true for "not for attribution," or promises to hold a story until an agreed-upon time. These commitments deserve some further examination:

(a.) *Off the record.* A reporter should not agree to accept off-the-record information unless that information cannot be otherwise obtained, and unless the information provides critical background that will enable him to write about other items in their proper context. Once such an agreement is made, however, it is unethical to report the material, or to use it as leverage to obtain it from another source without the permission of the initial source. A point of order: The reporter must agree to accept the off-the-record condition *before* the information is provided. If a source inadvertently discloses confidential information, then, on realizing his error, adds, "but that's off the record," the reporter is not obliged to abide by that.

(b.) *Not for attribution.* If a reporter agrees to accept material on the basis that the source will not be identified, then he is bound to protect that source, regardless of the consequences. Some reporters have been jailed for contempt of court for refusing to disclose sources. While the price is steep, the alternative of identifying confidential sources is professional suicide. However, a reporter should not accept this condition unless there are no alternatives to obtaining the information.

Another problem stemming from "not for attribution" is that some wily officials use such a condition to influence the public while escaping responsibility for their statements. A common example is that of using non-attribution to safely float "trial balloons"—potentially controversial proposals that are aired to gauge public reaction. If reaction is negative, then the proposal can be withdrawn without political damage to the unidentified official. If it is positive, then he can come out of hiding. In short, the news media is manipulated in a highly questionable manner.

Human Decency

The potential for the misuse of the power of the press to aggravate human suffering is vividly illustrated by Nazi Germany's press, which cruelly whipped up a froth of hate against Jewish citizens. The pattern has been repeated, even in the American press, as venom or prejudice against minority citizens has been fanned or reinforced by the news media.

Perhaps the best general summary of ethics in this area is: If a reporter has personal prejudices against a racial, ethnic, religious, ideological, or provincial group, he should leave them at home when he drives to work. Such bias, when it influences the reporting and writing of news, is a major violation of ethics.

Bias creeps into stories in subtle ways, even when the reporter attempts to abide by ethics. Let's examine the problems of bias toward:

1. *Racial or ethnic groups.* The most glaring example is the existence of editorial policy to limit coverage of community news in minority neighborhoods, or to ban inclusion of wedding announcements, organizational news, or even photographs depicting a racially mixed group. While many such policies have been discarded in recent years, bias can continue to creep in. Here are some ethical "don'ts" for reporting minority news:

(a.) Don't use offensive terms in reference to minority groups, even facetiously—and even when you mean no harm. To people who have suffered discrimination for generations, use of such demeaning terms is no laughing matter.

(b.) Don't needlessly reinforce minority stereotypes. Besides the obvious lack of taste entailed, such usage simply distorts the truth. Italian-Americans detest the "Mafia" stereotype, Irish-Americans deplore the hard-drinking image, and Mexican-Americans, Black-Americans, Polish-Americans, Chinese-Americans, and the countless other identifiable racial and ethnic minority groups are rightly offended by stereotypes that belie the decency and valuable endeavors of the majority.

(c.) Don't allow the racial or ethnic origin of the principles involved in an event influence coverage—unless it is a vital factor in the event. If a minority member is a victim of a crime, the value of the story should not be influenced, unless the crime itself involved racial or ethnic aspects that contributed to the event. Yet, if an event hinges on racial significance, then it must be reported fairly. Examples:

The city names its first black police chief.

A prominent Jewish citizen is barred from membership in a civic organization because of discrimination.

A racial dispute occurs within the Fire Department.

(d.) Don't "patronize" minorities. If a minority member official is a scoundrel who misuses public funds, it is no less a crime. Some reporters overreact in their desire to demonstrate their great virtue of being unbiased, shamelssly siding with any minority member involved in the news, and pointedly overlooking misdeeds that, if committed by a non-minority official, would constitute a major scandal. A variation is the media creation of a "spokesman" for a minority community. The idea that one individual can speak for the highly diverse collection of individuals in a minority community is as ludicrous as someone speaking for all white citizens.

It should also be noted that one majority segment of the American population also qualifies for treatment under the same guidelines set for minority citizens: women. The growing awareness of problems of sexual discrimination has emphasized the journalistic need of avoiding stereotype depiction of women. While many male reporters may struggle with the culturally-ingrained image of "a woman's place," it may serve to abate a lingering problem of "editorializing" that has plagued journalism for many years in the form of references to the "cute blonde" or "attractive woman." Unless the male reporter is equally willing to use such adjectives to describe men as "cute blonds" and "attractive man," his discrimination is showing when he uses them.

2. *Religion.* While religious bigotry has mercifully abated somewhat in modern times, as evidenced by the election of a Roman Catholic and, later, a devout Southern Baptist president, the problem lingers. An individual's religious beliefs are a matter of serious business. Religious tolerance has never been one of man's overriding virtues, as witnessed by warfare, pogroms, and oppression throughout history—including current history. Even the most subtle derogatory reference to a religious group can fan human emotions to a dangerous point. With this in mind, the reporter must:

(a.) Refrain from making critical remarks about or indulging in ridicule of a religious belief. If a religious group transgresses against public law or order, then the action, not the beliefs, of the group is the issue.

(b.) Avoid religious stereotypes. President Carter endured some measure of distrust and even ridicule from those who held a negative image of Southern Baptists—even when parts of that image did not reflect the church's beliefs nor its practices. President Kennedy was suspected by some of being subject to political domination by the hierarchy of his church —which wasn't so. Former Secretary of State Henry Kissinger was darkly accused of being biased toward Israel because of his Jewish ancestry—until he was publicly embraced by Egyptian President Anwar Sadat after even-handed diplomacy.

(c.) Refer to religious and religious leaders by their proper names and titles. Misuse is often offensive to the devout members of that body.

3. *Obscenity.* Regardless of a reporter's personal standards of the conversational use of certain words, the newspaper is a form of mass communication to a very broad spectrum of people. While standards constantly change—in the late-nineteenth century, it was considered outrageously improper to use the term "leg" in print—the reporter should refrain from using words that are offensive to community

standards. While "damn" and "hell" have become widely acceptable in print, terms that are considered blasphemous or biologically overly explicit are taboo. Keep in mind that the function of the newspaper is to communicate accurate information to the general public. A word with high-shock potential may detract from the message that is being conveyed.

Another form of obscenity is that of violence. While a police reporter is obliged to compile and convey information necessary for the public to comprehend the nature and extent of the accident or crime, lurid details of gore or savagery serve no real purpose other than to titillate some readers and sicken others. Reporting of gore is, perhaps, a carry-over from the era of sensationalism, in which newspapers routinely carried such detail, often illustrated with pictures of mangled bodies. Many modern newspapers have established editorial policy to spare readers from such ordeals.

Plagiarism

This is perhaps the most commonly violated ethic of journalism: that of printing (or broadcasting) stories as written by other reporters.

The simple use of another reporter's story as a source of information does not necessarily constitute plagiarism. Facts cannot be copyrighted; they can be used by anyone. In fact, normal reporting practices in the writing of a follow-up story allow for the use of a competitor's story as a source of information. Yet, a prudent reporter always verifies his competitor's information, and a competent reporter acquires additional information on his own.

Plagiarism occurs when a reporter copies another's story—or a significant part of it—verbatim, claiming it as his own.

This breach of ethics has instigated many heated, sometimes amusing, battles between journalists. One broadcaster routinely plagiarized newspaper stories, reading them on the air verbatim—typos and all. Once, a reporter sought diabolical revenge against a competitor who often swiped stories from his desk drawer in the police press room. This shady practice is also a form of plagiarism: Stealing information that another reporter gathers, before the story can be filed, thus "scooping" him. The aggrieved reporter gleefully composed a lively story about a sniping incident, then he left the copy in his desk drawer. His competitor filed the story.

In conclusion, the basic ethics of journalism are widely upheld by most reporters, for both moralistic and selfish reasons. A quick glance at the listing of major ethics items illustrates why. The flagrant and repeated violation of any one of these items will, in time, seriously undermine the reputation of the newspaper, the integrity of the profession of journalism as practiced in that locality, and the credibility of the work of every individual journalist in town. Thus, each reporter has a vested interest in the ethical conduct of other reporters.

SUMMARY

Legal and ethical restraints do not pose a problem to any competent reporter. Within the framework of the law and ethics, a reporter can acquire and publish any news story without fear of reprisal. In fact, the extra care that a journalist must take to abide within that framework greatly enhances the reliability of the given story when it is published, and serves to safeguard against careless errors that the reporter would regret personally, even without legal penalties.

Yet, to successfully operate within this framework, a journalist must carefully acquire a basic understanding of the limitations. Excessive caution born of uncertainty or misinformation about restraints is far more hampering than the laws and ethics themselves.

EXERCISES

1. Name the form of libel associated with each of these examples:
    a. The city's number one policeman secretly operates a bookmaking organization with direct links to organized crime.
    b. According to Councilman Joseph Black, City Manager Oscar Phillips "is a chronic alcoholic."
    c. State Sentar Andrew Owens routinely accepts large bribes from lobbyists who represent industries.
2. Assuming that the allegation is false, identify the libel defense associated with these examples:
    a. The newspaper prints a correction and apology in the next issue.
    b. The reporter verified the information with two different sources, then confronted the "victim," who refused to comment on the allegation.
    c. The information was stated on the floor of the United States Senate.
    d. The information was stated during a court trial.
    e. The information was included in an editorial concerning the public performance of an elected official.
3. Discuss the ethical consideration affecting:
    a. A close friendship between a reporter and a policeman, when the newsman witnesses needless brutality toward a prisoner by the officer.

b. A humor columnist who writes a light-hearted account that gently pokes fun at a woman Epsicopal priest's Celebration of Holy Communion.

c. A "rip-and-read" television reporter who reads a story from a newspaper without attributing it.

d. A reporter who accepts information off-the-record from one source, then uses it as an edge to press another source into leaking it.

6 | Tricks of the Trade

The reporter's notebook is one of the most essential tools of his trade. Into that small pad pours a flood of raw data that will give the journalist the material he needs to write any given story.

Although sizes and shapes vary with individual preferences, a favorite style is a small stenographer's notebook that fits snugly in an inside pocket of a sports coat, or in a purse. This convenience is important, because a reporter is rarely without a notebook.

Despite its small size and inanimate nature, the notebook often terrifies journalism students. After being warned of the dangers of libel and the strong ethical responsibility of maintaining accuracy (see Chapter 5), many students question their ability to accurately copy down information—especially direct quotations—from a steady stream of data and thoughts rendered in conversational speed. Indeed, it is humanly impossible to capture an entire conversation in notes without considerable stenographic training. And even the most seemingly innocuous omission can create great misunderstandings.

Suppose that a harassed ancient reporter had failed to catch and record all of the *nots* when Moses read the newly engraved Ten Commandments to the Children of Israel? The world would be in even worse condition today.

With such dangers in mind, reporters have, over the years, developed a simple and effective technique for accurately capturing information in their notebooks. A proficient reporter can conduct an intensive, hour-long interview and write a long story, filled with direct quotation, without misquoting or misstating the facts. The system is modified to fit each reporter's individual style and background, but the essential characteristics are common.

Here is a note-taking system:

1. When listening to the news source, concentrate on catching

and jotting down the essential points. In a normal interview, the source will offer elaboration after each key point. As he elaborates, the reporter may listen with "half an ear" as he uses the time to jot down the vital information or quotation.

2. If the source is providing information or quotations at a pace that exceeds the reporter's ability to scribble it down or understand it, then the reporter may slow him down by requesting elaboration. Some reporters often ask "throw away" questions aimed solely at slowing down a rapid-fire flow of facts. Still another technique is to tell the source candidly that you are afraid that you may not have copied down the information correctly, and ask him to repeat it. Please note that this technique is generally applicable to most newsgathering situations, and not just to formal interviewing.

3. After obtaining all needed information, take time to recheck facts and direct quotations with the news source. Make sure that you *understand* the information. Later, when you write, the raw information may be worthless if you don't know how to fit it together in proper context. Most sources appreciate a reporter's desire to be accurate by rechecking.

4. In jotting down the information, the reporter should:

(a.) Develop his own "shorthand" style. Frequently used words may become a symbol or a standard abbreviation. For example, *with* becomes *w*; *without* becomes *w/o*; *city hall* CH; *police* is *p*; *suspect* is *s*; and so on. Articles, such as *a, the, an*, may be omitted from notes, and later filled in by the natural sentence flow.

For example, a police reporter may jot down these notes:

Schulte: "3 S arm w revol. held up store & escap. w $3,000 noon Th."

Translation: "Three suspects, armed with revolvers, held up the store and escaped with $3,000 at noon Thursday," Lt. Richard Schulte, Chief of Detectives, said today.

You may wonder where some of the above information came from. Remember, the police reporter took the notes. The reporter is very familiar with all major police news sources, including the chief of detectives. He can quickly fill in the full attribution as a matter of course while typing. In fact, he may have a standard abbreviation for each routine news source. Schulte may become Sch.

(b.) Jot down only the key words. Assuming that any news story will be written within a few hours after notes are taken, a reporter can easily train his memory so that, with the help of key words, he can remember a quotation verbatim.

Example:

Mo: "City in good fin shape desp reckl accus by Sm. We hav $2M cush in spec emerg, conting acct. Sm knws fulwl that no dang bankrt. It is self-s pol statem, full lis & ½ trus."

Translation: "The city is in good financial shape, despite the reckless accusations by (Councilman Joseph) Smith," Mayor Moore said at a morning press conference today. "We have a $2 million cushion in a special emergency, contingency account. Smith knows full well that there is no danger of bankruptcy. It is a self-serving political statement, full of lies and half-truths."

A note of warning: If, for some reason, there is a delay in writing the story, the reporter should take time to type out the full quotations before his memory fades. Frequently, a reporter is unable to read his own notes after a few days.

While most newsgathering situations allow reporters to scribble their notes freely and openly, sometimes notetaking becomes complicated.

A city hall reporter may be in the midst of a friendly chat with a bureaucrat in a coffee shop. Then, unexpectedly, the bureaucrat may inadvertently disclose some crucial information about a very newsworthy situation. The reporter faces a problem: The bureaucrat is unaware that he is spilling the beans, and the newsman must carefully conceal his excitement and interest so that the source will continue talking. If the reporter eagerly pulls out his notebook to jot down the information, then the source is immediately advised of his blunder. The flow of information may stop abruptly.

Similarly, if the bureaucrat is knowingly leaking the information under the guise of innocent chatter, he is obviously attempting to protect himself from the "who-leaked-it" inquiry that his supervisor may conduct when the story breaks. If he is seen talking with a reporter who is furiously scribbling down information, then he may face dire reprisals from his bosses when word filters back to them.

The reporter's only options are:

1. Arrange a later, private conversation with the source so that notes can be freely taken. If the leak is unintentional, however, this option is nonexistent.

2. Carefully memorize the most important information as the conversation proceeds and, as soon as the source leaves, jot it down. The drawback here is that the risk of error is considerably greater, and the chances of getting a direct quotation are limited by the keenness of the reporter's memory.

Using a variation of the second option, the reporter may jot down the information, then confront other knowledgeable sources for confirmation or denial, and for direct quotations.

For example, a reporter may have a casual conversation with an engineer from the city planning department. The conversation occurs in the city hall coffee shop, with other officials sitting at nearby tables.

"Boy, have I had a rotten day," the engineer complains. "I'm caught right in the middle of the overpass fight between my boss and the county engineers."

"Yeah, that's a real mess," the reporter says sympathetically, as he silently ponders, "Overpass? What overpass?"

"I made a beautiful design that clears up the congestion at the railroad tracks by Central Station, and it only costs $600,000. That's half the cost of the county plan," the source says grumbling.

"Tell me about your design," the reporter urges soothingly. "I know that you do better work than those clowns over in the county."

The game continues, with the reporter feigning only a friendly, sympathetic interest, and the source pretending to be unaware that he is leaking the story. Both players are well aware of the game: The disgruntled engineer is protecting himself while forcing the issue into the public limelight. The reporter is gathering the ammunition he needs for a good story.

After the conversation, the reporter says, "If you don't mind, I think I'll dig around to see if I can do a little story on this. Can you show me your design?"

"It's up to you about the story, but you will have to ask my boss," the engineer says righteously. "I'm not allowed to give out any information. If it's okay with him, you can see the design."

As the engineer leaves, the reporter jots down the vital information, then hurries to the office of the Director of Planning. Armed with the engineer's information, he can place the Director in the unenviable position of having to confirm the facts and thus become the attributable source, to deny the facts and thus be vulnerable to later public exposure, or to refuse to comment. In such cases, a refusal to comment is essentially a tacit confirmation.

Many other newsgathering situations can hamper notetaking. An investigative reporter may prowl around the city, carefully concealing his identity as he seeks information in an "undercover" role. The presence of a notebook would quickly reveal his occupation, perhaps endangering him, so he must rely on his memory until he can return to his office to make notes. A police reporter who accompanies detectives on a wild, nighttime automobile chase may be far too busy holding onto the armrest for dear life to take notes, asuming that he can scribble legibly in a darkened car interior to begin with.

Notetaking is an essential tool in reporting, yet a reporter must acquire a capability of discerning and remembering important information when it is impossible to use that tool. Note-taking cannot become a crutch. The real storage place for information is the reporter's memory and mind. The notebook is simply a useful key to unlock that memory.

As an alternative means of recording information, reporters may, on occasion, use a tape recorder instead of—or along with—a note-book. Electronics media reporters generally depend more on this gadget than newspaper reporters, because the use of a recorded statement from the news source may be played on the air to add to the effectiveness of the report.

Newspaper reporters, particularly the older reporters, use tape recorders only in special circumstances because of some drawback:

1. Under deadline pressure, use of tape information wastes valuable time. If, for example, a reporter used a tape recorder in covering a speech, he would have to listen to the speech again to pick out key quotes. If an interview is taped, then the reporter must fiddle with the recorder to find vital parts of the interview. If a reporter is skilled in note-taking, the use of a tape recorder is not only superfluous, it is a hindrance in writing the story.

2. A tape recorder intimidates many news sources. The engineer who leaked the story to the city hall reporter would have been un-nerved by the mere presence of a recorder. He may trust the reporter not to reveal his source, but if his voice is taped, then hard evidence exists to prove that he leaked the story, even though it is unlikely that the reporter woud let anyone else hear his voice.

3. A tape recorder immediately puts the news source on guard. The source knows that a slip of the tongue or a sensitive, off-the-record remark may find its way to the tape. Even when the recorder is off, an unscrupulous reporter can quietly hit the "on" button without warn-ing. Still another factor is that human vanity is often injected. The subject may be so intent on avoiding grammatical errors for the benefit of the tape that the flow of information may be impeded.

4. The darned contraptions don't always work. Many reporters can woefully recall horror stories about tape recorders that conked out in the middle of a critical interview or ran out of tape at the wrong time. The human error of pressing the wrong button can be disastrous. And a dead battery can cause a reporter's face to glow a deep red as he tries to explain the missed information to an unsympathetic city editor.

With such drawbacks in mind, it's little wonder that many news-paper reporters simply refuse to use tape recorders.

Yet, when used intelligently, a tape recorder can be a valuable tool:

1. For stories written in question and answer format, the tape recorder is ideal. The reporter simply reads a question and allows the subject to answer it as he likes. The Q & A format requires a verbatim use of quotations, which may try the abilities of even the most skilled note-taker. The information may be edited later to delete conversational banalities.

2. Sensitive, or potentially libelous accusations are best recorded,

particularly if the source is likely to deny making the statements later.

3. In general interview situations, a tape recorder may be used as a backup to note-taking, if the reporter judges that the source will not be intimated by the gadget. In such cases, a good practice is to inform the sources that the recorder is in operation, then place the machine so that it's out of sight. As the interview proceeds, the source may forget about the tape recorder.

As a matter of ethics, the tape recorder should not be used unless the source is aware of its presence and of the on-the-record nature of the interview. The ethical considerations governing the use of recorded material in news stories are identical to those governing the use of notes:

1. When a reporter approaches a public figure or legitimate news source in his occupational capacity as a reporter, anything the source says may be considered usable unless the reporter specifically agrees to allow off-the-record information.

2. Persons who are not public figures and who are not accustomed to dealing with news media should be clearly warned that their remarks may be used in news stories and attributed to them.

3. Information obtained by a reporter who is acting "undercover" must be handled with extreme care:

(a.) If the information comes from a public figure engaged in activity that has a bearing on his public role, then the reporter may print information and quotations, even though the official was unaware that a reporter was nearby.

(b.) Information or remarks by private citizens in a public place may be used if necessary in a story, but the source should not be identified unless permission is obtained.

(c.) Anyone engaged in illegal activities is fair game. A bartender who is accepting gambling bets may be identified and quoted if the reporter can substantiate the illegal activity in court if necessary. Without such solid proof, the reporter is risking libel actions.

(d.) Innocent remarks made by people in a crowd may be quoted freely, but attribution should be made only with the person's permission. A reporter who is covering a disaster may pick up remarks from the crowd of onlookers for use in painting a vivid picture of that disaster.

Telephone Techniques

Besides pen, notebook, and tape recorder, another vital tool in reporting is the telephone. Although most people are fairly familiar with this common gizmo, a new reporter soon learns that newsroom use is far different from home use.

When a major story occurs near deadline time, the telephone

suddenly looms as the only practical means of getting essential information from the scene of the event to the typewriter in time to process it for print. Professional teamwork between the reporter at the scene and the rewrite man in the newsroom must occur in the dictating and assembling of the story through telephone wires.

A veteran reporter and a veteran rewrite man, working together over the telephone, can calmly and efficiently put together a top-quality story under even the most frantic circumstances.

First, let's look at the techniques of dictating a story to a rewrite man:

1. Be calm and coldly rational, regardless of the sometimes hysterical chaos at the scene of a story. A reporter who allows himself to become caught up in the event can rarely operate efficiently in rendering information.

2. Write a lead for the story in your notebook before calling the rewrite man. The lead will often help the reporter organize his thoughts and identify essential information.

3. When the rewrite man is ready, read the information slowly and distinctly. If a word is likely to be misunderstood, spell it out. Spell out all names, unless a name is so commonly known that the rewrite man knows the spelling.

4. If the story is written (common in out-of-town assignments) before dictation, read the story in phrases, stopping after each phrase to allow the rewrite man to catch up. You may be able to hear his typewriter.

5. If a given bit of information should be checked, caution the rewrite man. For example, if the victim's name "rings a bell," ask the rewrite man to check clippings to determine whether the person is more newsworthy than is evident. The victim of a hit-and-run accident may have been a notorious gambler.

6. Don't waste words. If the rewrite man is a close friend, don't inject idle conversation into the gaps between phrases as he catches up. Keep the conversation terse and matter-of-fact.

7. Don't hang up until the rewrite man is through. He may have additional questions to ask that may fill "holes" that you overlooked, or he may want to doublecheck information you provided.

On the other end of the telephone, the rewrite man has his techniques, too:

1. He must learn to wedge the receiver between ear and shoulder so that he may use both hands in typing. To the considerable relief of sore-necked rewrite men, many newspapers now provide operator-styled headsets.

2. Use the brief time necessary to put paper in typewriter to learn the general gist of the story:

"What do you have?" the rewrite man asks.

"Hit-and-run fatality—maybe deliberate," the reporter replies.

3. Establish a rhythm of dictation-typing. Lift the paper guide from the carriage of the typewriter so that the clatter of your typewriter is magnified. This will help the reporter adjust his dictation to your typing speed.

4. Type as rapidly as possible and signal the reporter with a "yeah" each time you want him to resume dictation. A crisp "whoa" will slow him if he is going too fast.

5. Listen closely to information as you type. If the reporter neglects to spell out a name, stop him and request it. If he has missed a critical bit of information, question him. Lead him through the story.

6. If the reporter seems shaken or excited, calm him down. Neither of you can do the job if communications are threatened by his excitement.

7. Read back any questionable information. If a word is difficult to understand, even when spelled out, ask him to spell it phonetically:

"The victim's name is Eric Zuessman," the reporter says.

"Spell it," the rewrite man demands.

"Z-U-E-S-S-M-A-N," the reporter obliges.

"Phonetically," the rewrite man says, as he eyes his version of the name suspiciously: "Tuessman."

"Z, as in zebra, U as in ultra, E as in elephant, S as in Sam, S as in Sam, M as in Mouse, A as in apple, N as in noodle," the reporter says.

8. Before hanging up, check with the city editor for instructions, then, if possible, take down a telephone number where the reporter can be reached for the next several minutes.

Besides being a vital means of transmitting stories from the scene to the newsroom, the telephone is also a tool to save wear and tear on shoe soles. If a breaking story requires information from several sources, located throughout the city, a reporter can use the wonderful contraption to touch all bases without leaving his desk, thus saving time and travel.

Perhaps a spokesman for the Fraternal Order of Police accuses the city of endangering the lives of officers by refusing to purchase new police cruisers.

"They are saving money at the risk of our lives," Sergeant Paul McAdams charged. "The cruisers are now, on the average, six years old. They are literally falling apart. In the past six months, three officers have been injured in accidents resulting from mechanical failures. We cannot continue to provide a high level of protection for the public without safe and adequate equipment."

After obtaining the necessary additional information from the sergeant, such as the circumstances surrounding the accidents and possible police actions in protest of the situation, the reporter must quickly get "the other side." He is thirty minutes away from the final deadline. He quickly calls the chief of police, the mayor, the city manager, and several members of the city council to obtain information for a well-balanced story. He may enlist the help of other reporters who aren't working on deadline stories to split the list of needed respondents.

The technique of using the telephone to gather information under intense deadline pressure is tricky. Most people rightly expect a bit of formal courtesy from a caller—even a reporter. And few people can resist the temptation to ramble and engage in non-related conversation.

The reporter doesn't want to offend the news source, but he must meet his deadline. His only option is to firmly control the flow of conversation, after explaining briefly his need to be somewhat brisk.

To illustrate the problems and techniques, let's say that the reporter calls the mayor to obtain his reaction to the Fraternal Order of Police spokesman's accusation:

"Mayor Greene? This is Lou Coles from the *News*. I just received a statement from the F.O.P. that may interest you. I'm on deadline, so I would appreciate your reaction. Here's what Paul McAdams said . . ."

"McAdams said that?" the mayor says angrily. "He's just trying to stir up trouble. Ever since he's been on the force, he's been a troublemaker. A few years ago, he . . ."

"Excuse me, mayor, I hate to interrupt, but I'm really pressed for time. Can I call you back after deadline for additional background? I may be able to use it tomorrow. For now, I would appreciate your response to today's charge," the reporter says, as pleasantly as possible.

"Yes, well, okay," the mayor says. "I believe that McAdams' statement is irresponsible, inaccurate, and hysterical. We carefully studied the police department's request for new cruisers and rejected it only after considerable soul-searching. We must operate on the money that our citizens provide. The money is simply not in the budget. Every department in the city is operating on an austere budget. We value our policemen, but they are not deserving of any special treatment. Their vehicles are operable . . ."

Standard Informational Sources

With the overriding requirement for speed and accuracy in mind, a reporter must be aware of several standard sources of reference at his disposal. Here are the basic, standard references used by most reporters:

1. *The Telephone Directory.* This masterpiece of assembled information provides a highly reliable source of information about virtually everyone in the city. The correct spelling of the name of the

victim can be quickly verified, along with his or her address. The means of obtaining additional information, a home telephone number, is simultaneously provided.

2. *The City Directory*. Normally published by a private firm for advertising revenue, this directory not only provides an alphabetized listing of names, addresses, occupations, and members of the household; but it also provides a cross-reference by street address. Persons who do not have telephones may also be listed in this publication.

The value is considerable. Perhaps there are six Joseph E. Smiths in the telephone directory, and the reporter is seeking information about an accident victim. Joseph E. Smith, who is an attorney. *The City Directory* identifies the correct Joseph E. Smith by listing the occupation. Next of kin are also listed.

Perhaps a reporter hears a police radio broadcast calling officers to respond to a disturbance at 5830 Lakeview Street. He may quickly check the directory to determine the names of the occupants of the home and names and telephone numbers of next door neighbors. With a few quick telephone calls, he can learn the nature of the disturbance and take steps to gain story information.

3. *The Reference Library* (newspaper morgue). Most newspapers maintain an elaborate system of filing story clippings for future reference, often supervised by a professional librarian. Clippings are normally filed by subject and by name of each person involved. Additional reference materials, such as encyclopedias, atlases, out-of-town telephone directories, and other publications, are normally available in the "morgue."

A standard procedure of many reporters is to check the morgue for files on any person or subject suddenly thrust into the news. For example, a reporter who is writing obituaries may routinely check files against a list of names of deceased persons. A routine death may take on new significance. A reporter once discovered that a young woman who had died on the previous day had made several, sometimes spectacular, suicide attempts in the past few years. Cause of death wasn't included in information from the funeral home, so he called the coroner's office and found that she had finally succeeded in killing herself. Further investigation disclosed that her family had unsuccessfully tried to have her committed to a mental institution. The routine obituary became an excellent, page-one story of personal tragedy and institutional ineptitude.

Investigative reporters may spend hours in the morgue, looking for bits and pieces of information to tie together a tangle of seemingly unrelated information. Perhaps a reporter discovers that a bartender also serves as the neighborhood "bookie." If he is attempting to piece together the structure of a major gambling organization, he would check the clippings on the bookie and learn of previous arrests on gambling charges. The files may provide the names of others arrested with him, background on the gambling operations, and clues to help determine just how important the bartender may be in city gambling circles.

A city hall reporter, who is writing a major story on a proposal to place an ordinance to increase city income tax rates on the ballot, would check files for information on previous attempts. The information that similar proposals were soundly defeated may help readers discern the improbability of a tax increase.

Meeting Deadlines

At this point, you may perceive that the major thrust of using all of these tools is to obtain information accurately and quickly. Speed is a vital factor in reporting because of the normal intensity of deadline pressures.

A reporter soon learns that the demands of his job are humanly impossible—unless he uses his time with extreme efficiency. A police reporter may face the task of gathering information and writing stories on half a dozen or more significant, breaking stories in the span of five hours. A city hall reporter may emerge from a city council meeting with a major story in note form, half an hour before the final deadline. Let's examine two diverse—and actual—situations in which a reporter faced almost impossible deadline obstacles.

Late one morning, a city hall reporter learned of an impending, major city hall reorganization. His sources, though reliable, could not be quoted directly. As he hurriedly shuttled from office to office to glean bits of information about the reorganization, major facets of the new structure began to take form. At 10:30 A.M.—one and a half hours before the final deadline—the city manager had scheduled a press conference on another topic of minor interest. During the press conference, the reporter was able to draw a general confirmation from the city manager to the effect that a reorganization was in the works. He refused to elaborate, but the reporter had already obtained many details. He listened with half an ear as other reporters asked for information that he had already obtained. As time was wasted on such unproductive questions, the reporter busily devised a lead for his story and began to outline its structure.

Then, his attention was suddenly pricked when another reporter asked for a progress report on the impending selection of a new police chief. The reporter was well aware of the search for a chief and, through his sources, had learned that the city manager planned to select either the present assistant police chief or an out-of-town candidate for the job. His sources were very close to the city manager.

"Jim, can you tell us whether you will select from inside the department or go for an outside candidate?" the reporter asked innocently.

The city manager replied that the job would be filled by a present member of the police department. That was all the reporter needed. As soon as the press conference ended, he privately confronted the city manager with the name of the assistant chief. The city manager confirmed the information, but refused to do so publicly.

It was 11:15 A.M. when the reporter left city hall on a dead run, heading for the newsroom. He already had the lead for the reorganization story in his notebook, along with the story outline, so he concentrated on the police chief selection as he ran. By the time he reached his typewriter, he had formulated the lead for the police chief selection story. Enroute, he alerted the city desk that both stories were coming, so that the city editor could notify the news editor that two major stories were coming at the last possible minute. Deadline was 12 noon. The reporter handed the city editor the first story at 11:45 A.M., the second at 11:59 A.M. The time that he saved by composing as much of the stories as possible during "wasted" moments—during unproductive moments of the press conference, and during his dash back to the newsroom—gave him the necessary edge.

In another situation, a police reporter found himself faced with half a dozen breaking stories one morning. As soon as he learned of the stories, he listed them in descending order of importance so that, if he was unable to get to all of them, the most important stories would be covered. He used every possible moment efficiently. If he had to wait a few minutes to interview a detective, he used the time to scribble down another story in his notebook. The final story on tap was a press conference at which the chief of police was to announce major policy changes. The press conference was scheduled for 11 A.M.

As time permitted, he rushed to the small press room at police headquarters and dictated stories from notes to a rewrite man. As other developments came later in the morning, he called back to update the stories. When the press conference began, he had dictated all other stories. The press conference continued until 11:30 A.M., and he ran back to the newsroom to write the final story of the day.

If the police reporter had unwisely waited to return to the newsroom before writing his stories, most of them would not have been ready by the deadline.

In still another actual instance, a reporter was assigned to cover a speech by a nationally known political figure. The speech was scheduled to begin at 10 A.M., but it was delayed until almost 11 A.M. However, the reporter had the foresight to obtain an advance copy of the speech and, along with information from the clipping file, he had written a rough draft of the story. The speech did not end until

11:40 A.M., but the reporter managed to meet his deadline by rapidly accommodating the speaker's digressions from the prepared text and inserting audience reactions.

The race against the clock is replayed daily by every beat reporter. The professional frustration of a reporter who loses the race after doing his best is acute, but even the most hard-nosed editor can forgive such a loss. Yet, a reporter who consistently misses stories because of inefficiency may find himself assigned to writing obituaries for the remainder of his career. Even the best reporter loses occasionally, but never frequently.

While deadline situations are so varied that there is no universal approach to beating the clock, some general guidelines are helpful:

1. *Don't panic.* If a reporter is to have any chance of meeting a seemingly impossible deadline situation, he must retain his wits. Panic or frenzy wastes valuable time by inducing indecision or the tendency to thrash about in every direction. A calm, controlled approach is a must.

2. *Be organized.* In each of the preceding examples, the reporter's ability to organize his time and efforts with maximum efficiency enabled him to meet his deadline. He quickly organized his actions by priorities and controlled his efforts so that they were directed at meeting those priorities.

3. *Use every moment wisely.* In every situation, a momentary lull occurs that can be used for thinking, scribbling, or even fact-gathering. In the case of the city hall reporter, he composed a lead and organized his story during a lull in a press conference, then mentally hashed out another lead while returning to the newsroom.

4. *Be decisive.* Lengthy wavering in the face of a critical decision may be deadly. Make a decision quickly and stick with it—even if it's the wrong decision. Perhaps, due to second thoughts, a reporter may question his decision to pursue one story instead of another. If he ponders too long, he will get neither. In another application, be decisive as you write. A reporter under intense deadline pressure cannot spare the time to contemplate a blank piece of paper as he waits for inspiration, or for an angel to whisper a lead into his ear. As soon as you have paper in the typewriter, start typing. Most reporters opt for a simple, easy-to-write, summary lead, unless otherwise inspired immediately.

5. *Plan ahead.* If you know that an important story will break on deadline, assemble background information in advance, written as an insert if possible. Try to clear your schedule of other stories before the event begins. The police reporter's handling of stories before the important press conference is a case in point. He was able to concentrate solely on the last-minute story and stay a few minutes longer at the event, which continued well past his deadline. In

another example, the reporter who covered the speech would have been unable to write a full, informative story if he had not written a draft from the advance copy.

SUMMARY

The tricks of the trade discussed in this chapter are, by no means, comprehensive of all the professional techniques used by reporters. Each newsperson quickly develops his or her own approaches and shortcuts.

Reporting is a profession that constantly demands ingenuity and adaptability on the part of its practitioners. It requires a healthy dose of common sense and logic, as well as the ability to be the only person in the room who is not thrashing about in hysteria in a given disaster or happening.

Perhaps a lesson can be drawn from the experience of a radio newsman who provided on-the-scene coverage of a tragic fire. The newsman was so shaken by the tragedy that his voice broke repeatedly during his broadcast. His sentences were ungrammatical garbles, his information was scrambled and, at times, contradictory. He lost his professional composure and his audience—and his career suffered.

Reporters are not superhuman. They may also feel immense sorrow and frustration from a tragedy. Yet, a true professional will perform with a cool detachment until his job—his service to the public—is done. Then he can indulge in the human tendency to cry, laugh, or simply sit in a shell-shocked trance.

EXERCISES

1. During the next class meeting, each student will take copious notes of the lecture, including direct quotations, and turn the notes in at the end of the class (to be returned later).

2. If facilities are available, divide the class evenly and give each half a different story. Then, using telephones and typewriters, have each half take turns dictating and receiving stories.

3. Using a tape recording of a speech or a meeting, have the class take notes and write a news story based on the speech or meeting. Notes should also be collected.

7 | Interviews

With a kindly smile and mischievous eyes peering through the wire-frame glasses that gave his face a grandfatherly countenance, the police chief slyly offered the new police beat reporter a frustrating lesson on the perils of interviewing a veteran public official.

The reporter was well prepared for the interview. He had amassed a depth of background material on various issues that concerned the police department. He had carefully planned his questions so that, in the allotted half hour, he could delve into the most pressing and interesting matters. And he knew exactly what information he wanted to obtain, preferably in the form of direct quotations.

The department was suffering severe racial tensions between black and white police officers. Black officers charged that they had been routinely denied promotional opportunities, and that hiring procedures were stacked so that minority citizens had little opportunity to become policemen. White officers angrily countered that minority policemen were simply trying to obtain easy, "give-away" promotions —at their expense.

Before the reporter entered the office, the chief had anticipated ticklish questions. While he understood the reporter's desire to pinpoint his views on the problem, the chief knew that he could not afford to be publicly "cornered"—not yet. He wanted to wait until the current mood of tension and anger subsided a bit before taking action, so that his plans to remedy the problem could be greeted by cooler heads. A premature disclosure of his intentions of promoting and hiring more black officers could escalate existing tensions to a dangerous level.

The reporter, who had not interviewed the chief before, was hampered by a conflict between his desire to obtain the story that he knew was there and a genuine admiration and sympathy for a reputedly honest, competent official who was faced with a predicament. Moreover, he was a bit awed by the power of the city's top policeman —a man who could be a dangerous adversary for a new beat reporter whose informational sources were still very tentative.

The interview progressed so smoothly that the reporter was soon lulled by the charm and cooperativeness of the chief. Not only did he answer the reporter's questions, but he elaborated at great length and took pains to explain even the foggiest background material.

As twenty-five minutes passed, the reporter amassed several pages of interesting notes about secondary, less controversial issues. Then, a glance at his wristwatch provided the startling realization that only five minutes of the interview time remained. The chief was, at that point, expounding at length about a new policy of stricter enforcement of parking violations. Nervously, the reporter waited for the chief to reach a logical pause so that he could squeeze in the important question concerning racial tensions. Finally, he interrupted apologetically and asked his question:

"Chief, the black officers claim that discrimination has curtailed hiring and promotional opportunities for blacks. Do you consider their complaint to have merit? Also, what are you going to do about the situation?"

The chief glanced at his watch and frowned. "That's a rather difficult question to answer in one minute—that's what we have left— but I'll try to oblige.

"I cannot judge the merit of the complaint at this point, because the black officers have not made their complaint to me. They have voiced their concerns to the public through news media, but they haven't taken the opportunity to visit with me about them. I have an open-door policy with my officers, and I take considerable trouble to encourage them to see me when they have some sort of problem. We also have official channels, which . . ."

The reporter, finally alert and desperate, interrupted again. "I'm familiar with your open-door policy, but can't you comment on the charges that have been made publicly to the effect that your department has a racist structure?"

"I hate to address a charge that has not been made through official channels, because there's a tendency for distortion through public media," the police chief retorted. "I will say that a police department is manned by human being—and we have four hundred persons working together. It would be absurd to say that none of them, black or white, are racist. Given even a basic understanding of American history, it would be equally absurd to say that any public institution is totally guiltless in a system that historically has resulted in certain discrimination against black Americans. Indeed, there may be some vestiges of such discrimination that continue to exist in any institution, including the police department. If the problem exists—and I don't really know whether it exists or not—we will take corrective steps."

Before the reporter could even mutter a "yes, but . . ." the chief's secretary entered to announce that another appointment was scheduled, and that a visitor was waiting to see him. The dejected reporter left the office with his head ringing with double talk. As the door closed behind him, the chief chuckled happily, relishing his easy victory.

A postmortem on the reporter's inept performance reveals that his defeat was due to a total lack of control over the interview. The chief had filibustered through the easy question because the reporter allowed him to drift and digress at will, using up precious time. While the reporter's good manners in not interrupting the chief are commendable, a firm but polite "excuse me, but to return to the question . . ." would have ended the official's cunning game.

The difficulties of conducting a formal interview are illustrated by this example. An interview is, in a sense, a contest of wits, wiles, and wills between reporter and interview subject. This matchup is often trying for both participants, as a clever official, who has successfully dealt with reporters for many years, tries to withhold the information that an experienced and intelligent reporter is seeking.

Some important variables affect the interview process, such as the relationship between reporter and official. If the official is friendly and cooperative, then the interview is a simple, straightforward event in which two reasonable people engage in an honest and open discussion. If the official is hostile or reluctant, then the event becomes a duel. Between those extremes lies the bulk of journalistic interviews.

RESEARCH

Well before the reporter leaves for the interview, he should do his "homework," by assembling background material on the person to be interviewed and on issues that should be pursued during the session.

A beat reporter may need only a few minutes to assess his notes and scan clippings. In performing his job daily, he becomes—and stays—thoroughly familiar with important officials and major issues on his beat.

Many interviews, however, are conducted by reporters who have had little contact with the subject of the interview and little knowledge of the issues. In such cases, the research stage is critical to the success of the interview. The reporter must learn as much as possible about the person to be interviewed—his personal and professional background, his character, his competence, and such. Moreover, the reporter must quickly and fully comprehend the issues and newsworthy circumstances concerning that individual, and the full implication of those issues and circumstances.

To compile this research, the reporter may use these sources:

1. *The reference libary* (morgue). Clippings of news stories about the official can provide not only biographical data, but insight to his character, competence, and professional tendencies.

If, for example, a gubernatorial candidate is in town, a reporter assigned to interview him could become thoroughly familiar with his ideology by reading articles detailing his platform. Insight to his character and personality can be gleaned from other stories.

2. *Other reporters.* Perhaps other journalists on the staff are personally familiar with the subject, especially if he has been a newsmaker for some time. Friendly briefings from colleagues not only provide background, but professional insight to the official's techniques in dealing with newsmen.

3. *People who are in professional contact with the interviewee,* or those who are in conflict with him. To gather background before interviewing the mayor, a reporter may contact city councilmen, high city hall officials, political opponents, and others who encounter him routinely.

As a result of this research, the reporter should have a solid "feel" for his interview subject, even if he has never met the official. He should also have a clear understanding of all issues and situations that could pop up during the interview—even unanticipated ones.

FORMULATING QUESTIONS

With research completed—either through extensive preparation or by everyday beat exposure—the reporter's next task is to prepare his questions in advance. It is essential that he not only know what information to seek, but also how to word questions carefully in a manner that will pry loose that information. In the latter instance, the timing of the questions and the staging of the truly important queries can sometimes be imperative.

The questions themselves should organize the plan of attack, the approach to retrieving information. A well-structured set of questions will allow the journalist to exercise tight control over the interview, regardless of the tactics used by the reluctant subject to avoid giving an answer.

General guidelines to use in compiling questions are:

1. Decide exactly what information you want to extract. Write down each important item.

2. Carefully word questions so that they will *precisely* request each of those important informational items.

3. List those questions in descending order of importance.

Now, armed with that list of targets and tools for striking them, the reporter's next step is to decide the most effective plan of attack for presenting those questions. That plan will vary greatly with the tone of the interview and the anticipated degree of cooperation from the subject.

Friendly or Cooperative Subjects

If you anticipate that the subject will respond freely and openly, then the arrangement of the questions and their wording is essentially established by the initial draft, in descending order of importance.

A typical example of such a case occurs when an official *wants* to convey information to the public. The detective in charge of the robbery squad may be concerned about a sudden outbreak of armed robberies. He may seek out a reporter to suggest that "somebody is going to get killed if the public doesn't learn how to react to robberies. Too many people are trying to resist the robbers, and some of them have already been shot."

An interview with the detective, then, would be straightforward. Both the policeman and the reporter share the common objective of informing the public about a dangerous situation.

In preparing for such an interview, the reporter can quickly assemble background information on the robbery outbreak from clippings. After listing his informational objectives, the reporter prepares his questions in descending order of importance, so that the time available for the interview will be used with maximum efficiency.

Cautious, Unpredictable Subjects

The police chief in the previous example illustrates this broad category. While friendly and polite, the chief could not extend full cooperation because of circumstances. At times, almost any public official will seek to withhold information or avoid making commitments during an interview, for a host of logical reasons. The chief may be concerned about public safety. A city manager may avoid discussing a planned reorganization, for fear that premature disclosure may be politically and managerially troublesome. A school board official may try to withhold information about a contract proposal to the teachers' association because public disclosure could unbalance sensitive negotiations. The reporter, on the other hand, is expected to provide aggressive beat coverage by producing news stories before his competition can acquire them. Unless convinced that disclosure of secret information would be detrimental to public safety and welfare—and not simply an irritant to an official's ulcers—he is expected to ferret out and break such news.

Besides the pressure of competition and editor's expectations, the desire to dig out and disclose information that is being withheld from the public—for whatever good reasons—is also fueled by principles. As a matter of principle, a beat reporter tries to maintain a reputation for being able to sniff out secrets so that dishonest or unscrupulous officials may be deterred from misdeeds. If, for example, an official devises a scheme to embezzle public funds, he would be more likely to initiate the plan if the beat reporter was lethargic and uninspired, rather than aggressive and capable.

With such an interview expected, then, the reporter must prepare for battle. After completing research, the journalist carefully designs his pattern of questions so that the official is more likely to be trapped into answering the question that really counts.

Instead of brazenly opening with the key question, the reporter may start with easy ones in an effort to loosen up the interviewee, prod him into talking fluently, and erode his defense. Frequently, such an approach will succeed in giving the "opponent" a false sense of relief that the reporter is not seeking the truly sensitive information. Toward the middle of the interview, however, the journalist will casually toss out the question designed to lead the official into the real subject.

Another effective technique is the bluff. A reporter may decide that his best chance is for a "frontal assault," particularly if his research has provided strong but unconfirmed information about the nature of the official's secret.

If, for example, the city hall reporter is convinced that a major reorganization of city hall bureaucracy is being quietly planned, he may be able to project a likely scenario of the new structure by combining sketchy information from his news sources with his own logic and understanding of city hall life. In interviewing the city manager, he may unleash his bluff from the start:

"Your new organizational structure really turns everything topsy-turvy. I've been able to construct the plan from various sources, but I simply want to get a few comments from you to round out the story.

"I was intrigued to note that you are chopping the number of city departments down from fourteen to six, thus saving a great deal of money. *Can you give me a good, ball-park figure on the amount you expect to save?*"

The question (in italics) is boldly set up by the reporter's brief, triumphant disclosure of conjecture in the form of fact. The success of the ploy hinges greatly on whether his specific projection of the reduction in the number of departments is correct, or at least very close.

Now, let's move to the other side of the desk and check the city manager's position. If the figures were correct, then the city manager is trapped, even before he speaks the first word. Although he may suspect that the reporter is bluffing, he knows that the journalist has some solid information with which to bluff. His options are bleak and limited:

1. If he denies the reorganization plan or the specific figures, then his credibility with the public and with the press will suffer when the plan is announced and his deception is disclosed.

2. If he refuses to comment, the reporter can go ahead with the story, by carefully emphasizing that the information is tentative and unconfirmed by official sources. The city manager's refusal to comment would be included and emphasized in the story, so that the readers could judge the significance of his refusal. From the official's viewpoint, such a course would possibly result in some distortions and inaccuracies, give rise to dangerous rumors, lower employee morale through uncertainty, and generally cause even worse problems than premature disclosure of the real plan. Many readers may translate "no comment" into "yes, it's true, but I can't or won't admit it."

3. Confirm the initial information (a reorganization is being planned, and it will reduce the number of departments to six), then regroup to try to fend off other questions about specifics as the interview progresses.

At this point, you may astutely note that the question asked for dollars savings, not for confirmation. The question itself is, however, of secondary importance. It is merely a vehicle to force the official to confirm the reorganization.

If the city manager says, "I can't give you a figure," the response only delays the inevitable.

> Reporter: "But you do plan to save money through reorganization?"
> Official: "I don't believe I have mentioned any reorganization."
> Reporter: "All right, then. Do you confirm or deny that there will be a reorganization of departments? Secondly, do you confirm or deny that this reorganization will reduce the number of departments to six?"

The outcome of the duel is certain. It was ensured by the initial bluff. The sparring may continue for a few minutes, but the reporter knows that he will emerge with the story.

Both approaches, the "soft" start and the bluff, can also be used in dealing with another category of interviewees: hostile subjects.

Hostile Subjects

One of the most unpleasant duties of a reporter is to conduct a formal interview with a hostile official. When a journalist discovers or strongly suspects damaging information about an official, the interview becomes far more than a stimulating duel of wits; it sometimes becomes a vicious struggle, with the official's political or professional career at stake.

If, for example, a reporter has gathered evidence that a judge has accepted bribes and maintained secret ties with organized crime, then his investigation will sooner or later culminate in a face-to-face inter-view confrontation, in which the judge would be allowed to explain or respond to that evidence.

Picture yourself as that reporter. You are sitting in the judge's chambers, ticking off the particulars of your findings, as the official's face reddens with outrage, or pales in shock. You are confident that you have established his wrongdoing beyond any doubt, and you are utterly convinced that the man has betrayed public trust. His sins against the people are being coldly, professionally recounted, and they hammer his human dignity mercilessly.

Yet, despite this conviction, and despite the professional satis-faction that comes from a successful investigation, you also see a man who is being destroyed by your work. You know that he is a devoted family man, and that his family will suffer. You know that he may well go to prison, if convicted of these charges. You know that, despite his crimes, he has performed unselfishly, quietly, to assist many beneficial community projects.

In short, the taste of victory is tainted by genuine human sym-pathy for the man who is trapped and exposed and professionally destroyed by it—even though he brought it on himself.

That unnerving sympathy, while understandable, is dangerous to the reporter. His opponent, the official, isn't constrained by such tender emotions. He is cornered, and his only recourse is to fight back with all of the considerable power that he has accumulated with the public trust that he has betrayed.

Fortunately, any reporter who is competent enough to uncover such misdeeds is normally competent enough to complete the job with a good interview.

The research stage of the process occurs simultaneously with the investigative reporting. As each count of wrongdoing is uncovered and carefully documented, crucial questions evolve naturally. By the time the investigation has reached the confrontation-interview stage, the reporter should have a vivid picture of the official, and a full grasp of each item that will be discussed.

The basic format of the questions is simple: Present the evidence, then ask the official to confirm or deny the charge. Then allow him to explain his actions, so that if the evidence is refutable, the official can explain to the public. The difficult part is make absolutely certain that evidence for each accusation is solid and provable.

One first-rate investigative reporter always assumes the role of the accused and tries to refute his own evidence before confronting the subject. If he finds any shaky or questionable documentation, he either bolsters it with further research or discards it temporarily.

"I don't want to give him any room to wiggle," the reporter explained. "I've seen some very good stories knocked down because of one loophole. If ninety percent of your material is solid, he can still discredit your reporting by proving, and focusing on, the ten percent that's off base."

When questions covering each facet of the alleged misdeeds are compiled, the reporter must then decide on his basic approach so that he can list his questions in the most effective arrangement. Common approaches include:

1. *A direct, blunt accusation at the beginning.*

Example: "Judge, I have found solid evidence that you have accepted several bribes in return for acquittals, and that you have maintained strong, personal contacts with Jim O'Hara (head of a huge gambling operation). I assure you that I can prove these allegations, but I want to give you the opportunity to comment on them."

The strategy is aimed at stripping the subject of his defense through shock and surprise, and establishing very firm control of the interview from the outset. If, indeed, the reporter has amassed such evidence, and if the subject is guilty, then the stunning, unexpected announcement may render the latter helpless.

A danger to this plan is that the judge may be well aware of the reporter's investigation, and he may have spent much time preparing for the interview. A brazen counterattack may reverse the advantage:

"I'm aware of your efforts to libel me, and I assure you that if you print a word of that trash, you and your newspaper will be sued. I have several witnesses to your brash statements, to the effect that you are 'going to get' the judge. I also suggest that witnesses that you pull out of the gutter, circumstantial evidence that cannot be considered binding even in a kangaroo court, and my personal choice of friends—which has no bearing on my judicial judgment—will not suffice."

Even the most experienced reporter would be seriously undermined and shaken by such a ploy.

2. *A sympathetic approach.*

Example: "Your Honor, I have found some very disturbing allegations that concern you. While I would prefer to ignore them, they are beginning to stir some damaging rumors that smear your reputation. I would like to present these allegations, and give you the opportunity to put those rumors to rest."

If the judge has prepared a tough counterattack, the sympathetic approach may throw him off balance. A fierce denunciation of the reporter and his investigation would, in this context, constitute a classic case of "me thinks thou dost protest too much." It also establishes a civil and polite tone for discussion of explosive allegations, and focuses the interview on the issues and not the subterfuge. Also, the approach may lull the official into the comforting delusion that the reporter is a spineless dullard, who can be deflected from the story. As the interview progresses, however, the "dullard" slashes through any defense based on this false assumption.

The drawback to this approach is that if the official is astute enough to perceive the ploy, he may use it to gain critical time with which to adjust and design his defense. This is particularly undesirable if the official wasn't aware of the reporter's investigation. Also, the official can quickly turn the ploy around:

"I appreciate your consideration in giving me the opportunity to confront these allegations," he says smoothly. "I've heard such rumors, and I've long awaited an opportunity to allay them."

With such a deft stroke, the interview tone has suddenly become one of "let's get our wits together so that we can deny those nasty rumors."

3. *A camouflaged approach.* If a single, less serious transgression is involved, then the reporter may choose to conceal his main objective during the early stages of the interview, casually tossing out the blockbuster question when the time is right.

Example: After asking several questions about the large backlog of cases awaiting trial, the reporter may say: "Oh, by the way, I understand that you play golf with O'Hara every Saturday morning at the country club. Do you consider such association with a noted gambler to be proper?"

If the guilt by association factor is the only substantial fruit of the investigation—if other allegations cannot be established—the reporter may consider such a one-shot ploy. The casual approach may elicit a reaction without alerting the judge to an interest in the full scope of his alleged misdeeds, if the reporter plans further investigation.

As will be discussed in later chapters, however, premature confrontations are generally unwise because they may initiate a coverup.

The approach is more commonly used to elicit responses to single, isolated misdeeds. For example, a city hall reporter may have found that a councilman filed an exorbitant expense account after an official trip to Washington, where he attended a meeting. The interview may focus on the results and significance of the meeting, yet the reporter may be more interested in the expense account abuses than in the substance of the meeting.

After asking several questions about the trip, the journalist may ask:

"I noticed that you filed an expense account listing $3,000 for total costs, including $1,200 for miscellaneous expenses, for your three-day stay. Can you explain how you managed to run up such a tab?"

INTERVIEWS WITH NON-PUBLIC FIGURES

At times, a reporter must interview someone who is not accustomed to dealing with journalists. Perhaps a person is entering the public spotlight for the first time by seeking public office or through advancement to a position of responsibility.

In one respect, the reporter has a clear advantage, in that the person is not experienced enough to offer a stiff challenge in the interview. Yet, that advantage is often tempered by the person's shyness, suspicion, or reticence. The interviewee may be so afraid of the reporter that he is reluctant to say anything of substance.

Let's say that a local dentist is seeking a city council seat. Although the dentist has been active in community affairs in his neighborhood, and has held many offices in such activities as PTA, church vestry, and neighborhood associations, he has never before achieved city-wide prominence.

The reporter's resources for conducting pre-interview research are limited. There are no newspaper clippings about the man on file. Normal news sources know little about him. He has only today announced his intention to seek the office, so no campaign material is available. The reporter can only contact neighborhood people who have served with him in various activities, and low-level politicians who may have been in contact with him as they represented his precinct.

Such sketchy resources produce only very general questions, about the candidate's views on current issues, his motives for running, and his general background. The main thrust of the interview is to determine just who the person is, and what he has to offer his fellow citizens.

In arranging interview questions, the reporter must take into account the candidate's inexperience and anticipate his anxiety in that initial public exposure.

Perhaps the most effective technique is to fashion the interview into the format of an informal chat, weaving the important questions into a fabric of congenial discussion. The tone is established by the reporter's initial question, accompanied by a warm smile:

"I can't help but wonder why anyone with such a constructive and lucrative profession as dentistry would condescend to get involved with politics. Can you tell me why on earth you are willing to run?"

The question, although presented in a friendly, light-hearted manner, stabs at the heart of the interview. Simultaneously, the underlying flattery should boost the candidate's confidence somewhat, as the reporter seems to think that the dentist is *condescending* to run.

The greatest obstacle to a successful interview with a non-public figure is that of overcoming reticence. The reporter must create a warm and friendly atmosphere, winning the confidence and trust of the citizen, in order to facilitate a flowing discussion.

To emphasize the need, imagine yourself as the dentist-candidate. You sincerely believe that you can offer your talent and integrity to make your city a better place to live. At the same time, you know that you are extremely vulnerable, and that the journalist who is sitting before you is quite capable of exploiting your inexperience and destroying your candidacy before it ever gets off the ground. You are nervous, unsure of yourself, and suspicious of the reporter.

The journalist frowns, gazes contemptuously at you, and asks:

"Why on earth are *you* running for city council?"

The question is an invitation for a hostile or defensive remark. You are angered by the reporter's seeming contempt, and deathly afraid that he is about to portray you as the town fool. Instinctively, you "clam up" by giving him as little information as possible.

While the reporter may, indeed, portray the candidate as the "town fool" by dutifully reporting his shallow, inept answers, he has failed to meet even the most minimal standards of reporting. His job was to obtain a full and accurate account of the candidate's positions and political character. His brow-beating approach squelched any chance of obtaining a deeply probing look at the man and his offerings, and distorted the dentist's candidacy into an ugly caricature.

Interestingly, the basic question is the same in both approaches: Why are you running for office? Yet, the initial approach was positive and encouraging, carefully designed to extract a substantial answer, which could lead to a fair and realistic examination of the candidate.

In such interviews, many reporters allow for several minutes of casual chatting before even broaching the first question. A friendly discussion of a topic of mutual interest, such as the performance of the local baseball team, or the miserable spell of weather, can put the citizen at ease while giving the reporter a chance to assess him casually.

A good variation is to find something interesting about the citizen, which doesn't directly relate to the substance of the interview. Perhaps, while chatting with acquaintances before the interview, the reporter learned that the man is an avid fisherman—an interest that the reporter shares.

After exchanging amenities, the reporter begins:

"I understand that you and I have something in common—a love for fishing."

For five minutes, the conversation focuses on favorite fishing holes, techniques for presenting a dry fly to a hungry trout, and the virtues of various lures. By the time the real interview begins, the candidate and the reporter may be chatting like old friends.

Then, with a chuckle, the reporter says, "I could discuss fishing all day, but my editor will wring my neck if I don't return with a good interview. He doesn't understand that fishing is more interesting than politics."

With this variety of interview styles in mind, the need for flexibility in designing interview questions is apparent. The format in which the questions are arranged—where should the most important question fit in?—is a crucial factor. The packaging of each question is important, as is illustrated in the "why are you running?" example.

Yet, there are some basic guidelines that are generally applicable to writing questions for most types of interviews:

1. The prepared questions should be designed to *lead into* general subject areas and guide the flow of the interview. Normally, a reporter cannot anticipate the specific answers to his questions, thus his impromptu follow-up questions—those not listed in advance—are the critical tools to extract specific information. In short, each question should have a fairly broad focus, which would be narrowed to more and more specific probing with follow-up questions.

2. Each question should be designed with a clear objective in mind. Extraneous questions should be eliminated. For example, while interviewing the police chief about racial tensions and major policy changes, it would hardly be wise to insert a question such as: "Do you think the police image as portrayed on television is a positive influence on police morale?"

3. Say exactly what you mean when you write the question. Don't leave room for misinteptretation or evasion.

4. Phrase the questions forcefully. Imagine the police chief's glee if the reporter asked: "Do you think that there's a chance that white officers may be upset if you find that the black officers' complaints have merit?" The chief would have a huge opening to filibuster at will, or curtly close the door by replying, "How should I know?" Better stated, the question should say: "Since white officers have already reacted bitterly, how do you intend to deal with their discontent?" Follow-up questions can explore the alternatives as they arise. Since the reporter cannot confidently anticipate the chief's leanings, a pre-planned question based on such an assumption is foolish.

5. After formulating the questions, assume the role of the interviewee and read them through his eyes. While the reporter is obviously limited in his ability to anticipate reactions, the process may enable him to weed out weak or extraneous questions, or spot flaws in his strategy.

CONDUCTING AN INTERVIEW

While various approaches to different types of interviews have already been discussed, let's examine some specific guidelines for conducting an interview with a public figure, then apply those guidelines to a realistic example.

1. Maintain firm control of the interview.

If a reporter loses the struggle to control the interview, the official succeeds in assigning him the role of a public relations agent. The official, not the reporter, determines what information will be included in the story, and you can rest assured that the information will be favorable and conducive to his goals and purposes.

The battle for control of the interview is conducted with several elements:

Time. A reporter must control the amount of time spent in discussing any aspect. As noted in the case of the police chief interview, an astute official can firmly take command by expounding on secondary items.

In fact, there's no reason why a reporter should lose this struggle. Few humans can talk for more than a few seconds without pausing slightly to catch their breath. That momentary pause is an ample opening for a reporter's polite but firm interruption to shift to another topic.

Evasion. This is the most troublesome element. An official can verbally dance around a specific commitment or item of information for several minutes, always appearing to be on the verge of getting to the point. An untimely interruption may actually hamper the flow of information, yet a reporter cannot afford to allow the dance to continue indefinitely.

Prestige. The relative advantage of the reporter/official matchup may hinge somewhat on the degree of public esteem that each enjoys. Some of that prestige is inherent in each profession: A reporter is the agent acting on behalf of—and with the authority of—a respected newspaper; the official carries the full authority of his elected or appointed position. The inherent prestige of a reporter from the *New York Times* would give him an advantage over, say, a minor local official in a midwestern city. The prestige of the Governor of California would be a weighty obstacle for a small-town reporter to overcome, should he interview the governor.

Prestige, however, can be exuded through professional confidence. It's a subjective quality, and a small-town reporter may arbitrarily decide that he's every bit as important and powerful as the governor.

Prestige is a factor only when one of the two adversaries is awed or overly impressed by the other. Any factor that places one participant in a position of dominance—as opposed to a sense of professional equality and mutual respect—can tip the control of the interview.

From the reporter's viewpoint, it is essential that he not feel inferior to the interviewee. He must project a professional, confident self-image so that he can maintain parity.

Agenda. The reporter and the official may have strongly conflicting notions about items to be covered during the interview. A strong-willed official may have a mental list of topics that he intends to expound upon. While a reporter may gain useful information from items that aren't on his agenda, it is imperative that he lead the official through subject areas in which he is interested. Then, if some time remains after the reporter has explored his agenda, he may allow the official to talk about anything that is on his mind.

2. Establish the desired tone of the interview at the outset.

Normally, the tone most conducive to the extraction of information is one of cordial, even intimate, casualness. Few officials would be candid and cooperative if a reporter projected an attitude that he was St. George in shining armor and the official was a fierce dragon.

Even if the two are obviously adversaries, an experienced reporter will try to disarm his opponent. Time permitting, a reporter spends a few minutes establishing this casualness through trite chatter, with the goal of relaxing the official and establishing a pattern of informality that is conducive to unfettered talkativeness. Once the official is talking freely, the reporter can smoothly, gently swing into the interview.

Exceptions, however, abound in special circumstances. As noted earlier, an unavoidably hostile or sensitive interview may require a direct, frontal assault of accusation coupled with evidence.

3. Engender a feeling of trust.

Few officials will be candid when they have misgivings about the integrity of the journalist. Much of this trust is based on reputation and previous relationships. But in an initial interview in which neither participant has previous experiences in dealing with the other, trust must be quickly established.

A reporter can often create a feeling of trust by projecting concern for the official. If, for example, the interviewee makes a potentially damaging remark through an innocent slip of the tongue, the reporter may say:

Excuse me, but I'm afraid you may have misstated (so and so). Is that what you meant to say? I want to get it right."

Such displays of honesty and concern may greatly enhance the grateful official's candor. However, it should be noted that, as his foremost consideration, a reporter is obliged to serve his readers. If the damaging slip of the tongue is an absentminded lapse into candor, the reporter may be obligated to print it. Example: If a public official uses a derogatory term to describe minority citizens, and if the reporter is convinced that the slip reflects his racial attitude, he should include the ugly quotation.

4. Use the prepared questions as an outline.

After focusing the interview on a desired topic, the reporter must be ready to ad-lib with follow-up questions to fully explore the area, especially when important, unanticipated information comes forth. A general question about police plans for combating rising crime may evoke the unexpected announcement that a new tactical patrol unit will be formed to bolster protection in high-crime areas. The reporter must then follow up with questions that elicit a clear definition of the unit.

5. Take time to get it right.

If the official offers a complicated response, the reporter should make certain that he understands. If a particularly attractive quotation is offered, the reporter may ask the official to repeat it, or he may read his notes back for confirmation. Such painstaking steps to ensure accuracy serve not only to avoid distortion, but they also contribute to the official's feeling of trust for such a conscientious reporter.

6. Don't interrupt the flow of interesting, pertinent information.

If the official has been lulled into casual candor, an untimely interruption may break the spell. Wait until he has finished before asking for clarification or repetition. No one can speak for long without digressing into less important or repetitious material. Use such interludes as an opportunity to catch up with your note-taking, and to organize your thoughts for follow-up questions, before interrupting.

A reporter should be cautioned against keeping too tight control over the flow of the interview. Interruptions should be made only when it becomes apparent that the official is digressing in an attempt to control the interview, or if a long-winded official has become more intent on hearing the sound of his voice than on offering information.

7. At the end of the interview, offer an open-ended question, such as:

"We seem to have covered my questions. Do you have anything to add that may further clarify the issue?"

Frequently, the response is negative or only moderately interesting. Yet, at times, such an offhanded invitation has triggered surprising responses. During the interview, the official may have had fleeting thoughts that were interrupted, then lost. The final, open-ended "jogger" may revive a concept that otherwise would have gone unsaid. The opportunity is normally worth taking, since the reporter can wait until the interview time has expired before tossing out the question amid closing cordialities as the official's secretary impatiently holds open the door.

8. Throughout the interview, be as courteous as possible.

Despite the gruff, abrasive image of a reporter that many people hold, most professionals prefer to be civil and polite, for both the sake of human decency and professional technique. It simply enhances the flow of information.

Also, it is obvious that a reporter who is tossed out of the office for gross provocation after two minutes acquires less information than his colleague who conducts a civil and cordial thirty-minute interview.

APPLYING INTERVIEW TECHNIQUES

Now that interview methods have been examined, let's take another try at interviewing the police chief to examine the application of the methods.

As a new police beat reporter, you must conduct considerable research to prepare for your adversary. After reading clippings in the morgue, you contact leaders on both sides of the critical issue, both black and white officers.

From the black officers, you obtain these major items:

1. Although black citizens comprise 38 percent of the city's population, only 9 percent of the city's police officers are black.

2. None of the 47 command-level officers on the force is black.

3. Only 7 percent of all black applicants for police jobs have been accepted during the past 5 years, compared with 20 percent of all white applicants.

4. About 80 percent of the department's black officers are assigned to patrol black neighborhoods. Of these, all but 10 percent have black partners in their cruisers.

5. Quotation from Patrolman Leroy Simms, president of the Black Police Officers' Association: "We have, in effect, two separate police forces: one black and one white. You can talk to any black officer and find specific instances of discrimination or abuse from white officers. We have had all we can take; we've tried to work quietly to straighten this out for years, and got nowhere. A few white officers are color-blind, friendly. But they are precious few. The chief must make a stand now; he must be for or against us. If he's against us, or even if he's not for us, every black officer on the force will resign. We cannot support or belong to a racist organizaiton."

From the white-dominated Fraternal Order of Police hierarchy, the reporter obtains these items from Sergeant Gabe Powell, FOP president:

1. Promotions are strictly governed by civil service examination. Officers who score highest on written exams almost invariably win available promotions. No black officers have scored highly on such exams.

2. Hiring is also governed by civil service screening. Applicants who score highly on entrance examinations, who are physically fit, who have no criminal records, win the jobs.

3. Many black officers specifically request black partners. By custom, if two officers want to work together, that request is granted if possible.

4. Black officers are assigned to black districts "because we feel that they can better understand and serve black citizens."

5. A quotation: "Racism has no place in this department. We respect our black colleagues because most of them are fine officers. However, in fairness to everyone, we believe that hiring and promotion must be done on an open, fair, competitive basis. Several black officers have ample intelligence and capability to win promotions. I would like to see them do it. But we contend that rank must be earned, not awarded on the basis of black or white skin."

Note. As the issue unraveled in future weeks, the fairness of entrance and promotional testing became a major issue, as black officers contended that the tests were weighted to give those from a white cultural background a considerable advantage over those from the black culture. Yet, at the time of the interview, the reporter could not anticipate such arguments.

After gathering such background, the reporter then talks with his predecessor, a newsman who moved to the city hall beat after spending three years covering the police beat. After providing additional background and insight on the racial issue and the officers involved, the ex-police beat reporter provides information about the chief:

"He's the best chief the city has ever had; he's honest, competent, and progressive. As you know by now, many policemen dislike him because he has the courage to change old, traditional evils. My guess is that he will accommodate the black officers' complaints, but he won't move until he feels that the time is right. He can take the pressure.

"When you interview him, stay alert. He's the toughest official I've ever interviewed. His favorite trick is to filibuster on secondary questions. When you finally pop the big one, he can be amazingly elusive—he's got more moves than O.J. Simpson on an open field. The good thing is that when you do get an answer, you can trust him. If you nail him, he will be honest."

Preparing the Questions

Armed with such valuable information, the reporter can compile his questions accordingly. Forewarned about the chief's affinity for secondary issues, the reporter omits such openings by focusing his questions on the single subject of racial tension. After defining his informational objectives—what he *really* wants to find out, and spending several minutes composing and rewriting questions, he devises this list:

1. Black officers charge that hiring and promotional practices are discriminatory. Are you aware of any such discrimination?

2. I have verified figures that show that, while black citizens comprise 38 percent of the city's population, only 9 percent of the city's police officers are black. Can you explain this disparity? Do you consider this to be an indication of discrimination?

(Note: Question 2 is added on the assumption that the chief will sidestep the opening query. Even if he doesn't, it's a natural follow-up.)

3. Not one command-level officer is black. Can you explain why? Again, does this indicate discrimination?

4. I have also confirmed that about 80 percent of your black officers are assigned to black neighborhoods. Why?

5. Black officers threaten to resign unless you support their positions. Do you think that they're serious? What do you intend to do?

6. Many white officers are also upset, contending that black officers are trying to win appointive promotions at their expense. Would you consider appointive promotions? Are you concerned about tensions and hostility among white officers?

7. Have you seen any indications that racial tension is affecting the morale and the performance of your officers? What do you intend to do about it?

8. Patrolman Sims has charged that there are two separate police departments, one black and one white. Do you agree?

While other questions can obviously be formulated from background information, this list is more than ample for the brief half hour allotted. Also, the reporter doesn't wish to tip his hand by revealing all of his information. Instead, he plans to use the background for tactical effect in follow-up questions.

Note that most of these questions are multiple. In many instances, the reporter may choose to wait for the answer to the initial question before asking the subsequent one.

The Interview

After exchanging customary cordialities, the reporter quickly sets the stage.

Reporter: "Chief, I know you must be concerned about racial tensions within the department—so is the public. I don't envy your position, but I have to ask a few questions to clarify things a bit. Perhaps we can allay some of those dangerous rumors that are flying round."

Chief: "Although I am aware of tensions, I may have trouble answering questions about the situation, since no one has officially presented me with the problem through channels. I have enough real problems on my mind, without looking for new ones. For example, our firearms policy is so ambiguous and confusing that our officers have no idea of when they can use their weapons. That's dangerous, not only to the officers, but to the public. You can quote me. It's high time that we . . . "

Reporter: "Excuse me for interrupting, but that's not the story I'm here for. After we cover the racial issue, I would, however, like very much to get those views. I'm afraid I have a one-track mind, too many subjects confuse me. (Smile and laugh)

"Now, black officers charge that (asks Question 1)."

Chief: "I am not aware of any specific instances of discrimination, but I don't doubt that it could exist. After all, with four hundred human beings in our department, it would be absurd to contend that none of them is racist—black or white. The department is a microcosm of society; it reflects that society which, unfortunately, contains racist elements. Racism is an ugly, brutal thing that can't be tolerated . . . "

Reporter: "But you are not personally aware of any discriminatory practices that are established by departmental policy or procedures?"

Chief: "No, I'm not aware of anything like that. But I would be a fool to say that they don't exist at this point, before I have looked into it. If we have any discriminatory practices, I will certainly end them. But, at this point, none has been brought to my attention."

Reporter: (asks Question 2)

Chief: "If your figures are correct, then it certainly implies that discrimination has been at work. However, it may be that the culprits are history and society. Historically, black citizens were indeed denied police jobs and promotions for many, many years. I've been on this force for twenty-seven years, and I've seen it. But, in the past several years, a concerted effort has been made to remove such barriers. Those figures may reflect a lag between implementation of equal opportunity policy—the city decreed such policy six years ago by law—and a response from the black community. Many blacks, understandably, are suspicious of our institutions. Among blacks, police have been viewed as oppressors for generations. They have been kept outside our ranks. Now that the door is open, many may be reluctant to walk in. As for society, educational opportunities have, in the past, been so inferior in the black community that young blacks simply lack the training to successfully compete for jobs and rank. It's a terrible tragedy, but I don't think you can necessarily point the finger at us. Again, if discriminatory practices exist within this department, I will correct them."

Reporter: "I've also verified that only seven percent of all black job applicants are hired, as opposed to twenty percent of all whites. Why do you suppose this occurs?"

Chief: "I would like to think that it's because of educational disadvantages among blacks, rather than because of departmental practices. I will have to delve into the matter and determine whether it's us or education."

Reporter: "Then you do intend to investigate the alleged discrimination?"

Chief: (Unhappily aware that he has stepped into a trap): "Yes, at the proper time, I will investigate. That proper time, however, will be after black officers have made their charges directly to me, rather than through public media. I continue to practice an open-door policy toward officers who have legitimate complaints. I sincerely urge both black and white officers to take advantage of this. If they're unhappy, I certainly want to know about it, but I must hear it from them, not you."

Reporter: "Assuming that the allegations prove valid, will you take affirmative action on behalf of the black officers?"

Chief: "I operate on facts, not assumptions, so I can't comment on such conjecture until I can examine the facts."

Reporter: "Here's a fact, then. Not one black officer holds command-level rank. (asks Question 3) Can you explain why? Does this indicate discrimination?"

Chief: "At this point, it only indicates that black officers are not being promoted. I don't know the reason, but I intend to find out. If discrimination exists, I will put an end to it. If there are other circumstances that are blocking blacks from promotion, I would be willing to work with those officers to find ways of alleviating those circumstances."

Reporter: "Even at the risk of aggravating hostility among white officers?"

Chief: "I will not give any officer, white or black, an unfair advantage over others in promotions. When I make a decision after investigating the situation, that decision will be in the form of fair and impartial action. If any officer is unhappy about it, whether he be black or white, he can either console himself to accept it, or resign. Personally, I don't care which alternative he accepts. I'm not fixing to put up with soreheads, whether they be black or white soreheads."

The interview would, of course, continue through the remaining questions, but the example should be sufficient to illustrate techniques of a successful interview. Compare the latter example with the initial interview at the beginning of this chapter.

Such a comparison quickly shows how, in the final example, firm control enabled the reporter to obtain truly significant material.

The stage was set effectively when the reporter implied sympathy and understanding in his remarks prefacing the initial question: "I don't envy your position, but . . ." He quickly followed with a suggested incentive for cooperation: "Perhaps we can allay some of those dangerous rumors . . ." While neither ploy could be expected to deceive the perceptive chief, they helped to establish the proper tone of cooperation.

The battle for control was waged with the initial question. When the chief assumed his filibuster tactic, the reporter politely but firmly cut him off, adding a touch of self-depreciating humor to arrest any anger that may have resulted. The chief, of course, got the message: The reporter was too alert for the tactic. Delay and digression were removed from his arsonal.

The chief was still far from defeated, however. His next move was to formulate foggy, philosophic answers to unpleasant questions. The reporter allowed him to indulge for a few moments before abruptly stating a still sharper, more specific follow-up question.

For a while, the dual continued on equal terms, with the chief continuing to elude specific comments on the problem. Then, the official stumbled by stating that he would have to "delve into the matter." The reporter pressed his advantage home by turning the statement into an admission that an investigation would be conducted— something that the chief had tried to avoid. From that point on, the official was far too preoccupied with defending himself from the on-slaught of sharp questions to indulge in the fancy verbal footwork needed to battle for control of the talk.

The results of the interview were, by no means, one-sided. While the reporter emerged with meaty material that, in essence, was a very strong commitment to investigate and correct any discriminatory practices within the department, he failed to pin the old chief down on several highly sensitive points.

Although he revealed considerably more than he had intended to disclose, the chief protected his explosive personal leanings: After twenty-seven years on the police force, he knew that countless subtle ways existed to give a friendly subordinate an advantage in seeking a promotion. He knew that blacks had not been on the force long enough to learn the system. He knew that announcements of police job vacancies were far better advertised in the white community than in black neighborhoods, thus giving whites the inside track in seeking jobs. Knowing all of these factors, he was strongly inclined to do all in his power to help the black officers.

The chief's secrets remained unsaid because he knew that a premature announcement would seriously damage his chances of rectifying the problems.

An important point can be drawn from this: No reporter, despite his skills and competence, can force an official to provide complete information. The final example was a successful interview, yet major secrets remained unsaid. Perhaps, whenever a reporter savors a successful interview, he would be well advised to examine his material in postmortem, reading between the lines for clues of missed opportunities and deflected questions. He may thus be better prepared for the next interview session.

SUMMARY

In the example illustrating interview techniques, some procedural methods weren't readily applicable. Unfamiliar words, concepts, and terms weren't involved, so the reporter wasn't required to request clarification or definition. At times, the reporter may have requested a restatement for quotation purposes.

The interview is an art form in journalism that is acquired, then polished by experience as well as talent. It is inconceivable that any notable reporter could attain a top-rung position without mastering this art.

EXERCISES

1. You have an exclusive interview with the President of the United States. Outline the procedures you would follow in researching background for the interview, and in composing and arranging the list of questions. List ten questions that you would ask the President, and in the order which you consider most effective.

2. Class exercise: Redistribute the lists of questions so that each person has a set other than the list he or she prepared. On a separate sheet of paper, critique the questions to determine:

   a. The effectiveness of the arrangement of questions.

   b. The virtues and flaws of each question asked.

8 | Speeches

The speaker's white teeth sparkled in a smile that stood out in contrast with his suntanned face as he gazed over the hostile audience that was jammed into the auditorium.

The smile—or perhaps boyish grin—carried a warmth, a charm that began melting the frosty crowd response even before he spoke the first word. Local folks had long considered him an arch political enemy, a symbol of a brand of liberalism that they despised. They had come out of curiosity, not admiration. Many simply wanted to see the enemy with their own eyes.

As the speech continued, a noticeable change of atmosphere became apparent to reporters covering the event. Applause, at first coolly polite, became warmer, then exuberant. The senator's message contained little newsworthy substance, or even exciting rhetoric. Style, oratorical skill, and awesome personal charm caressed the hearts of the audience and evoked a simple human affection for the man.

During the question-and-answer session at the end of his speech, the senator finessed even the toughest questions with self-deprecating humor and wit.

"If I don't know the answer, I'll find out for you," he promised the questioners. "Please state your name and address before you ask your question so that I can contact you later."

The performance ended with a standing ovation. Nervous police officers edged onto the stage to escort the senator through a side exit. After all, the man was despised locally.

To their horror, the senator nimbly jumped down from the stage and began a grand, triumphant exit down the center aisle. The startled crowd hesitated only for a second, then converged en masse to try to shake his hand, to see this amazing man close up. Many had tears of emotion in their eyes as they followed him outside.

The setting: The University of Alabama, 1966.

The speaker: Senator Robert Kennedy.

Even a veteran reporter covering such a speech would be hard pressed to capture the impact of the event. How can a journalist convey that an audience underwent a personality change through an almost magical spell of charm? Set in cold type, the senator's words would appear almost shallow, perhaps even dull.

A decade later, a Southerner delivered a far more substantive speech before a national audience in a moment of victory. Like Senator Kennedy, the Southerner was blessed with a charming, toothy smile—a cartoonist's dream. Yet, his low-keyed, droning style failed to spark an audience that was largely composed of ardent supporters.

The setting: Democratic National Convention, New York City, 1976.

The speaker: Jimmy Carter, who spoke to accept the party's nomination.

The contrast between these two speeches illuminates a serious obstacle in developing a pat technique for speech coverage. The *real* story may or may not be found in the speaker's words, or in the circumstances of the speech. Style can far overshadow substances, and setting can, at times, exceed all other newsworthy considerations. In some rare instances, such as the Kennedy speech, the crowd's reaction may be the story.

To cover a speech effectively then, a reporter must first be well prepared, primed for the event through research, so that he can perceive the significance of the message he hears. Secondly, he must be acutely alert for what *happens*, and not so blindly intent on the prepared and anticipated event that he fails to note unpredictable developments that sometimes overshadow the speech itself in importance. In short, a reporter cannot allow his attention to become so riveted to his pre-released copy of the speech that he fails to perceive the *real* story.

In covering the Kennedy speech, let's assume that a reporter had an advance copy (which, in the actual case, wasn't available), and that he lazily followed the speech, line for line, making corrections when the senator deviated from the text. While laced with bright rhetoric, the speech offers little newsworthy substance. Yet, the reporter mechanically records the verbal proceedings, then packages the words into the common framework of a speech story:

1. Most important or interesting quotation or paraphrase, plus setting.

2. Transition (often a passage to put lead quote in context).

3. Additional material related to the lead, including more background on the setting or audience response.

4. Second most interesting or important quotation/paraphrase.

5. Elaboration of Item 4.

6. (The quote-elaboration cycle continues.)

The result of such uninspired coverage would be a story of only moderate interest even to local readers, who are curious about the famous person in town. Nationally, the speech would be worth only a few lines—at the most—deep inside the major newspapers.

The reporter, in this instance, would have been both unprepared and asleep at the switch during the speech. With even a minimum of preparation, he would have been aware of the underlying significance of the speech as an event with extraordinary human significance:

1. In 1963, President John F. Kennedy had sent federal marshals and "federalized" National Guardsmen to the University of Alabama to ensure the enrollment of two black students, as Governor George C. Wallace "stood in the schoolhouse door" to symbolically bar their entrance. He judiciously stepped aside after the military show of force. Robert Kennedy was then the United States Attorney General. During that turbulent summer, the Kennedy name was unpopular in Alabama. Hostility still lingered in 1966.

2. Senator Kennedy was a liberal, the arch-enemy of traditional Southern politics.

3. Although moderate and liberal views had begun to make inroads, the student body and the community were overwhelmingly very conservative. The audience had come to boo, not cheer the senator.

Forewarned by such research, the reporter would have been acutely alert to the real story: the ideological confrontation between Robert Kennedy and his audience. The dramatic result would have been an exceptional story about a speech that became a happening.

With this lesson in mind, let's examine the techniques of speech coverage.

PREPARATION

The preparation for coverage of a major speech begins in the newspaper morgue. The reporter should read all available material about the speaker, the prospective audience, and the setting of the speech. If an advance copy of the text is available, then he should carefully read and analyze the text, underlining key passages.

As a time-saving technique, some reporters write a background passage in advance for insertion in the story that will be written later. The speaker's biographical background isn't likely to change before the speech, nor is the information concerning the location, sponsoring organization, and so on.

Other reporters carry the preparations a step further: They draft the entire story from the advanced text and background material, leaving space to insert standard passages concerning crowd size and reaction. This technique may be beneficial in cases where extremely tight deadlines follow the speech, but it has some major drawbacks:

1. Most speakers deviate from the prepared text at times. Occasionally, a speaker is inspired to dramatically announce that "I am going to discard my prepared text, and speak from my heart." The audience may love him for it, but reporters who had already drafted their story are quite naturally livid.

2. The reporter is strongly committed to cover the speech in the pre-established manner, regardless of what later transpires. This can greatly influence coverage. The story that results may be about what was supposed to have happened, rather than what actually occurred.

Reliance on the acquisition of an advance copy of a speech is unwise for another good reason: Except for major public figures who are backed by professional staffs of speechwriters and public relations persons, very few speakers offer advance copies. In fact, local figures often speak from hand-written notes jotted down hurriedly. Many excellent speeches result from this slap-dash style of preparation, and such speeches deserve professional coverage. It may be noteworthy that President Lincoln's great Gettysburg Address was scribbled on the back of an envelope. An advance copy is, then, a convenience and a tool, and not a necessity.

Coverage of local speeches by lesser-known figures poses still other problems for the reporter. The speaker may be an authority in a given field, but his fame may not have spread to the newspaper morgue. Moreover, the organization hosting the speaker may have had little previous public exposure. The problem, then, is to acquire background material about both the speaker and the organization.

Many such organizations have publicity chairpersons who can, when contacted, provide a written or verbal background of both speaker and host. The reporter should contact organization officials to obtain this material, and, if possible, a copy of the program agenda.

BEFORE THE SPEECH

Arriving at the location well before the speech is to begin, the reporter should acquire needed secondary information beforehand, so that he can concentrate fully on the speech when it is delivered:

1. *Note the physical setting of the event.* If it's a political speech from the county courthouse steps, the reporter should jot down a description of weather conditions, facilities (is there a podium? a bank of microphones? a platform?), and atmosphere (banners, placards, a country-western band).

2. *Note the composition of the audience.* Is there a predominant age group (mostly young adults or elderly?), social class (a $100-a-plate dinner?), mode of clothing (minks and tuxedoes, coveralls, white collar?), occupation (farmers, attorneys, politicians, students?), race, or ethnic group.

3. *Note the size of the audience.* Estimating a crowd is often difficult, even in an auditorium. When the speech is given outdoors, to a standing, milling audience, crowd estimates are challenging, even to experts. However, a few methods have proven fairly effective:

(a.) *A seated audience.* First, find out the total seating capacity. If the facility is filled to capacity, or overflowing into the aisles, then the reporter can use the number of seats as a base, then make a minor adjustment to accommodate those standing, or perhaps the few empty seats. A simpler approach is to write: "The 15,000-seat auditorium was filled to capacity, with several hundred people standing in the aisles." The essential message is clear to the reader: The speaker had a very large audience, and his popularity (or notoriety) was such that many were willing to stand.

A problem occurs when the audience rattles around in a large facility, with many empty seats. Unless people obligingly sit tightly together in the first few rows, allowing the reporter to count the number of seats per row and multiply by rows filled, the newsperson must mentally divide the auditorium into sections according to crowd density, then estimate seating in each section. The total estimate could have a significant margin of error.

(b.) *A standing audience.* A large, milling crowd is very hard to measure. Unless the reporters can find a vantage point offering an overview of the crowd, only experience and intuitive feel (translation: a wild guess) is available. However, with a good vantage point, the reporter can sometimes derive a good estimation by focusing on a section of the crowd with representative density, carefully assessing the approximate number within that section, then mentally using it as a yardstick. If the representative section contains about a thousand people, and if it occupies about a tenth of the crowd area, then the crowd is roughly ten thousand people.

Still another technique is to mentally compare the crowd with other assemblies, at which an accurate estimate had been made. Perhaps the reporter judges the crowd to be about the same size as the one that attended a high school football game earlier that week. He may recall that twelve thousand people were registered by turnstiles at the game.

The final "safeguard" for reporters who are desperate to obtain a crowd estimate is to consult police. Experienced officers are frequently able to provide reasonably close estimates. However, dependence on secondhand sources for crowd estimates at political events is risky.

If, for example, the officer is politically attracted to the speaker, he may be exceedingly generous in his estimate. The opposite is also possible.

Why should a reporter take such pains to estimate the audience size? Because it is an important indication of the speaker's popularity or public stature, and of the newsworthiness of the event. In covering a political speech, crowd estimates are especially vital because they add or detract from the politican's "standing." In a campaign, drawing power is an indication of the candidate's strength.

One particularly shrewd state politician discovered an effective way of inflating crowd estimates at his speeches. Long at odds with a certain large newspaper, he inserted this remark in his speech:

"That lying newspaper is determined to undermine our campaign. You can tell it when you pick up the newspaper tomorrow and see that they estimate this crowd at three thousand. Look around you; any fool can see that we have ten thousand people here."

The reporter covering the speech had, of course, completed his estimate earlier: three thousand people. The candidate knew that the crowd consisted of three thousand people, yet the reporter was neatly trapped into detracting from his newspaper's credibility by reporting an honest appraisal.

If that wasn't enough, the candidate soon added a new twist in a later speech. The reporter was casually standing at the front of the crowd, taking notes, when he was startled to hear the candidate say:

"Ole (his name) is the reporter for that lying newspaper. (The candidate pointed an accusing finger at him.) Why, I know why you have trouble estimating crowds; you can't see from down there."

Then, the candidate walked down to the reporter, grabbed his arm, and happily led him to the podium for a better view. "Now, what do you say? Don't you see ten thousand people out there?"

4. *Note the mood of the audience.* As the speaker is introduced, the reporter should note the mood of the crowd and the reception that it accords the speaker. A crowd invariably has its own unique personality derived from the "chemistry" of its composition. The identity of each individual, his personality and opinions, is quickly melded and shaped into a group composite. The crowd may be hostile, friendly, happy, sorrowful, or possessive of any other human emotion, as dictated by the prevailing mood. At times, a crowd may be schizoid, when it is sharply divided into different factions. A political convention, or a sports event at a neutral site may be conducive to such a split personality.

The mood of the crowd should become evident with the first reaction to the speaker. The reporter should carefully assess the meaning or the implication of the reception: Polite applause may indicate that the audience isn't sure whether they will like or dislike the speaker; loud applause mixed with boos and catcalls strongly forebodes a volatile, schizoid crowd. The reporter should also remember to compare the actual reaction with what was reasonably anticipated. Lukewarm applause for a candidate speaking before an audience heavily composed of normally fervent supporters may bode ill times.

5. *Note any manipulation of the audience.* Shrewd public figures are well aware of the rudiments of crowd control. Given the objective of winning a warm, vocal display of affection that will enhance their public standing, such public figures may resort to crowd-pleasing or controlling ploys. A reporter should be cognizant of more common crowd-control tactics, and alert to report their use. The readers should know whether the crowd's reaction was spontaneous or carefully evoked.

Among the more common manipulative methods are:

(a.) *Staging.* A warm and receptive atmosphere is created before the speaker even appears at the podium. In a rural area, a country-western band may stir up a happy, festive crowd mood. At an urban rally, a popular entertainer or star atholete may precede the speaker to "warm up the crowd." Supportive placards and banners may be strategically placed to establish a mood of prevailing approval for the speaker. Attractive women campaign workers may mill through the crowd, passing out bumper stickers and heart-warming smiles. A lesser known speaker may heap praises on the main speaker and ear-scorching criticism on his adversaries before the speech.

While all of these devices have acquired a legitimacy through use over the ages, they establish a *context* for the main speech and the crowd reaction that greets that speech. The readers should be offered that context.

(b.) *Crowd-stacking.* As a particularly prevalent practice in urban political campaigns, the speaker's campaign staff imports carloads or even busloads of vocal supporters to speeches in less enthusiastic areas of the city to create the illusion of unexpectedly strong support in that area. If the imported supporters are of the same racial and ethnic stock as the indigenous population, it is very difficult for a reporter to perceive crowd-stacking. Yet, if an amazingly large number of Irish-Americans appear at a rally in a predominantly Italian-American area of the city—or vice versa—then crowd-stacking may be at work. Another means of discovering the tactic is to confer with neighborhood political leaders, who may be more able to spot a large influx of outsiders. As a final precaution, the reporter may scan parking areas to discover whether buses or out-of-town cars are present. By noting the bus number and the name of the bus firm, later checking may document that the speaker's organization provided mass transportation to the site.

(c.) *Plants.* Even without mass importation of supporters, a speaker may sprinkle some vocal supporters in the audience to "season the crowd." The supporters act as cheerleaders, cueing the crowd to applaud. Sometimes, a "plant" may be given a brief speaking part. At a critical moment in the speech, he may bellow: "We love you Charlie!" or some other inanity designed to draw "spontaneous" applause. In recognizing a plant, a reporter may note that the same person delivered the same spontaneous message at the same point in the speech two days earlier in another town. Or, he may recognize the plant as a low-ranking campaign staff member.

(d.) *Hecklers.* The difficulty in assessing the nature of a heckler during a speech stems from the problem of determining from whence he came. He may be a local loudmouth acting on his own, or a plant by an adversary, or even a plant by the speaker's organization. If he's loud and local, neighborhood or town political leaders probably know him—people who are vocal enough to heckle at a speech normally exercise that outspokenness elsewhere.

If the heckler is an outsider, the speaker's response—or lack of it—may indicate his origin. If, for example, the heckler asks a pointed, embarrassing question that seems to fluster the speaker, drawing no direct response or, at best, a weak retort, the heckler is surely from the other side of the political fence. Yet, if the heckler lacks venom, and if his taunt evokes a brilliant, unhesitating response, the reporter's suspicions may be legitimately aroused.

Why would a speaker plant a heckler? A nasty, contemptuous heckler may create a strong feeling of dislike for himself and sympathy for the speaker. If the speaker, who is well primed for the heckle, responds to demolish his heckling friend with an effective put-down, then his standing among the crowd is considerably enhanced.

It should be noted, however, that an effective, spontaneous response may only indicate a quick wit. Many national political figures are masters of the devastating retort, their skills honed by years of political debates. If the reporter can ascertain that the heckler is a plant, then that item should be well emphasized in the speech story. Yet, mere suspicions should be withheld until verified.

(e.) *Crowd inflation.* A television film that shows a smiling speaker standing before a great throng of people can contribute greatly to the coveted "bandwagon" effect, giving a candidate the appearance of being a certain winner. Yet, closer examination may reveal that the speech was carefully staged outside the gates of a great industrial plant at quitting time, when thousands of workers were sure to pass by. Many workers would be drawn to the crowd by curiosity, not fervent support, thus vastly inflating the speaker's actual drawing power.

In summary, the moments before the speech begins should be well used by the reporter to glean information that will set the context of the speech. While it is naturally in the interests of the public figure to create an atmosphere to enhance his image, the reporter's task is to give the readers complete and accurate information necessary for them to accurately and knowledgeably digest the speech, both as a message and as an event.

Perhaps it should be noted that such alert, comprehensive coverage has become an exception, rather than a journalistic routine, even for major speeches by top-ranking national figures. All too commonly, reporters lazily act as stenographers during the speech, mechanically scribbling down words and raw reaction, then transcribing the notes into speech-story format. Yet, a speech is both an event and a message, with the former often outweighing the latter in potential significance to the readers.

COVERING THE SPEECH

When the speaker finally reaches the podium, the reporter should have already gathered several pages of notes. He should be well tuned in to the crowd, aware of the likely response so that he can accurately assess the real impact of the speech on the audience.

His final pre-speech notes should concern the crowd's greeting and the speaker's physical appearance:

1. How does the crowd respond as he reaches the podium?
2. Describe his facial expression. Is he smiling?
3. Note his clothing. How is he dressed for the occasion?
4. Note his mannerisms as he faces the crowd for the first time. Does he raise his hands above his head, forming victory "V's" with his fingers? Does he stand woodenly, nervously waiting for the applause to fade? Does he slowly scan the audience, assessing the mood and composition? Does he nervously squirm or pace, or casually lean against the podium?

As the speech begins, the reporter must focus his attention on three aspects of the event: the message, the speaker, and crowd reaction and behavior. The concentration necessary to accomplish this three-fold feat isn't unlike that needed to juggle three balls simultaneously:

1. *Following the speech.* Whether blessed with an advance copy of the speech, or condemned to scribble madly on clean note paper, the reporter must perceive, assess, and process each word and thought uttered by the speaker as he delivers his message.

An advance copy of the text simplifies matters. The reporter may follow the speech, word for word, on that copy, underlining significant points and noting digressions, omissions, or corrections. He should particularly note significant changes and, later, try to discover why the departure was made. Many reporters make separate notations in their notebooks, even with the advance copy, to briefly outline major points and significant crowd response. This technique later allows them to quickly retrieve major points without having to wade through insignificant passages. They may note the basic message, underline the passage in the advance copy, then key the page number beside the notebook notation for quick retrieval. A few reporters tape record the speech as a backup to their notes. But, under deadline pressure, it is generally impractical to rely solely on a tape recorder, since the entire speech would have to be replayed later. Besides, to suffer through a droning speech once is sufficient for most reporters. Still another valuable technique is to note the manner of delivery of key passages. Did the speaker harangue the audience in making the point? Did he dramatically drop his voice? Such description adds to the context of the message and brightens the flow of the writing itself.

Without the luxury of an advance copy, the reporter must employ all note-taking tricks (see Chapter 6) to succesfully record the newsworthy utterances of the speaker. In one sense, the absence of an advance copy can be beneficial: It forces the reporter to concentrate on the content of the speech, analyze and digest it, and apply a selectivity in note-taking that will enhance his speed in writing after the speech. Armed with note-taking techniques, such as key-wording and makeshift shorthand, a reporter can effectively capture the message by:

(a.) Keeping an ear tuned to exceptionally good phrases for direct quotations. Most of the notes are, of necessity, paraphrases. Yet, even with an advance copy, no self-respecting reporter would use a vast abundance of direct quotations in the story, since a professional journalist should be able to improve a given part of the message by rephrasing it in a clearer, more concise journalistic style. However, if the speaker provides a good sprinkling of well-phrased quotations, the reporter should jot them down verbatim, for judicious use in the story. A good blend of quotations throughout a speech story adds an aura of authenticity, and even serves to break the monotony of the reporter's style or writing—even the best writer's style becomes monotonous after awhile through a consistent preference for certain words and phrasing techniques.

Through practice, many reporters can remember a quotation verbatim for several minutes after hearing it. This allows them to continue taking rough notes until the speaker digresses or bogs down in unimportant detail. Given a momentary dull lull in the speech, the reporter can quickly jot down the quotation before he or she forgets it.

(b.) Being selective in note-taking. Once the reporter has taken sufficient notes to capture a given point, belabored, detailed explanation and examples may be omitted. Many good speakers are, by nature, also good teachers, who use the technique of repetition and redundancy to clearly convey a concept. If a reporter understands the message, he can often rest his cramped hand as soon as the speaker says, "In other words . . ."

(c.) Keying notes to indicate any material missed, so that after the speech, the reporter can contact the speaker to obtain information omitted from notes. On occasion, any reporter may fail to catch an important item through human error or, perhaps, simply because of inability to hear the speaker's words. While the reporter may frequently be unaware of the omission, the speaker often provides a clue. For example, the speaker may preface a listing of items with: "There are four good reasons why this legislation is vitally important . . ." If the reporter's notes contain only three reasons, then there's a good chance that an item has been missed. When such an omission is found, the reporter should note the need for additional information in an easily recognized manner—perhaps a large-lettered, printed and underlined notation: "Get fourth reason." A variation of this method is to tear out a piece of paper to list possible omissions and areas needing clarification or verification, for doublechecking after the speech.

2. *Covering the speaker.* The manner in which the message is delivered may have a strong bearing on the meaning and context of that message. The reporter is obliged to jot down observations about the manner of delivery, when such observations can influence clarity and context.

For example, the speaker grins puckishly as initial applause fades, then proclaims, in an obviously tongue-in-cheek manner: "Either I am underrating myself, or Abe Lincoln's theory that you can't fool all of the people all of the time has just been shot down."

Without the addition of a brief description of the context—the manner in which the remark was delivered, readers may be startled to see one of the most brazen political confessions of all time.

Body language can convey a great deal of the non-verbal message. A remark that is punctuated by the sound of a fist slamming angrily on the podium, delivered in a voice quivering with rage, or subdued in silent fury, can alter the meaning of the message. Like many ordinary folks, some speakers "talk with their hands," making gestures, pictures, and measurements to help convey their message. The reporter can capture this visual message:

> Congressman Jones accused his opponent of uttering a "tiny little lie." He extended both arms to their extremes to illustrate the size of the alleged falsehood, as the audience laughed in appreciation.

The full context leaves the reader little room to misinterpret the speaker's sarcastic use of the word "tiny."

3. *Crowd reaction.* The crowd is the reader's proxy in determining how to react to the speech and to the speaker. The effect of insertions describing crowd response is similar to that of canned laughter on a television situation comedy: Your audience is given a cue.

If the reader is aware of the composition of the audience—predominantly young, of a general background that is associated with liberal political views, for example—he is cued on how he should react. If he is a liberal, and the liberal audience applauds, then the speaker's remarks may tend to be received favorably. If he is a conservative, the opposite may be true. Crowd laughter tells the reader that a remark was made in a joking manner. Mixed applause and boos alerts the reader to a controversial assertion.

The crowd reaction, then, serves as an emotional barometer, which should be carefully checked throughout the speech.

A closely related factor is the peculiar "chemistry" between the speaker and the crowd. In the earlier example of the Kennedy speech, that volatile chemistry provided the real story, as the senator's personal charm not only neutralized cool hostility, but, at least for a moment, magically created a personality change in that strange, often unpredictable beast called a crowd. A gifted speaker can sense the mood of the crowd and adjust his style according to woo them.

AFTER THE SPEECH

As the speaker's final word is uttered, and the crowd response is duly noted, the reporter's final task is to reach the speaker for clarification or elaboration. As noted earlier, the reporter may be concerned about note-taking omissions, or about foggy points in the speech that demand clarification.

Perhaps more importantly, a brief interview after the speech provides the journalist the opportunity to be more than a mere conduit of information from speaker to reader. Keep in mind that a speech is a carefully prepared rendition of material that the speaker calculates to be favorable. A speech is often the ultimate public relations medium —free, highly favorable publicity.

During the brief post-speech interview, the reporter should not only obtain material omitted and elaboration of points, but should firmly seek to penetrate questionable assertions:

1. Any allegation detrimental to an adversary. A less scrupulous speaker may sprinkle "cheap shots" at his opponents throughout his speech, stating rumor or suspicion as fact, and half-truths as full truths.

By blindly printing such allegations, the reporter not only risks a well-deserved libel suit, but he also allows himself to be used as a propaganda outlet.

If, then, an allegation is either made or implied, the reporter is obliged to demand substantiation of the charge. For example:

"I'm not saying that my opponent is immoral," the politician may glibly assert with a wink and a grin, "but we've all heard about those wild parties in Washington."

But, of course he *is* implying that his opponent is immoral, yet stopping just short of the point of committing provable slander. The reporter, then, should ask:

"Do you know of any instance in which the congressman attended a 'wild' party in Washington? If so, can you prove it?"

2. Questionable material presented as fact should also be scrutinized. Perhaps the same candidate said in his speech, "Throughout my political career, I have always championed environmental causes, even long before they became a popular public concern."

In the research performed before the speech, the reporter may recall contrary evidence. He should force an explanation:

"Sir, you described yourself as being a champion of environmental causes. Yet, as a state senator, you were criticized for opposing every piece of environmental legislation presented during your terms. Can you explain this apparent contradiction?"

After such an interview, the reporter should also take another step to ensure accuracy and fair play—if time permits. If damaging charges or questionable assertions are made, the reporter should make an effort to contact the speaker's adversaries and offer the opportunity of rebuttal. Not only does this step serve in the interest of fairness, but it also provides the reader with both sides of the question so that he can judge for himself.

SUMMARY

The steps and techniques of speech coverage, as provided in this chapter, should lead to an abundance of information from which to choose when the reporter sits before the typewriter. Perhaps most of the information gathered will be discarded during the writing stage, yet a thorough, comprehensive approach to the coverage of any news event worthy of as much as a column inch of news space enables the reporter to write a truly accurate account. The magnitude of the particular speech, and the time available to the reporter for coverage are variables that generally dictate just how thorough coverage can be for a given event. The news value and the resulting space allotment determine the comprehensiveness of the final account.

The overriding objective of speech coverage is to gather all material necessary to convey the speaker's message, and in a context that keeps distortion to a minimum, and to provide the reader an honest, clear account of both the message and the event surrounding that message.

EXERCISES

1. Assume that your governor is campaigning for re-election. He is speaking at a local campaign rally tonight. Outline your steps in covering the speech (assuming that no advance copy is available).

2. Class project: Each class member will cover a speech, designated by the instructor, then submit notes and other material gathered prior to, during, and after the event.

3. Estimate the size of a standing, milling crowd at a designated site on campus. Explain how you derived that estimate. Then estimate the size of a seated crowd at a designated event on campus. Explain your methodology.

9 | Press Conferences

By all appearances, the city manager is grossly overmatched against the pack of reporters that fills the city hall conference room, as he makes himself available for his monthly press conference.

His adversaries include several television and radio news reporters who cover the city hall as one area of their large newsbeats, and city hall beat reporters from the city's two large daily newspapers, specialists who spend their entire efforts probing the nooks and crannies of the city manager's domain. Each reporter is armed with a list of questions about the various crises that the city government faces. In general, the reporters are bright, alert, and well prepared. But, so is the city manager.

The press conference opens as the city manager reads a lengthy, carefully prepared statement that supports a large city income tax increase, which is already on the ballot for a referendum in an upcoming election. The statement, which outlines the city's financial crisis, is so bleak and threatening that it would have brought tears to a miser's eyes. Among the consequences that the city manager offers in the event that citizens reject the tax increase are:

1. A 25 percent reduction in police manpower. "I don't have to tell you that every citizen will face a greater threat of crime if this occurs," the city manager adds. "This city may become a dangerous place to live."

2. A 25 percent reduction in fire department manpower, and the closing of one fifth of all fire stations. "The fire chief assures me that we will retain minimum resources for routine services, such as a single house fire. Yet, he warns that a single major fire could so drain available manpower and equipment that much of the city would be stripped of fire protection until that blaze could be brought under control. If two major fire occurred simultaneously, we could not fight

both. I did a little research and found that simultaneous major fires have occurred three times in the past five years."

3. Weekly garbage pickup would be curtailed. Trash would be collected every other week. "Health officials warn that infestation of rats would probably increase considerably, along with the threat of disease."

As the city manager continues his listing of assorted catastrophes, reporters scribble down new follow-up questions concerning the prepared statement. Suddenly, the doomsday list takes priority over all the subjects reporters had carefully researched before the conference.

As the statement ends, the city manager assumes a statesman-like, weary countenance, then invites the reporters to begin their questioning.

"Bill, the list you read sounds like a blackmailer's threats," the first questioner notes. "Are you trying to blackmail voters into passing the tax increase?"

With an indignant glare, the city manager says, "I do not consider blackmail to be moral or ethical, and I resent your implication. I am simply offering citizens a realistic view of the alternatives they face when they choose between saving money and saving this city. I assure you that I am not, to my knowledge, misrepresenting this crisis. We cannot continue our present level of service without a tax increase."

The questions and follow-up questions concerning the statement fail to shake the city manager's assertions. His answers are calm, precise, and well supported by an inch-thick folder of studies and reports. Each reporter is given a copy to underscore dramatically the integrity of the assertions.

In short, the press conference has been cleverly transformed into a carefully staged "media event" under the firm, calculated control of the city manager. The unpleasant, penetrating questions that reporters had prepared to ask fall to the wayside—to the city manager's considerable relief.

Before the conference, the official had spent many hours assembling the data and preparing the statement. The day before the meeting, his public relations aide had grilled him during a dry run of the media event. Copies of the background material was carefully loaded with technical jargon and padded with tangential items to make them appear more impressive and less appealing to any reporter who might have been tempted to read the document. Even if a reporter had overcome his reluctance and read it, several hours would have been required before logical questions could have been formulated to refute or dilute the impact of the assertions. The reporters may have outnumbered the city manager, but the official easily routed his adversaries.

This hypothetical account illustrates the sad fate that all too often befalls reporters at a press conference. As noted in the chapter concerning interviews, *control* is vitally important in any matchup of journalist versus news source. A press conference is so easily manipulated by an official that any news that evolves from such events should be examined cautiously by both reporter and reader.

Despite appearances, the hosting official has several key advantages over his journalistic friends:

1. He has the "home field advantage." He can control the format of the event, the staging, and even the composition of the audience.

The format is especially important, since it regulates the nature of answers given. Some officials require questions to be submitted a day in advance, in written form, so that sufficiently self-serving answers can be prepared in advance. (Fortunately, few reporters accept such a condition.) Another format ploy is to arrange the program to permit a minimal time for open questioning.

The staging includes the time, place, and available facilities of the press conference. A particularly troublesome reporter who persists in asking embarrassing questions may find press conferences scheduled very close to his final deadline time, so that he has little opportunity to question the official's assertions or to disrupt the proceedings by raising unrehearsed topics. Or, the conference may be scheduled past his deadline, so that the favorable, managed "news" can enjoy free-wheeling media play for an entire news cycle, before the note of discord can be raised. Facilities can also contribute to staging. A plush, executive conference room, with well-cushioned chairs and a table laden with complimentary coffee and doughnuts can put the press corps in the proper state of mind to accept what is offered.

Some officials have, on occasion, used the heavy-handed tactic of excluding uncooperative reporters. While they can hardly bar an accredited journalist from a press conference, they can take pains to avoid informing him of the event.

2. The official faces a highly divided camp of adversaries. Each reporter present is competing with every other journalist. The intense, natural competition often precludes the logical progression of questions designed to penetrate past the facade of the official position and into the realm of truth.

Using the initial example, let's say that a reporter asks:

"The dramatic budget cutbacks that you listed all involve the most basic city services. Aren't there other areas, other programs that can be curtailed or terminated without such disruption?"

The city manager shakes his head sadly and says, "I wish that were true. Next question?"

Before the suspicious reporter can bore in with follow-up questions, a competitor has change the subject with another query. Evasiveness is a cherished tool of many officials. In the chaos of a press conference, it is a mightily effective ploy.

3. The official will be well prepared to answer almost any conceivable question. After establishing the date of the conference, he can carefully assemble his thoughts and positions, and rehearse responses.

The Positive Side

This negative depiction of a press conference has been assembled to convey the challenge that faces a reporter who attends such a media event. Despite such obstacles, even the most aggressive reporters have learned to accept press conferences as "necessary evils" in their quest for news. It should also be emphasized that many—perhaps most—press conferences are honest attempts by public officials to be responsive to the public's right to information. While, quite naturally, they seek to present information in a context enhancing to their official viewpoints, most officials try to maintain personal integrity by resisting the temptation to distort. Yet, a reporter should always fill the role of adversary, of public watchdog, by suspiciously examining the message of even highly respected officials with an established record of honesty.

Let's examine the advantage of a press conference:

1. Many top news sources are extremely busy people, who can spare only limited time to deal with news media. A police chief, who spends fifteen hours a day struggling with massive responsibilities can hardly be expected to set aside his work to chat with every inquisitive reporter who wants to interview him. Yet, the chief may sincerely want to inform the public of problems and circumstances that affect public welfare. The press conference is a legitimate vehicle for disseminating such information in a time-efficient, effective manner. It also provides reporters with a limited time of accessibility that they might otherwise have been denied.

2. In a crisis situation, in which many reporters are clamoring for an official position or statement on a breaking news event, the press conference is the only logical means of accommodating the press. If, for example, a major scandal occurs that implicates the mayor, then the mayor may hastily assemble a press conference by herding the waiting mob of reporters to a conference room.

3. The press conference may legitimately serve the public's right for information, even though it denies the individual reporters the satisfaction of an exclusive story. From the reporter's point of view, perhaps the most discouraging aspect of a press conference is that he must share the revelations with all of his competitors, even if his questions unlocked the most important items of information.

PREPARING FOR A PRESS CONFERENCE

When a beat reporter is informed of a scheduled press conference, he may immediately ask the public relations aide, "What topics will be discussed?" If he can pry an agenda from the PR person, then he can direct his preparations to cover those areas as well as the assorted other items of interest.

Before the conference, the reporter should scan clippings and reports on all issues and areas of interest that lie within the official's domain. Then, the reporter should prepare a list of questions in *descending order of importance*. In competing for the official's attention with other reporters, it is most unlikely that he can ask more than two or three questions. Yet, he may prepare a lengthy list on the chance that other reporters will ask the obvious, top-priority questions before he can gain the floor. In composing the questions, the reporter should carefully arrange the phrasing so that the query evokes only a specific answer, and not a curt "yes" or "no." Also, the question should be worded so clearly that the official cannot freely misinterpret, and answer according to his misinterpretation.

An aggressive reporter may take still another preparatory step, and that is contacting news sources close to the official to try to gain further insight on the nature of the information to be disclosed. Returning to the initial example, if a reporter had pieced together the general drift of the city manager's message before the press conference, he may have succeeded in devising penetrating questions or even contradictory material. At the very least, he could have gained valuable time to delve beneath the surface of the carefully packaged statement. Far better, he could have written an exclusive, well-informed story that would have appeared before the press conference, thus puncturing the well-laid plans of the official.

BEFORE THE CONFERENCE BEGINS

By now, it should be obvious that time is important to a reporter, and that a good journalist rarely wastes any. The normal ten- or fifteen-minute lull from the time the reporters straggle in until the official begins the program can be well used in prying assorted information from some unlikely news sources—other reporters.

An assembly of professional newsgatherers should be filled with bits of information, or even mother lodes of news. Since even reporters are people, and since people are cursed with a tendency to talk too freely, a sly journalist can frequently pick up many interesting items from unwittingly cooperative competitors, particularly those who can be goaded into the popular "I'm better informed than you" game. The reporter who graciously loses such matches of horn-tooting may take consolation in the items he picked up from the winner. A variation is information trading. Reporters may trade news items and insight, much as horsetraders swap their livestock. The object is to offer the least information in exchange for the most. It should be noted that in such exchanges a seemingly minor item offered by one reporter may be of major importance to another. Newsgathering often is akin to fitting together a massive jigsaw puzzle. In the context of other information a reporter has acquired, an offhanded revelation by another reporter may provide a vital missing piece.

PARTICIPATING IN THE PRESS CONFERENCE

After sharpening their wits on each other, the reporters should be well tuned up when the press conference opens. As will be discussed later, the means of performing effective coverage can vary considerably, depending on what transpires during the press conference. For now, we will examine routine coverage of a normal press conference, with these assumptions:

1. The hosting official is a reasonably honest, conscientious person who is seeking to disseminate—not manipulate—news.

2. The reporter's viewpoint is that of a journalist for an afternoon newspaper, which has a noon deadline. The conference is set at 10 A.M.

3. Despite the natural competition, an air of professional courtesy prevails, along with a common interest to extract an accurate, complete account.

4. Ample time is provided after the opening statement to accommodate not only questions about the prepared announcement, but also queries about other issues.

5. For the sole purpose of illustrating the techniques, we shall let the chief of police be the host. The techniques—not the hypothetical information—should be the central concern.

Opening Statement. As the official issues the opening statement to provide the information that, from his viewpoint, is the major objective of the press conference, the reporter should take notes in the same manner as he would during a speech. Direct quotations and careful paraphrases of major items should receive note-taking emphasis. However, even as notes are being collected, the reporter should quickly digest the material and formulate questions to expand or elucidate the statement.

Questions about the opening statement. Before pursuing other issues, the reporter should first raise questions about the statement.

Perhaps the police chief has announced that women officers will be permitted to accept patrol assignments and other duties previously limited to male officers.

"Although I'll admit that I have strong reservations about this, the city attorney informs me that we have no legal alternative other than to make this policy change. Despite my personal reservations, I intend to firmly enforce the policy and to remove any obstacles that curtail the opportunities for women officers."

The statement continues in length to explain the legal background of the issue, the problems of implementing the policy, and other related items.

The reporter for the afternoon newspaper glances at his watch to note that an hour and a half remains before deadline. As he quickly scribbles his questions, a television newswoman asks:

"Chief, have any women police officers requested street patrol duty? How many women officers do you expect to have on patrol when this policy is fully implemented?"

As the official finishes responding, a radio newsman asks:

"Do you anticipate problems with male officers?"

Frowning, the chief knows that the answer will be ticklish. By publicly anticipating problems, he fears that he will encourage disgruntled officers to create problems. He answers diplomatically, "Some male officers could be unhappy with the ruling. Policemen tend to be conservative about changes, and this is a big change that will take some getting used to. I hope that the men will suppress any reservation and give the women a fair chance. Next question."

Recognizing the smooth evasion, another reporter, who had gained the floor, discards his own question and asks:

"Chief, I don't believe you answered the question. Obviously, you don't want problems to erupt, but the question is: Do you anticipate problems with male officers?"

"Yes, I do," the chief responds unhappily. "Street patrol duty has always been a man's world, a dangerous world in which each officer must have confidence that his partner can back him up in a tough situation. If you were a policeman, facing two mean, belligerent drunks who were contemplating reshaping your head, how much confidence would you have in a one hundred and thirty-pound woman partner? I suspect that many male officers will resist being assigned a female partner. That's the kind of problem I anticipate."

The newspaper reporter presses the opening:

"Chief, you expressed personal reservations. Can you tell us the reservations you have about the assignment of patrol duty to women? Secondly, if you were a patrolman, how would you react to having a woman partner?"

"My reservations stem from my concern about the physical safety of each of my officers," the chief replies. "I really do care about what happens to my people out there on the streets. I am concerned that, in a physical confrontation, a woman officer could be seriously injured simply because of the vastly superior strength of a potential assailant. I am also concerned about the safety of male partners, who could be at a dangerous disadvantage in a fight without a physically capable partner.

"Now, before I answer the second part of your question, I must say that my reservations have been abated somewhat. Yesterday, I went out to the police academy to observe and, later, participate in an experiment. Policewoman Bonnie McLaughlin had challenged a two hundred and thirty-pound patrolman to a fight. Mrs. McLaughlin weighs a hundred and fifteen pounds. Using the extensive judo training given to all police officers, Bonnie wasn't even breathing hard after she threw her opponent and captured him with a wristlock. Now, I thought that the match was too sterile. A real street fighter would use a weapon, and use the element of surprise. So, without warning, I grabbed a baton and charged. My ancient body is still aching from the results—she had me flat on my back and disarmed before I knew what was happening.

"With that perspective, I still have some reservations, but I honestly wouldn't worry much about my own safety if I were a patrolman and Bonnie were my partner. If other women officers are equally skilled, then my fears may well be groundless."

The rival newspaper reporter is still dissatisfied, and says:

"Chief, even after that demonstration, you were still concerned enough to express reservations. We all appreciate your colorful anecdote. but I suggest that you are far from satisfied. Am I right?"

"I've answered this question fully and honestly," the chief replies angrily. "You can infer anything you want, only attribute it to yourself, not to me."

As time moves ever closer to deadline, the afternoon newspaper reporter decides to switch to other topics:

"Chief, a sixteen-year-old boy was fatally shot in the back as he fled from officers last week. Have you decided whether to take action against the officer who fired the shot? Secondly, does this incident seem sufficient to justify a review of your firearms policy?"

The questions and answers on an array of topics continue through the remaining time.

At this point, let's assess the conduct of the press conference to draw some guidelines for reporters participating:

1. As a matter of professional courtesy, assist other reporters in pinning down an evasive answer. If the official fails to offer a satisfactory response to a previous question, then the next reporter to gain the floor should restate the question and press for an answer.

Similarly, if a pertinent follow-up question to the previous response occurs to the next reporter, then he should pursue the matter. The benefits of such professional courtesy extend far beyond mere politeness:

(a). It prevents the official from maintaining firm control over the press conference through evasiveness and through playing reporters against each other.

(b.) The public's interest is far better served when reporters insist on complete answers to each question. Instead of merely accepting what information is offered, reporters extract the vital truth beneath the surface.

(c.) As a matter of self-interest, no reporter wants to see such succesful evasions of colleague's questions. If evasion is a viable ploy, then the official can use it to fend off your questions as well.

2. Ask only pertinent questions. Time is far too limited to be squandered on a reporter who poses a question only because he enjoys hearing the resonant sound of his own voice. If you haven't a good question, then simply listen and profit by others' questions.

3. Be cordial and polite when questioning the official. While firm insistence on a straight answer is often necessary, belligerent badgering is not. Furthermore, an official who has won a position of newsmaking prominence is hardly like to shrink in fear and 'fess up to an obnoxious reporter. More likely, he will simply dig in his heels.

4. Many reporters use a double-barrel technique in posing questions: They tag a follow-up question to the prime question to prod a full response. While the method is effective, reporters should limit themselves to no more than one or two tag-along follow-ups. First, a barrage of questions uttered in a single breath may confuse the official and evoke an incomplete mish-mash of answers. Secondly, the orderly pursuit of information can quickly degenerate into chaos if even one reporter hogs the floor to dominate the press conference.

AFTER THE PRESS CONFERENCE

If time permits, a reporter should carefully seek other sources of information before writing the story. In the example of the chief's press conference, the reporter would immediately try to obtain a reaction from both male and female officers. In contacting patrolmen, he may find that the chief vastly understated the potential for problems as, to a man, the officers vowed to resist working with female partners. On the other side, female officers may criticize the chief for expressing his reservations, and some may suggest that the chief is encouraging male resistance.

In seeking follow-up information after a press conference, a reporter may also try to corner the press conference host for additional, exclusive information. Some highly competitive reporters save their best questions until the official can be privately queried. In fact, few reporters who are seeking major, exclusive stories would even dream of posing a question that would tip other journalists to the story potential.

A few years ago, a television series about a reporter frequently depicted the protagonist at press conferences, stunning his competitors by posing questions that invariably informed them of a major, exclusive story that he was pursuing. No real reporter in his right mind would do so.

The necessity of non-participation at a press conference is especially relevant when the event occurs on the competitor's news cycle. If the same event had been staged after the noon deadline, the afternoon newspaper reporter would have quietly taken down the information uncovered by his rivals, then he would have sought fresh, substantial information for the story that would appear on the next day, after the morning newspaper had broken the news.

ALTERNATIVE PRESS CONFERENCE SITUATIONS

While most press conferences may fit into the general outline discussed previously, the precarious civility and order can easily be broken down if the hosting official is perceived as being hostile or dishonest in his presentation, or if the simmering rivalry between journalists boils over.

If the hosting official becomes openly hostile, then verbal warfare between the press and the official quickly ensues. In reality, this kind of breakdown in order is to the detriment of both reporters and the official. An angry, defensive official is unlikely to provide much printable information to the reporters. The lingering ill will can hamper even routine news coverage of the official's domain for several days. The official, then, may momentarily relish the discomfort of reporters who vainly seek information, but he must pay the penalty of failing to meet his objective of providing the information to the public that he had wanted to release.

A second type of breakdown occurs when the professional truce between competing reporters dissolves. At times, reporters yield to their deeply ingrained compulsion to beat the competition. If the hosting official has a sense of humor, he may be highly amused by the "cutthroat" tactics as:

1. A television cameraman casually unplugs a rival's electronics equipment during a critical part of the interview.

2. A newspaper reporter, aware that his rival is very close to

final deadline, filibusters with a long, involved question about a very minor news item, in hopes that his opponent will have to leave before more newsworthy items are covered.

3. A newspaper reporter making loud, obscene sounds or words throughout the proceedings to enrage broadcast reporters who are recording the official's words.

4. Television cameramen who carefully arrange lights to blind offensive competitors. (It is difficult to take notes when blinded.)

5. A gigantic newspaper photographer who, after being pushed aside by a television camerman, picks up the offender—camera and all—and calmly ejects him from the room.

While sometimes amusing, such displays can undermine the effectiveness of reporters at the event to a point where, as the conference ends, the journalists leave with only the packaged material offered by the official. Rivalry is vital to journalism, yet it should not be allowed to detract from that common objective of informing the public.

Still another alternative situation is an informal or impromtu press conference. These hastily assembled, casually conducted meetings are normally called to accommodate reporters seeking information about a fast-breaking news story.

The decorum and the resultant civility of a formal press conference are often missing, as deadline-pressed reporters try to gather information quickly, then run for telephones to file the story.

For example, let's say that a major union at the city's largest industrial plant staged a walkout to protest the firing of a union leader. As soon as news of the walkout reaches newsrooms, reporters rush to the union hall and to management offices to try to obtain information from both sources.

At the union hall, journalists may be forced to wait outside as union members hold a meeting to discuss the situation. After the meeting ends, the local union president emerges to meet with reporters standing outside. Journalists and photographers elbow for position as they crowd around the official, shouting questions. In short, the meeting melds the press into a classic "wolf pack" assembly.

A hapless reporter who becomes entangled in the pack loses control of his newsgathering operation. He has no alternative other than to jostle and shout with his colleagues. Information is gathered in the midst of chaotic conditions that are far from conducive to quality reporting.

A wise editor may beat the pack by assigning a team of several reporters to cover the action. One reporter must endure the pack environment to obtain the essential information from the top official. However, another reporter is freed to interview less exalted but equally informed officials to obtain far more information on an exclusive basis.

Still another reporter may talk with union members as they leave the hall to sample their reactions. The result: a far more complete account of a major event, a story that incorporates the essence of the press conference, yet goes beyond it.

Even a reporter working alone can beat the pack. Normally, the most important information is quickly unearthed in such situations. However, once assembled, the pack is slow to break up. They continue to press for more detail, more background, until satisfied that the official has given all that he can offer.

Importantly, a reporter should learn to perceive when to leave a press conference. As soon as the major information is received, a more resourceful reporter may slip away from the crowd and seek the exclusive interviews with secondary news sources. While such a move requires a calculated risk that major items won't be forthcoming after he leaves, the risk is often worth taking.

SUMMARY

The task of covering a press conference is deceptively difficult. On the surface, it appears that even the most incompetent reporter can easily perform the mechanical tasks of note-taking and of asking logical questions. Yet, truly professional coverage only begins with the conference itself. It extends to post-conference interviews with adversary or secondary sources who can expand or contradict the material offered at the conference.

In any news event—including speeches and press conferences—the *real* story may well lie in what is *not* said, rather than in what is said. In practical terms, a reporter makes a choice between two stories:

1. He can choose to write a straight account of the information that the speaker condescended to offer—information that has been sterilized of potentially adverse or contradictory material to form a distorted piece of propaganda.

2. He can use the offered information as a base, then use all of his reporting skills to obtain additional information that may radically change the account that is finally offered to the public.

In short, the newsperson must choose between performing as a public relations person for the official, or performing as a reporter for the public that will read the story with the sometimes naive assumption that truth is being served up.

EXERCISES

1. Class exercise: Invite a local official to visit the class to hold a press conference. Each student should prepare a list of five questions before the press conference. The official will begin with a statement announcing a newsworthy event (it may be fictitious), then open the floor for questions.

2. You are covering the press conference for an afternoon newspaper with a noon deadline. It's 11 A.M., and your rival from the morning newspaper is obviously filibustering to delay the flow of important material until after you leave. What would you do?

3. Reversing the roles outlined in Question 2, your rival faces a deadline. He has asked an important question, which the official evaded. The official then cleverly allows you to ask the next question. You must choose between redirecting your rival's question to insist on an answer, thus helping your competitor; or changing the subject. Which alternative would you choose? Why?

10 | Beating the Opposition

To passersby, the reporters who sat sipping coffee at a table in the city hall snack shop seemed friendly toward each other, swapping jokes and stories as they endured a momentary lull on the normally hectic beat. Occasionally, a city official stopped by to chat briefly, or acquire a new joke for his repertoire.

The appearance of camaraderie was both real and misleading. After sharing mutual frustrations in covering the complex beat, a genuine collective friendship had arisen from the experience. Yet, beneath that surface friendship, the competitive instincts of veteran journalists constantly prodded each reporter to find and disclose a story—any story—before colleagues caught wind of the event.

The most intense rivalry existed between two young, aggressive newspaper reporters, who routinely scored alternating victories. Close on their heels was a newswoman for the city's largest television news staff, who covered city hall as part of a much larger beat, and a radio newsman who had twenty years of experience and all the well-groomed news sources that come with such seniority. The final member of the group was a television newsman for the city's smaller station, who survived by "ripping and reading" stories printed in the newspaper, by pirating news aired by other television and radio journalists, and by winning the affection of city hall officials through constantly favorable and unaggressive reporting.

Because of the size and complexity of the beat, each reporter was able to stake out a "territory" of news sources who would loyally "leak" stories to their favorite reporter.

Before turning to the operation of the competitive system, let's examine the reasons behind its existence, and the benefits that the public reaps when highly competitive journalism is at work.

Reporter's View

From the reporter's viewpoint, the compulsion to beat the competition stems from both professional and personal pride.

Professionally, job advancement and even career survival may depend on a reporter's ability to score on news breaks. Editors demand a steady flow of exclusive news from any major beat, particularly one that produces as many page-one stories as city hall. If a reporter is unable to win consistently his share of competitive battles, then he will be shuttled to a less demanding beat or, perhaps, dismissed. On the other hand, a consistently superior performance on a top-level newsbeat can lead to rapid advancement in both pay and position.

From a personal viewpoint, most reporters take considerable pride in their professional abilities, especially that of newsgathering. A reporter once noted:

"This business has more emotional highs and lows than a roller-coaster ride. During a good week, when you clobber the competition, you're on top of the world, basking in the sunshine of page-one stories. Then, a week later, you lose a couple of stories, and you begin contemplating that comfortable public relations job offer that you turned down.

"I don't believe that anything can match the depressiveness of that stomach-knotting experience of picking up the competition newspaper and seeing a page-one story that you missed."

Perhaps an equally effective form of personal incentive is that many reporters simply relish the competitive *game*. Humans are generally competitive creatures who enjoy winning so much that they play tennis, bridge, bingo, or news reporting with equal intensity, determined to win out of love for victory. When caught up in the intensity of the work-game, they seek to score with the ruthless determination of a professional athlete.

The Public's View

From the viewpoint of the general public, such journalistic rivalry is normally a benefit. Spurred by the race for news, reporters aggressively sift through the beat, ever watchful for even the smallest sign of corruption or mismanagement that may lead to an exclusive exposé—under the appropriate by-line.

In cities where such intense competition exists—and not every city is blessed with rival newspapers and electronics media—it is less likely that wholesale corruption or governmental mismangement can thrive. Furthermore, potentially corrupt officials are less likely to yield to temptation when they know that "head-hunting" reporters are methodically searching for just such an exclusive story.

The public also benefits from a deeper, more thorough overall news coverage. Even if the city government is exceptionally honest and competent, rival journalists will press until they fully explore each issue, each problem, and each operation of city government, thus informing the citizen who is willing to take the time to become informed.

Such aggressiveness is, however, not without potential hazards to the public. The drive for exclusiveness greatly increases the potential for human error that can misinform the public. Reporters may be tempted to publish stories before they are fully and carefully researched, thus reducing the threat that a competitor may break the story first. This intensity can also lead to abuses. A simple, relatively insignificant human error on the part of an official can be blown out of proportion —officials refer to such instances as "cheap shots."

For example, let's say that the mayor dozes off in the midst of a long and dull city council meeting. To his considerable chagrin, a councilman finally must shake him to restore his consciousness for the next item of business. An overly aggressive reporter may rightly determine that the public has a right to know that the mayor was asleep at the switch. Faced with a deadline, he may leave before the meeting ends and file a story which contains a cleverly humorous reference to the mayor's lapse. The public would be amused and perhaps disgusted at the mayor's antics. The mayor would be embarrassed and enraged. Normally, a reporter should have no qualms about embarrassing an errant official, yet a journalist is obliged to print the truth in its proper context. Had the reporter been less eager to break the news item first, and more eager to obtain the whole truth in context, he would have hesitated long enough to recognize some warnings of mitigating circumstances: the mayor is normally alert and in full control of council meetings, thus the lapse was highly unusual. Also, the mayor appeared unusually haggard and weary before the meeting.

The truth in context was that the mayor had participated in 'round-the-clock labor negotiations with union offiicals representing city sanitation workers. The mayor had not slept a wink the night before because of his dedicated desire to protect his city from a crippling strike. The reporter had already learned that the meeting produced an agreement. He had filed a story that contained quotes from the mayor, and he had even noted that the mayor had participated in the meeting. Unfortunately, he did not take time to put the two events together in his mind. The critical, embarrassing story did not reveal the truth: a tired, overworked official's physical stamina had faltered, causing the understandable lapse. If the truth in proper context had been published, citizens would probably have lauded, not condemned the mayor.

From this example, then, it should be apparent that competiveness must be tempered with responsibility. The first duty of any reporter is to obtain and publish the closest facsimile to that philosophic reality called truth that is humanly possible to achieve. All the rewards entailed in being the first to report a news item are pointless if that report is inaccurate or misleading—even if the error goes undetected.

For an overview of how the "beat competition" operates, let's take a close look at each of the reporters. Keep in mind that these characters are created to represent common reporting styles.

Newspaper reporter "A" takes the hardline approach to reporting, preferring a no-nonsense frontal assault on news sources, distaining finesse. He has carefully established an image of driving competence and integrity by working relentlessly to obtain any given item that interests him. He chooses bluntness over tact, brushing aside the diplomacy of the city hall establishment, thus embittering some high officials who are sensitive about their high public standing. But he wins the confidence of others who value competence and integrity. He has built a network of news sources among those who admire his straightforward style. This reporter's greatest strength, however, lies in his ability to gain information from lower-ranking city employees who, perceiving his antagonistic relationship with many top officials, conclude that he is the person to be trusted to rectify problems and wrongs that they see. Reporter "A" is also popular among community activists who besiege city hall. The activists and lower-level city employees provide reporter "A" with a steady flow of tips for exposés and interpretative stories on community problems. Reporter "A" is, however, hampered by a general exclusion from top-level city hall sources who, in their personal dislike and distrust for him, take pains to deny him stories.

Newspaper reporter "B" exudes a personal charm in his soft-line approach to beat coverage. A genuinely sensitive soul, this reporter is all things to all people—a natural politician in his own right, who is easily the most popular journalist on the beat. He has systematically groomed friendships with officials at every level, and in every major functional area of city hall. Reporter "B" has also achieved a reputation of competence and professional honesty, even though his personal honesty is sometimes suspect because of his role-playing. He most frequently acts the part of a naive, "good ol' boy," who is a bit slow mentally. Yet, countless officials have bitterly learned that behind that image lies a quick and sometimes ruthless mind that thrives on errors made by those who carelessly underestimate him. His professional honesty is established by a spotless record of protecting confidential sources, of absolute fairness in dealing with all factions involved in any given controversy, and of delivering on even the most casual promise. This reporter's strength lies in his blanket, overall coverage of all segments of his beat. His friends freely offer such a flow of information that little substantial news escapes him. His weakness is that the delicate balance he maintains between friendship and professional obligation dilutes his aggressiveness. Also, the lingering suspicions about his *personal* integrity sometimes discourages sources from providing truly explosive news tips that could jeopardize their jobs.

The television newswoman is a realist, who knows that she can't spend enough time on the city hall segment of her large beat to compete successfully with the newspaper reporters in meticulously thorough coverage. She can't hope to unearth as many exposés, investigative stories, or secondary items, so she concentrates on establishing and mining a few carefully selected major news sources: a city councilman, the assistant city manager, the director of personnel, and other key decision-makers. Just as aggressive as her newspaper competitors, the newswoman offers the ego-caressing exposure of television cameras to entice officials into cooperating. Like reporter "B," her personal style exudes charm rather than bluntness, as she extracts information from officials who consider her to be a friend. Her strength is her iron-fisted grip on that small but important segment of news sources that she has staked out. Her weakness is that much of city hall is essentially out of her domain, as she must follow up stories written by competitors. Also, she must accept the professional limitation of her information medium: Because of the preciousness of time, television reporting rarely penetrates beneath the surface of a given news item. This inability to carry investigative or interpretive stories denies her many important, confidential sources in this area.

The veteran radio newsman specializes in gathering information from high-ranking career officials in the city hall bureaucracy. He has known many of them for more than a decade, befriending them long before they became department supervisors and policy-makers. The radio newsman operates as an unofficial member of the city hall bureaucray—his face is so familiar that officials often forget that he's a journalist. He escalates reporter B's friendly approach to a much greater extreme by becoming a close, personal friend of many officials —fishing, golfing, and dining with them. Although he does air unfavorable stories, he does so with great reluctance, especially when a fishing partner is embarrassed by the story. The radio newsman's greatest strength is in his vast knowledge of his beat, and the steady flow of information from the entrenched bureaucracy. His weakness is "cronyism," a tendency to become so personally entwined with the bureaucracy that his objectivity is suspect and his aggressiveness is feeble. At times, he seems more intent on defending the rascals who are exposed as wrongdoers than in informing the public.

The last and least member of the coffee table crew is the *"rip-and-read" television newsman*. With the instincts of a scavenger, this journalist drops by the newspaper offices to grab the earliest available editions. He rapidly scans the newspaper for stories pertaining to his beat, then clips them. At times, he extends the effort of calling officials to confirm the newspaper information but, more often, he simply reads them on the air—verbatim. Once, he was slightly embarrassed to learn that a line of type had been dropped from such a story, making the information nonsensical. He read the story, typo and all.

The scavenger does, however, work his beat in his own style. He never misses a press conference, broadcasts any interesting news release, and serves as a ready outlet for the official political line on any controversy. As a result of his unquestioning, ever-accepting readiness to broadcast favorable, often misleading city hall statements, officials provide a deluge of such self-serving fodder for him to pass on to his viewers. This newsman's strength is in the shear volume of his material: he acts as a public bulletin board on which officials can tack anything they wish. His weakness, of course, is that he is a propaganda outlet, not a journalist.

With the exception of the scavenger, the collection of reporters provides the public with an aggressive, thorough, and well-balanced journalistic view of city hall. Collectively, they comb through the great expanse of local government, effectively providing any interested citizen with more than ample information about his city government.

Each competitive style serves a purpose, both to the individual reporter and to the public at large.

Despite the differences, the reporters share a common trait: each has adapted professional style to personal character. A gregarious, "soft" approach is demonstratably as effective as the hard-nosed approach. In each case, the reporter realistically assessed personal strength and weakness, then learned an effective manner of operating with them.

In taking a more specific look at competitive techniques, each reporter, in an individual manner, sought to establish these necessities:

1. *A reputation conducive to trust.* Reporter A's aggressive honesty, reporter B's friendly earnestness, the television newswoman's selective bridge-building, the radio reporter's "cronyism," and the television newsman's all-accepting boosterism—all succeeded in winning the trust of at least some informational sources.

2. *A "territory."* Each reporter established and jealously guarded a segment of the news source "market." Few beats are so small that one reporter can win the respect and affection of each person in that area. Regardless of how strongly established a veteran newsman may be, a new competitor can invariably find officials who will be part of his territory.

With a sound reputation of trustworthiness and a solid territorial base, a reporter is then ready to compete in earnest with all competitors.

ADVANCE COVERAGE

For the purpose of illustrating techniques of competing, let's take reporter B's vantage point. Although he has a segment of the beat safely tucked away within his own sphere of news sources, a large common hunting ground exists in which all reporters compete on fairly even terms; and that is coverage of breaking news events, which cannot be confined to any single reporter's news sources. In competing for such news, he may group his coverage alternatives into three categories:

1. Advance coverage (news breaks).
2. Concurrent coverage (on-the-scene).
3. Follow-up coverage (after a competitor breaks the news).

A public meeting is a typical example of such a common-ground news event, which will be shared by all journalists. Let's shift the coffee-table journalists to the education beat for this example. The city school board will meet tomorrow night, in the midst of the morning competitor's (Reporter A) news cycle. Reporter B is, then, limited to either advance coverage or follow-up coverage. Naturally, he chooses the former alternative.

The morning before the meeting, he telephones the school superintendent to pry loose an advance story.

> Reporter: "Dr. Powell, I understand that the board will consider approval of a new teachers' contract tonight. Can you tell me the amount of pay increase entailed in the new agreement?"
>
> Superintendent: "I'm sorry, but that's confidential until the board acts. We do plan to act on the contract tonight, so you should find out then."
>
> Reporter (Scribbling down the official's confirmation): "I understand your position, but can you tell me whether the teachers' association bargaining unit has accepted the tentative offer?"
>
> Superintendent: "They've agreed to present it to their membership for referendum. Negotiations were, of course, difficult because of our budget restrictions, but I believe that their bargaining unit was finally satisfied that we made our best offer. You should talk with Max Goldfarb, the president of the teachers' association. Max can speak for them."
>
> Reporter: "Have you informally discussed the contract with school board members?"
>
> Superintendent: "Yes, I have, but I can't comment on those

discussions. I'd like to be more helpful, but I'm afraid I'm saying more than I should."

Reporter: "You have been very helpful, and I appreciate your kindness. However, may I ask whether you expect anything else of significance to come up tonight? I know you have been examining alternatives for increasing your budget through such means as a bond issue or property tax increase."

Superintendent: "We will discuss such alternatives, but we do not have the power to impose taxes or float bonds. We can only request such action from the county commission. I can't elaborate, so . . . ."

Reporter: "That's understandable. I'll talk to Max and a few of the board members to round out my story. Thank you for your help."

Armed with such a generous start, Reporter B subsequently learns the details of the contract from officials in the teacher's association, the amount of property tax increase to be requested through a school board source, and the probable outcome of the voting on both the contract and a proposal to seek a tax increase. Before the school board gathers for the meeting, members are startled to read a page-one story that begins:

> City teachers may receive a 7 percent pay increase next fall, paid for by a 2-mill property tax increase, if the Board of Education approves the proposals tonight.
>
> And approval seems almost certain, as 5 of the 7 board members told The Daily News that they support both measures.

The chagrin of board members is exceeded only by the anguish of Reporter A, who had smugly assumed that the story would fall in his lap.

An advance story is a great competitive weapon, yet it should be used with considerable caution. In this example, the board could have shelved the issues to "punish" the brash reporter, or the board could have voted against the measures. Despite such risks, the reporter would, in this instance, proceed confidently with the advance story because:

1. He has an accurate account of the situation as he submits the story, even though subsequent events could alter the situation and make his material dated. Even if the board reacts so negatively to the story that members reverse what was true at press time, the reporter has correctly informed his readers of the *impending* situation. If he exercises reasonable caution by following these rules for writing advance stories, his credibility cannot be damaged:

(a.) Do not *predict* the outcome; carefully specify that the material is a factual account of a present situation that is subject to change. For example, instead of writing that the board *will* approve the contract and recommend the tax increase, the reporter should use the term *may*. Early in the story, he should further emphasize the uncertainty in this manner:

> Although most board members indicated their intentions to support the proposals, only two members firmly committed themselves to vote for the measures, while three others suggested that they could conceivably change their minds by meeting time.

(b.) Attribute the source of the information, if possible. While some sources will demand the guarantee of non-attribution before offering information, the reporter should attempt to provide the strongest possible attribution within bounds of ethical considerations. If one of the five potential supporters allows attribution, then the story is much stronger, and the reporter is protected from future shenanigans by the disclosure. In this example, *board members* provides a strong indirect attribution.

(c.) Include any circumstances that may alter the likely outcome. For example:

> The situation could change drastically if the teachers' association rejects the contract proposal before tonight's meeting. Association officials were undecided about whether to call a meeting of members to consider the proposal before the Board of Education meets.

2. In assessing the situation, the reporter can logically conclude that the board has little alternative other than to proceed with the action. If the proposals are shelved, the consequences of facing angry teachers' association officials should far outweigh the fleeting satisfaction of torpedoing a brash reporter. If board members switch to oppose the measures, then they must bear even greater consequences. In summary, the story is safe.

CONCURRENT COVERAGE

At times, efforts to produce an advance story are fruitless. Perhaps the superintendent and board members refused to comment. Even though the reporter may personally expect those two major issues to erupt at the meeting, he cannot print an educated guess.

During the meeting, he must reconcile himself with the reality that his competitor will share the story. Let's alter the nature of the competition so that both newspapers have the same deadline—admittedly an extreme rarity, since few cities have two morning or two afternoon dailies. The competition, then, becomes a head-on match of reporting skills. The reporter, then, must attempt to win the match by:

1. Being better attuned to the significance of the board's actions than his competitor. Perhaps a seemingly minor event occurs: The contract proposal is approved despite a "no" vote by a member who has always strongly supported benefits for teachers. While his competitor mechanically records the voting, the alert reporter ponders the significance of this development.

2. Going beyond the surface information provided by the event. While the competitor casually returns to his newsroom to leisurely write the story from information that the meeting provided, the alert reporter lingers to corner the unexpectedly dissident member.

> Reporter: "Considering your past record of supporting benefits to teachers, I was surprised that you opposed the contract. Can you tell me why?"
>
> Board Member: "I felt that the offer was totally inadequate. The pay increase barely keeps pace with cost of living increases. Our teachers deserve far more, and I insisted on a ten percent raise. It's a matter of principle, which I could not in clear conscience abandon."
>
> Reporter: "Have you been in contact with Max Goldfarb? Do you expect the teachers to reject the proposal?"
>
> Board Member: "I informed my colleagues that Max has little hope that the membership will ratify the agreement. They proceeded with this measure in hopes of exerting public pressure on teachers to accept it. This isn't a real proposal, it's a ploy. You can quote me."

Thus, the astute reporter eventually obtains a far different—and far more accurate—story than his less ambitious competitor.

3. Being alert for less obvious, unrelated stories. The agenda for a formal, public meeting by a governing body may be loaded with seemingly minor procedural actions. Deeply buried in the trivia may be a measure approving payment to an architectural consulting firm "for services rendered." The sum may be relatively minor, yet the reporter may realize that something far more significant is afoot. When the board approves the expenditure without question or discussion—frequently, governing bodies informally agree on minor items before a meeting—the reporter's curiosity is peaked. After the meeting, he asks the superintendent about the item and learns that the board has been quietly assessing the feasibility of building a new high school. Until the reporter's discovery, they had succeeded in keeping their preliminary efforts secret.

FOLLOW-UP COVERAGE

By far the most undesirable alternative, follow-up coverage must occur when by either the wiles or good fortune of timing, a competitor breaks the story first. To again alter the example to accommodate this form of coverage, we shall say that the reporter fails to produce an advance story, thus the event falls solidly on his competitor's news cycle. Well before the reporter's story can be published in the afternoon newspaper, the morning newspaper will carry his competitor's account.

The prospect of writing a follow-up story does not, however, mean that the reporter may sit through the meeting in a semi-stupor, then rewrite his competitor's story the next day. Instead, the reporter should alertly resort to all of the competitive techniques discussed previously, and press the sole significant advantage that he possesses: ample time before deadline.

Typically, a morning newspaper reporter faces a final deadline sometime between 11 P.M. and 1 A.M. A lively, freewheeling public meeting that begins at 8 P.M. can easily drag on for hours, creating intense deadline pressure for the competitor. Even if the meeting ends in sufficient time to allow complete coverage, the competitor may not be able to provide depth.

The afternoon newspaper reporter, then, may concentrate on the *ultimate* story, as it will exist at noon the next day. The transactions during the meeting serve as background, as a bank of information that will be expanded and developed later.

During the board meeting, the members approve both measures after a heated debate. The meeting adjourns at 10:30 P.M., and the competitor hurries to his newsroom. Meanwhile, the reporter gathers the important information from the dissident board member and chats with other officials to piece together a vivid picture of the behind-the-scenes battle. He calls the teachers' association president for elaboration and confirmation. The president advises the reporter that he plans to present the contract offer to the membership the next morning, and allows that he will oppose ratification.

After writing a story that emphasizes these important new developments for the first edition's 8:30 A.M. deadline, the reporter can sleep peacefully with the knowledge that by the time his final deadline occurs at noon, he will be able to offer his readers an entirely new story that will emphasize not the meeting, but the teachers' rejection of the proposal.

ELECTRONICS MEDIA

While the newspaper reporters compete with each other on their own terms, competition between electronics media journalists takes on a different tone. All three reporters face the identical 11 P.M. deadline for their late news broadcasts.

The "rip-and-read" broadcaster is at a distinct disadvantage, since he cannot utilize either newspaper clippings or press releases. However, he is not without resources. He quickly corners the board chairman to obtain the official viewpoint. Holding the microphone out to the smiling chairman while his cameraman records the interview as they stand in front of the school administration building, the broadcaster assembles the pro-school board version of the event by allowing the chairman to act as a highly biased, amateur reporter of the event.

The veteran radio reporter obtains a less-favorable perspective by interviewing the superintendent—another old friend—and other full-time administrative officials, who woefully suggest that the new contract will bankrupt the school system. However, the reporter contacts both the board chairman and the teachers' association president to obtain a more balanced account for his report.

The television newswoman deftly uses her resources to utilize the little available time in the most profitable manner. Like the newspaper reporter, she senses that a behind-the-scenes battle had occurred between board members. Ignoring the spotlight-seeking chairman, she interviews another member who is her prime source and discovers that the board is bitterly divided. Although the time factor allows only a brief peek behind the surface of the news, she offers her viewers the most substantive account.

It should be emphasized that the example of competitive coverage of a public meeting typifies the general styles and approaches used in reporting most breaking news events. The example could have as easily been a major fire, homicide, political rally, or almost any other event.

SUMMARY

Assuming that reasonably competent rivals are covering the same newsbeat, no reporter can expect to consistently break all major news stories first. The deadline cycle alone removes many stories from his grasp, while territorial emphasis by rivals will, to at least some degree, remove still others. Yet, even allowing for such handicaps, a reporter should be able to compete successfully by:

1. Carefully establishing a network of reliable sources in all

functional areas of the beat, including those areas where a competitor may excel.

2. Being ever alert to the often subtle signs of hidden news.

3. Learning all of the workings of each function on the beat, the people who manage those functions, and the current condition of each function at any given time. For example, a city hall reporter should be highly knowledgeable of every service performed by city government, including everything from problems of garbage collecting to the intricacies of a complex bidding document for a billion-dollar development.

4. Constantly looking beneath the surface of any news development in search of the *real* story that often lurks behind the scenes.

5. Simply working a little harder and a little longer than the competition on any significant news development that occurs.

If the process of competition appears to involve an uncomfortably high degree of physical and mental effort, then the preception is correct. Yet, most competent reporters find that the pain of exertion is far less agonizing than the peculiar, stomach-churning anguish of seeing a rival's exclusive story splashed across page one of the competing newspaper.

EXERCISES

1. You are the city hall reporter for an afternoon newspaper. City council is meeting tonight—on your rival's news cycle. You learn from a somewhat reliable source that the council may discuss discontinuing city trash collecting service for budgetary reasons, allowing private firms to operate in place of municipal service. How would you compete with your morning rival?

2. Unconfirmed information indicates that the county's supervisor of highways has been accepting bribes from contractors in return for construction contracts. You also learn that your competitor is investigating. An hour before your final deadline, you locate a courthouse deed that shows that the supervisor purchased a large parcel of land from a contractor at a suspiciously low price. You are unable to reach either the supervisor or the contractor. Would you write a story based on the information you have substantiated? Explain your reasoning.

PART TWO

NEWS COVERAGE

ASSIGNMENTS

Armed with the tools of reporting, as offered in the preceding chapters, the next step is to apply them to standard reporting assignments, such as newsbeats and specialties.

The methodology of covering a newsbeat remains essentially the same, whether used on police beat, courts beat, or city hall. The object in each instance is to pry loose information that is of interest, importance, or significance to the readers, whether that information must come from a person in the occupational role of policeman, judge, or mayor. Although each newsbeat is steeped in its own occupational peculiarities, news almost always comes from people. Basic approaches to extracting information from people remain generally the same, although they are adapted to the occupational environment of the beat.

To illustrate the application of reporting techniques, several diverse news assignments will be discussed in the following chapters. As noted in Chapter 2, many other news assignments exist at most newspapers, but this representative sampling is selected to offer a broad overview.

11 | Police Beat

It's your first day on the job as police reporter for a metropolitan newspaper. As you walk down the corridor of police headquarters to the small pressroom assigned to working reporters, you feel a little uneasy as you glance at the grim-faced, gun-toting men who pass you in the hall. The atmosphere is that of a businesslike, masculine world populated by men who have learned to be suspicious of newcomers.

If you're lucky, the previous police reporter had established a good working relationship with the officers, which may carry over. Regardless, you must establish your own rapport, your own system of covering news, if you are to succeed as a police reporter.

Perhaps frequently, young reporters are equally suspicious and aloof toward the policemen. Stories of police brutality, corruption, callousness, and general incompetence have created an extremely negative image of law enforcement officers. On the other hand, policemen often perceive an image of brash, pushy reporters who become troublesome pests at the scenes of disasters, who can destroy an officer's career with a single misquote. Worse, policemen may perceive all reporters as "bleeding-heart liberals" who invariably side with the arch-enemies: the criminals and troublemakers.

With such mutual image problems, it's little wonder that antagonisms can quickly arise between policemen and reporters. A reporter who unwisely falls into an antagonistic relationship may pay the heavy price of being isolated from his prime news sources and, eventually, he may be replaced on the beat.

Instead of being antagonists, policemen and reporters can find incentives to establish a good working relationship.

From the reporter's viewpoint, it is essential to create a network of informational sources among the officers who are actually involved in case investigations. No reporter can adequately cover the police beat with only press releases and official records as an informational source. Official press releases are invariably self-serving and shallow. Police records provide only the barest details on a given case. Perhaps equally important, a reporter must rely on a network of non-official sources to truly keep him informed. If a stakeout is being conducted to trap would-be bank robbers, a friendly tip can place the reporter on the scene for vivid, complete coverage of the arrest. If a major narcotics raid is planned, a good police reporter, using friendly tips from detectives, will be on hand. If racial tension exists between black and white officers, a reporter who has developed rapport with officers of both races can probe deeply into the causes, consequences, and subtle manifestations of this serious problem.

What does a reporter have to offer in building this relationship? The answer is publicity for officers who perform effectively, for problems that concern officers, for policemen's viewpoints when they affect morale or performance. This does not mean that a reporter must become a public relations person for the police—although some newsmen have overreacted to the need to groom sources to the extent that they become "one of the guys." A more effective and ethical approach is to carefully build a reputation of independency and integrity. Most officers can differentiate between fairness or objectivity and hostility, even when a given story may be unpleasant for them.

At times, the interest of a reporter and the interest of a policeman must be in conflict. A detective may seek to withhold information about an investigation from the public so that a wrongdoer won't be alerted by the newspaper. A reporter must seek to piece together the most accurate and complete picture of the crime that he can uncover. Yet, even under such a strain, a relationship of mutual respect and understanding will weather the momentary conflict.

With these factors in mind, let's create a good, effective police reporter:

After several months on the beat, the reporter has mastered a broad range of police procedures, organization, and terminology. He understands the nature of each major crime, and he knows police procedures for investigating it. He is fully aware of problems within the police department, and he knows where to find ample information about both sides of a given controversy. He knows the intricacies of the department's organization, and the basic routine of each element, from the complaint clerk to the police chief.

A good police reporter knows his city well. If a shootout is occurring on Summit Street, he can quickly find the location. In fact, before he reaches the scene, he is well familiar with the neighborhood. He knows the city's trouble spots—the bars that are common scenes of violence, the hangouts of "street people" and thugs, and the atmosphere or character of all the major neighborhoods.

The reporter also knows people. He can comfortably chat with detectives and uniformed officers, sip coffee with merchants who face crime problems, commiserate with mugged victims, or converse in street language with junkies, prostitutes, muggers, pimps, and all-around hoodlums.

By nature, the reporter is aggressive and conscientious. He has attained a reputation of objectivity, fairness, and competence among policemen. Most officers like and respect him, yet corrupt or brutal policemen fear and despise him as a lingering threat. Because of his proven integrity, many officers freely provide tips of major police activities, and they talk openly about problems within the department. He rarely loses a story to his competition, and, moreover, he is able to provide a depth and insight to his reporting that informs his readers not only of individual crimes, but of the significance of crimes and the crime problem.

All and all, the police reporter serves a much more important role than that of mechanically gathering and writing information for public edification. Among those functions that are rarely found in a job description are:

1. He is perhaps the only truly neutral watchdog available to protect the public interest in guarding against police abuse and corruption. Although most police departments have some sort of internal investigatory apparatus to root out misdeeds by officers, these in-house bureaus are often hamstrung by departmental politics or by an understandable tendency to side with the officer whenever circumstances allow. A reporter has no such restraints. If corruption or brutality exists, he can objectively delve into it and expose it to the public.

Perhaps surprisingly, a reporter may find ample help from honest, conscientious officers on the force in his efforts to expose wrongdoers. Some officers may be much more likely to pass tips of corruption on to a trusted reporter than to the department's investigators because there may be less likelihood of reprisal's and more likelihood of corrective action.

2. The police reporter may serve as a bridge between patrolmen and the public. Problems that affect the performance of a patrolman should certainly concern the public that the officer protects. Policemen often have legitimate complaints that somehow fail to be communicated to the public. If, for example, manpower is dangerously low during the evening shift, a reporter can effectively convey that problem to the public by interviewing officers, by observing a frustrating backup of calls in the dispatch center, by riding with officers to witness their burden, and by talking with victims of crimes who weren't able to receive police help when they wanted it. Perhaps racial tensions are undermining morale. The reporter could investigate and write a balanced story explaining the problem and the sources of the friction.

In such instances, the public may be unable or unwilling to rectify the problems, but, at least, the public is aware of them so that they can assume responsibility for either forcing corrective action or for enduring less than adequate police service.

3. At times, the reporter may be a mediator. Within most large police organizations, officers may tend to fall into organizational or social cliques that, at times, may be hostile toward each other. If the reporter is respected and trusted by all groups, he has access to the fine points on all sides of any dispute. In the process of gathering information for a story, the reporter may carry information between groups—either consciously or by circumstance. By the time the story is written, each side has gained a better understanding of the roots of the dispute. Thus, in simply doing his job, the reporter may also lay the foundation for a settlement.

4. A reporter serves as a bridge between patrolmen and high-ranking officers. Perhaps patrolmen are unhappy with a training program at the Police Academy. While command officers may be aware of some grumbling, they may lack a means of clearly assessing the full impact of the situation on morale. A newspaper account that defines the full nature of the morale problem and gives the root causes may relay vital information to police commanders that will enable them to take corrective action.

5. A police reporter can influence police policy. Untrained private security guards may be a source of danger to the public, particularly in the capricious use of firearms. A tip from concerned officers may spark an investigation by the reporter. The resulting story, which would expose dangerous practices by private security guards, could instigate strong new policies on regulating the training and procedures for such guards as a requirement for a license issued by the police department.

6. The police reporter often serves as an "ombudsman" for private citizens who become lost in the organizational maze of the police department, or who find that police are unwilling or unable to meet their needs.

If a citizen thinks that he was mistreated or roughly handled by policemen, he may go directly to the reporter to lodge his complaint. The reporter can either steer the citizen to the proper official if he knows that the official will handle the complaint properly, or he can investigate the complaint himself and write a story to force action. This function produces two benefits. First, the reporter often gains exclusive stories of police misconduct in the process of helping a citizen; second, the reporter's assistance invariably wins new friends for the newspaper.

With such demanding responsibilities, the question still remains: How does a new police beat reporter establish his knowledge and reputation so that he can provide full and effective coverage for his newspaper?

1. The first part of the answer is attitudinal: The reporter must project a friendly, sympathetic image to policemen. By relating on a personal, human level with policemen, the reporter can diminish some of the natural, occupational hostility that may exist.

2. He must demonstrate a real interest in the functions performed by even the lowliest police department employee. In lulls in reporting activity, he may chat with the burglary squad sergent about the nature of burglary, the methods that police use in solving such cases, problems that hamper successful investigations, and the nature of the enemy—the run-of-the-mill burglar. The reporter can move from squad to squad, and from function to function, in talking with officers. In the process, he is alert for feature story possibilities. A feature about how the homicide squad functions is not only a legitimate story that will help educate the public, but it helps the reporter learn valuable information about investigative methods. And, in still another valuable offshoot, the officers receive a bit of public limelight. The reporter, whose by-line is on the story that is clipped and filed in the officer's scrapbook, may be regarded by the officer in a friendly light.

Establishing contacts among uniformed officers may be more difficult, because their day-to-day jobs are less glamorous than those of detectives, and because the sheer number of street patrolmen may hamper efforts to get to know them.

However, a reporter can penetrate this area by spending time riding around with officers on patrol. Because of deadline pressure, such excursions are impossible during normal working schedules. Yet, perhaps on his own time, a reporter can spend, say, a night a week riding with a different patrol crew.

Obviously, the technique of writing feature stories to break the ice is limited in the case of such rides. Each patrol crew performs essentially the same function. Instead, the reporter must concentrate on getting to know the officers and on learning the fine points of police patrol work.

In still another ride-along area, narcotics and vice detectives can educate a reporter to a lifestyle that he may not have been aware of. Abundant feature stories and in-depth stories can flow out of rides with such detectives.

In such a situation, a new reporter became interested in a strange institution called "boot joints." A boot joint is a place where gambling—usually craps—and illegal liquor sales take place. Friendly vice officers arranged to educate one new reporter by offering a well-known boot joint proprietor a half hour of "free time." In this gentlemen's agreement, the detectives took the reporter to the boot joint and showed him a game of craps in progress.

3. In establishing himself on the beat, the reporter must carefully maintain his fairness. The reporter who was trusted by the officers who set up the boot joint experience could have turned on them by writing a story detailing the agreement. The officers would have been reprimanded for such a breech of police policy. In another instance, the reporter was privy to a major narcotics investigation, in which two detectives were posing as corrupt officers "on the take" in order to gather evidence. A premature story could have endangered their lives. A reporter must also know how to differentiate between an honest goof and incompetence. While riding with uniformed officers, he may see an officer make a blunder that allows a suspect to escape. Unless the crime is, in itself, newsworthy, and the officer's blunder stems from real incompetence, a story would serve no purpose other than embarrass the policeman. Human errors occur on any job —even reporting.

This does not mean that the reporter must become a tacit accomplice to police misdeeds that may occur in his presence. A good practice is to tell the officers early in the ride that, while you won't take "cheap shots" by printing stories about minor goofs and you will accept general conversation as being off-the-record, you are a reporter. As a reporter, you are obliged to report incidents that are seriously adverse to public interest. Most officers will appreciate such candor.

After establishing this clear understanding, a reporter who witnesses brutality or corruption has no alternative other than to report it.

In summary, by investing a great deal of extra time and effort in establishing personal relationships with individual officers, and in learning police problems, methods, and general character, the new police reporter can soon establish both the reputation and the competence he must have to provide first-rate coverage.

POLICE ORGANIZATION

With the nature of the police reporter's position in mind, let's return to the new police reporter's problem of learning to cover news on his beat. The first step is to determine the size, shape, and structure of the department, and the separate functions of key officials and bureaus within that organization.

Although organizational structures vary greatly among police departments, here is a typical, traditional structure for a medium-sized metropolitan force:

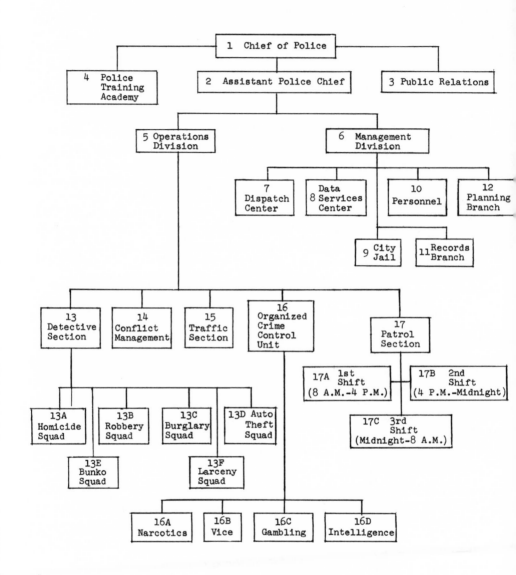

CITY POLICE DEPARTMENT

Two common variations of this organizational arrangement are the use of precinct stations (mini-departments serving large areas of the city), and the trendy "team policing" structure, in which uniformed officers perform complete investigations, eliminating the detective branch. For the purpose of learning the basic functions within a police department, we will use the traditional organizational model. Basically, the duties of the components are:

1. *Chief of Police.* The chief is generally responsible for the performance of all police functions. He must answer to the city government for all police matters, and he must enforce and institute the dictates of that government. Often, he is the man in the middle—caught between the frequently conflicting viewpoints of policemen and city politicians.

From the reporter's viewpoint, this is a critically important area of coverage. Whenever the chief makes a significant decision, it is news. Whenever he offers even a spurious opinion, it is newsworthy. Yet, this understandably busy person is often hard to corner for interviews or even brief statements. It is essential for the new reporter to establish some means of communicating with the chief when an authoritative, official statement is called for.

2. *Assistant Police Chief.* He may function largely like the United States Vice President—a man behind the scenes, except when the chief is away. Yet, the assistant chief is the second best source for official statements, and he is often acutely aware of problems and situations within the department that are newsworthy. He is an excellent source to be groomed by a reporter.

3. *Public Relations.* A senior officer or a civilian professional is given responsibility for dealing with the press. The public relations office churns out news releases on departmental matters, sets up press conferences, schedules interviews with the chief, issues police press passes, answers press queries, and generally serves as a bridge—or wall—between the press and the chief.

4. *Police Training Academy.* The academy trains new recruits in often rigorous courses to prepare them for street duty, conducts continual firearms training for all officers, and provides continuing education and training for officers at each level. The academy may be a fertile source of feature story material and, at times, hard news may break there when officers are disgruntled over individual training programs.

5. *Operations Division.* All "front-line" police functions, such as detective work, uniformed patrol, traffic control, and special police details are directed under this division, which is commanded by a senior officer.

6. *Management Division.* The flood of police paper work is controlled by this division. It is responsible for handling reports, directing

police response to citizen calls through the dispatch center, keeping records, computer operations, general organization and program planning, and the operation of the city jail. In short, all of the desk work is in this bailiwick.

7. *Dispatch Center.* This is the nerve center of the department. It receives and assesses hundreds of calls for police help, then dispatches police officers to handle the request. In dramatic situations, such as a bank robbery in progress, the dispatch center resembles a military headquarters, with the senior officer directing the placement of cruisers converging on the scene to block escape routes.

8. *Data Services Center.* With modern computer equipment, this center provides up-to-the-minute profiles of crimes in each section of the city. For a reporter who is working on an in-depth story about any crime problem, this center is a source of voluminous accurate material. It also serves to identify areas with a high incidence of a given crime so that officers can plan special tactics to abate the problem.

9. *City Jail.* Policemen detain persons arrested there, usually for a brief time until their arraignment. After arraignment, when bond is set, the prisoner is normally either freed on bond or transferred to a jail designed to accommodate a longer stay. A reporter may often find stories on disgraceful jail conditions. Suicides and violence may occur frequently.

10. *Personnel Section.* This section handles personnel records and actions concerning police officers. Although it rarely produces newsworthy events, it can provide photographs and, at times, information about officers who are in the news.

11. *Records Branch.* All reports of crimes are processed in this branch. Often it is physically combined with the "counter-sergeant" function, in which an officer performs the jack-of-all-trades duties of accepting complaints from citizens who walk into the department; accepting offense reports taken by officers on the street; taking telephone calls from citizens who need assorted directions, advice, and counsel not officially provided by police; and simply providing a good listening ear for someone who has a personal problem. The counter sergeant provides reporters with current offense reports, sometimes tips them about specific major crimes, and serves as an unofficial quick source of information about any police action. The records of crimes are in the public domain, thus any citizens or reporter can request to see them. Arrest records are not considered public record, yet, with good sources in the records section, a police reporter may have access on a confidential basis.

12. *Planning Branch.* Normally quiet and uninteresting to reporters, this branch plans many new police programs that, on occasion, can be controversial.

13. *Detective Section.* Experienced officers, wearing civilian clothes, perform the "glamor work" of investigations in solving major crimes. Television has given the public a severely distorted image of the day-to-day work of police detectives. TV detective heros enjoy more action in a single, hour-long episode than most detectives encounter in twenty years. Most detective work is drudgery: A detective interviews the victim, scans the reports of evidence technicians, talks with witnesses, and then settles down in his arm chair to wait for an informant to provide the name of the criminal, or for a uniformed officer to arrest the villain for another crime (the criminal subsequently confesses). Sometimes, the detective quickly pieces together tidbits of information that lead to an arrest soon after the crime. But, with the passing of each day, the chances of solving the typical crime decrease.

This isn't to imply that detectives aren't vital news sources. A friendly detective can provide essential details on any major crime under his investigation. Moreover, there may be a major difference between being able to arrest the suspect and being able to identify him. For example, a veteran burglary sergeant can frequently identify a burglar by his methods of committing the crime. Yet, being able to gather enough evidence for an arrest is a far different story.

Let's look at some of the detective specialties:

13A. *Homicide Squad.* A police reporter *must* have a functional relationship with homicide detectives. Murder is always news, and often page-one news. Whenever an "unnatural" or suspicious death occurs, homicide detectives are on the scene. Since murder is, fortunately, a less frequent crime, homicide detectives often handle assault and sex crimes as well, although in larger departments, these cases may be assigned to special units.

13B. *Robbery Squad.* These detectives investigate both armed robberies and "strong-armed" robberies, depending on the means that the criminal used to force the victim to surrender property.

13C. *Burglary Squad.* All cases of illegal entry and removal of property are investigated by the burglary squad. This crime is so common in most cities that all but the most unusual or costly burglaries are deemed unnewsworthy. Yet, a burglary is one of the most frightening crimes—an armed criminal is in the victim's home.

13D. *Auto Theft Squad.* Because of the sheer volume of such crimes, these detectives concentrate more on breaking up rings of thieves than on solving individual thefts. An auto theft is newsworthy only in unusual circumstances.

13E. *Bunko Squad.* Professional check-bouncers, embezzlers, and "con artists" keep these detectives busy. Bunko squad officers frequently seek to publicize a particular "con game" that is actively fleecing local citizens.

13F. *Larceny Squad.* Although the act of simple theft is essentially the same, the classification of a larceny crime may be either as a felony (major crime) or as a misdemeanor (minor crime), depending on the value of the goods stolen. Shoplifting is one of the most common forms of larceny.

14. *Conflict Management.* Specially trained officers work with street gangs, activist groups, and neighborhood associations to try to settle disputes before they escalate into major police-citizen confrontations. Several departments now have such specialists. When racial tensions rise, this section is involved.

15. *Traffic Section.* These officers enforce traffic and parking laws, and conduct special programs and projects to provide smooth and safe traffic flow. Investigators may also handle reports of fatal accidents.

16. *Organized Crime Control Unit.* Many departments have established such an elite detective branch to deal with crimes often tied to organized crime. Major arrests by these officers make significant news stories—particularly if the reporter can be on hand for the raid. This unit is valuable, also, as a source of background material and as a means of making contact with characters on the fringe of the "underworld" who can provide information for in-depth stories on crime problems. Prostitution, gambling, and narcotics activities are policed by this unit.

17. *Patrol Section.* This is the heart of the police department— uniformed patrol officers. These officers are usually first on the scene of any crime, disturbance, or disaster. They render immediate assistance, take down the details of the complaint, then turn over the information to detectives for follow-up investigation.

BEAT COVERAGE

The new police reporter must quickly and methodically familiarize himself with the functions of each of these organizational entities within the department and establish informational contacts. Yet, before getting into the techniques of setting up beat coverage, let's look at the prime news commodity that the reporter must harvest and sell: crime news.

Although any crime committed has at least some potential news value, the flood of crimes that occur in a normal city in any twenty-four-hour period is such that only the most interesting, consequential, or significant crimes can compete for newspaper space.

The police reporter must exercise a great deal of judgment, based on his understanding of crimes and of the nature of his city. If homicides are very rare in the reporter's city, then a marital quarrel that ends in a fatal shooting becomes page-one news. Yet, if a city suffers through a hundred or so murders in a given year, such a killing becomes "routine news," and the story is worth only two paragraphs deep inside the newspaper. The frequency of even such a tragic crime makes reporters and policemen equally callous after awhile. One police reporter, after learning of a homicide, greeted the investigating detective and asked, "Is this a routine homicide or a good one?"

Although the selection of items to cover is subjective to a large degree, most reporters use these general criteria:

1. *Importance of crime victim.* If the police chief's home is burglarized, then a routine burglary becomes page-one news. If the mayor's automobile is swiped, then a good story is obviously there.

2. *Value of property.* Almost any self-respecting burglar can steal $500 worth of goods from a home. A reporter may set monetary value guidelines for each type of crime, depending on the situation in his city. For example, the minimum amount for a significant burglary may be $5,000.

3. *The criminal's method of operation.* Can a ten-dollar armed robbery be page-one news? It can be if the robber was nude. Unusual, kinky twists to a crime can elevate its value greatly.

4. *The nature of the crime itself.* All else being equal, most reporters rank crimes in a descending order of interest:

(a.) *Homicide.* By all human values, the taking of a life is the ultimate crime in society.

(b.) *Armed robbery* (especially bank robbery). A direct threat of harm is implicit in the presence of the knife or revolver used to force the victim to hand over money or property.

(c.) *Sex crimes.* This category ranks high, even though there is great variation with the nature of the act. Child molesting, rape, and assorted perversions are not uncommon.

(d.) *Burglary.* The victim is not directly threatened, unless he confronts the burglar. Also, the crime is extremely common.

(e.) *Grand larceny.* Although the amount varies from state to state, a simple theft of money or property above the legal limit escalates the crime from petit larceny (a misdemeanor) to grand larceny (a felony).

(f.) *Auto theft.* Most auto thefts are juvenile joy rides or the work of petty criminals who strip the car of parts, then leave the hulk for recovery.

(g.) *Assaults.* This crime is woefully common. On a given day, a long line of assault victims may lead to the desk of a hapless detective who handles routine complaints. Only a small percentage of victims press charges after the arrest has been made. Most assaults occur in family quarrels.

Some so-called "victimless crimes" also have considerable news value:

(a.) *Major drug raids.* Arrests for the sale of "hard" narcotics, such as heroin or cocaine, are newsworthy, especially when the suspect is caught with a large amount of drugs on hand. Marijuana arrests are so common that the amount of drugs on hand must be significant to warrant coverage in most cities.

(b.) *Prostitution arrests.* Normally, the arrest of a prostitute is hardly newsworthy. Yet, a crackdown that results in many arrests is significant.

(c.) *Gambling arrests.* Generally, it depends on how big the arrest is. If a neighborhood bartender is arrested for taking bets, the significance is low. If a large gambling organization is smashed, it's major news.

5. *The identity of the suspect.* If the mayor's son is arrested for auto theft, if the suspect in a burglary is eight years old, if an eighty-year-old grandmother is nabbed shoplifting a tennis racquet, then the story is newsworthy.

6. *Crime patterns.* A single burglary may not be newsworthy, but a great wave of burglaries in a single neighborhood can be. A series of armed robberies by the same suspects is interesting. If "routine" crimes can be tied together, the significance grows vastly.

With these general criteria in mind, the reporter is ready to gather information about newsworthy crimes. The degree of detail will, of course, depend on the value of the story and the length that the story warrants. Here are the basic informational items that a reporter should gather for a story on each crime:

Homicide:

Name, age, address, and sex of victim.

Date, time, and place of occurrence (address if possible).

Weapon used, and the number and nature of wounds.

Name, address, age, and sex of suspect, or description, if suspect is at large.

Relationship between suspect and victim, if known.

Motive, if known.

Circumstances of the crime: how did it happen?

Witnesses (for possible contact, not for use in print).

Date, time, and place of death.

Progress of the investigation.

Any other significant or newsworthy implications (importance or occupation of victim or suspect).

Connection with any other crimes. Note that in many homicides, either the victim or the suspect may be connected to other crimes of violence. In a typical case, the suspect in one murder, who was out on bail awaiting trial, became the victim of another murder.

Charges brought against the suspect.

Armed Robbery:

Amount of money/value of property taken.

Name, age, and address of victim; or name, nature, and address of business.

Name, age, and address of suspect, or description.

For banks and businesses, the names and ages of employees present.

Conditions of any people injured in the robbery.

Circumstances: how did the robbers operate, what happened?

Time and date of robbery.

Progress of investigation.

Charges against any suspects.

Description of weapons used.

Burglary:

Value and nature of property stolen.

Name, age, and adress of victim; name, nature, and address of business.

Date and time of occurrence (also address, if different from victim's address).

Means of entry.

Name, age, and address of suspects; description, if available.

Circumstances.

Sex Crimes:

Name, age, address, and sex of victim (may be withheld by newspaper policy).

Name, age, and address of suspect; description.

Nature and extent of injuries to victim.

Progress of investigation; charge.

Circumstances.

Connection with other crimes.

Date, time, and place of assault.

Fraud:

Name, age, and address of each victim.

Value of property taken.

Date, time, and place of the crime.

Circumstances: explain clearly how the culprit operates.

Progress of investigation; charge.

Name, age, and address of each suspect; description.

Connection to other crimes.

Amount recovered.

Larceny:

Value and nature of property stolen.

Date, time, and place of occurrence.

Name, age, and address of victim; name, nature, and address of business.

Circumstances.

Progress of investigation; charge.

Connection to other crimes.

Amount recovered.

Auto Theft:

Value, make, year, and description of vehicle taken.

Name, age, and address of owner; name, nature, and address of business.

Date, time, and place of occurrence.

Circumstances: how did thief operate? How did owner happen to park there?

Address or location from which vehicle was taken.

Progress of investigation; charge.

Recovery: was it recovered? In what condition? Where, when, and how?

Drug-related Arrests:

Name, age, and address of suspect or suspects.

Nature and amount of drugs involved (if possible, street-value estimation).

Circumstances of arrest.

Date, time, place, and location of arrest.

Did the suspect resist arrest?

Charges filed against suspect.

Weapons found at the scene of the arrest.

Connection with other crimes.

Names of arresting officers.

Gambling:

Names, ages, and addresses of those arrested.

Date, time, and place of arrests.

Nature of gambling involved (bookmaking, numbers, cards).

Circumstances of arrests.

Police estimates of the size of the operation and money handled.

Did the suspects resist?

Circumstances of the arrests and of investigation leading to arrests.

Charges filed against suspects.

Connection with other crimes, or police actions (series of raids?).

Prostitution:

Names, ages, and addresses of those arrested.

Date, time, and place of arrests.

Circumstances of arrests.

Nature of the illegal operation: a house? a ring? street prostitutes?

Charges filed against suspects.

Related arrests (customers, pimps, accomplices)

Connection with other crimes (robberies are often a sideline occupation).

Did the suspects resist arrest?

The list of other possible crimes that a reporter may cover would be far too lengthy to allow continuation of such detail, yet these general outlines of information needed can be broadly applied with necessary variations.

Obviously, a reporter doesn't have time to pull out a checklist and painstakingly fill in the blanks for each crime he covers. Also, many of these items may be unknown or irrelevant for a given crime. The purpose of this listing, then, is to provide a feel for the thorough, systematic approach to information acquisition that a reporter develops through experience. In a short time, the process of picking out significant information becomes second-natured and not a conscious process.

Also, keep in mind that these listings cover only the basic, essential areas that should be routinely checked by the reporter. It provides information for the foundation of his story, but the fleshing-out process often requires considerably more research.

To apply these forms to practical reporting, let's examine the system that a reporter would use in gathering this information.

The first stop on a reporter's rounds after arriving at the police department is at the counter sergeant's position. A two-inch thick stack of offense reports is piled in a basket to accommodate reporters.

"What's happening?" the reporter asks the sergeant.

"We had a homicide last night, during a robbery," the sergeant replies. "It happened about midnight at a gas station over on Third Street."

With that helpful tip, the reporter scans each report. His practiced eye first takes in the nature of the crime, then moves on to parts of the report that contain information he needs to assess its news value. If nothing of interest catches his attention, he flips to the next report in ten or fifteen seconds.

Because of the robbery-murder, he is especially alert for armed robberies. He takes down information on each armed robbery that occurred overnight, especially others in the general area of the homicide-robbery. There may be a tie-in.

Half an hour later, he thanks the sergeant and leaves the counter with a half dozen stories in his notebook, including the robbery-homicide. He stops by the pressroom to call his city editor to alert him of the major story, then he proceeds to the detective section.

Two detective squads are involved in the investigation: robbery and homicide, with the homicide sergeant heading the joint effort. The reporter visits the sergeant's office.

"Good morning, Gene. Tell me about your homicide," the reporter asks.

"Which one?" the detective replies mournfully. "We have two now; a second attendant at the gas station just died of his wounds."

The reporter takes down this additional information, then seeks elaboration on the information he gleaned from the offense report. Detectives normally have far more information than that which is listed. The sergeant is cooperative and helpful, but he tells the reporter that he must withhold some information because premature leakage would hamper the investigation. The reporter, understanding the sergeant's position, is nevertheless obliged to extract all that he can. He takes down all the information that he pulls from his reluctant source, thanks him, then moves on to the robbery squad sergeant.

"Good morning, Jess. You had three other robberies just before the big one, all within a four-block radius. Do they fit together?" he asks.

"It looks that way," the sergeant replies. "We aren't sure yet, but the descriptions of the suspects match. Let me put it this way, if they're not connected, it's quite a coincidence, since the suspects at each robbery all wore black leather jackets, and they all rode motorcycles. It looks like we have a motorcycle gang on our hands."

The interview proceeds, with the robbery sergeant's information meshing with and supplementing the homicide sergeant's account.

When the reporter is satisfied that he has all available information on the crimes, he is troubled by a nagging thought: If a juvenile gang is on a robbery spree, there may be more to it than is apparent. He then visits the conflict management squad, whose specialists deal extensively with street gangs.

"Joe, are your kids misbehaving?" the reporter asks an officer who specializes in working with gangs.

"I'm afraid to answer that question; you'll get me in trouble," the policeman replies cautiously.

The reporter then tries a different approach.

"Can you tell me if I don't attribute it to you?"

"Yeah, we have a problem. The Devil's Riders and the Chain Gang are at war. If you're thinking that this could be connected to that homicide-robbery, I'm thinking the same thing. I've checked with my informants, and I have some information that I'll pass on to homicide. All I can say for sure is that we suspect that one of the gangs pulled the robberies. Witnesses saw one suspect with a "Devil's Riders" jacket, but don't jump to conclusions. No idiot would be dumb enough to wear his gang colors on a robbery. It may be a set up. Just say that we are investigating a connection."

The reporter asks several questions to learn about the nature and extent of the gang war and about the gangs involved. By the time he returns to the pressroom, he has taken the basic information listed on the offense report and has gathered material that expands the story to major, page-one story status.

During the remainder of the morning, the reporter checks out other, unrelated stories that he picked up from the complaint reports, using the same method of checking with investigators to broaden his information.

Still other stops must be made on his rounds. He visits briefly with the public relations officers to see if any announcements, press conferences, or releases are forthcoming. He checks with the traffic section to see if any serious accidents occurred. He calls the coroner for details on suicides, and he visits the offices of other detectives not involved in cases reported on complaints to see if he overlooked anything of interest.

Frequently, a police reporter's job is complicated by a host of assorted related responsibilities that fall into his area. In a medium-sized city, the police reporter must also cover fires and various other disasters, since police are normally involved anyway. Also, police work and organization has, in recent years, grown so complex that the reporter must spend considerable time covering the institution itself. Thus, during his routine, the police reporter must keep tabs on his other functions:

Fire Coverage

Most fire departments have a senior official in charge of releasing information to the news media. Well before deadline, the police reporter may telephone that contact to see whether any significant fires occurred overnight. In assessing the news value of a fire, the reporter uses these criteria:

1. *Estimated damage.* If the fire caused $50,000 or $60,000 in damage, it may be newsworthy. The damage criteria is, of course, set by the reporter.

2. *Deaths and injuries.* If the residents, employees, or firemen are killed or seriously injured, then the story is significant.

3. *Cause.* If arson is suspected, a small fire may be worth a story.

4. *Unusual circumstances.*

Firemen are also routinely involved in rescue work. The fire department spokesman can provide information on drownings, rescues, and miscellaneous industrial accidents that required fire department assistance.

Labor Relations

Many police departments have a recognized collective bargaining group to negotiate contracts and to represent the interests of officers. A Fraternal Order of Police (FOP) organization is a common bargaining group. In recent years, many police organizations have become outspoken and volatile in expressing the needs of officers. If a contract dispute is underway, the police reporter may spend considerable time covering the negotiations between police and city representatives.

Organizational disputes

Enmities and elaborate scheming for personal advancement are common in upper-echelons of any large organization such as a police department. Such feuding may directly affect police service. Moreover, any advancement among top-ranked officers is, in itself, news. The police reporter must be alert to such finaglings and, when provable, share the news with the public.

Special programs

Departments often try experimental programs to cut down crime, violence, and neighborhood problems. Perhaps a special sensitivity program is conducted by the police academy to help officers who have violent tendencies. Perhaps a special neighborhood police program attempts to abate crime by creating better relationships between citizens and police. These efforts deserve coverage.

Coroner's office

The coroner is a county official who must determine whether any suspicious or "unnatural" death is murder, suicide, or accidental. The police reporter should routinely contact the coroner's office to make certain he doesn't miss suspicious or prominent deaths that somehow eluded his attention as he checked police channels. Also, additional details about homicides under police investigation often can be found at the coroner's office. Significantly, a homicide isn't a homicide unless the coroner rules it to be one.

SUMMARY

Details of the complexities of police beat coverage—and the methods used to perform that coverage—could fill several volumes of textbooks. While this chapter provides a general overview of the world of a police beat reporter, it should serve only as the broadest guide to beat coverage. On-the-scene coverage of crime and disaster news is dealt with separately in Chapter 15.

The importance of the police beat within the framework of a reporter's career development cannot be overestimated. At one time or another, most reporters are exposed to this lively beat, perhaps in keeping with the age-old journalistic logic that it is an excellent "breaking-in" assignment. Perhaps the logic is partly based on the fact that the police beat is the most physically demanding assignment, thus requiring youthful vigor.

Physical stamina aside, the pressures of this assignment constitute an excellent test of a new journalist's potential. A noted columnist, when asked for career advice by a journalism student, suggested that the police beat is an excellent starting place. "If you can survive the police beat for six months, without costing the newspaper a libel suit, you are off to a good start."

EXERCISES

1. You are the new police beat reporter for a medium-sized metropolitan daily newspaper. While thumbing through the offense reports, you find a report of a homicide by arson. Where do you go to find additional information?

2. While riding around with two friendly uniformed policemen, you see them slap a handcuffed prisoner who uses abusive language toward them. Should you report the incident?

3. List each major contact you would make on a routine daily basis as police reporter. Explain why you would contact each source?

4. Class exercise: Make arrangements with a nearby police department for students to observe police officers at work.

5. Class exercise: Make arrangements for students to visit a fire station and, if possible, accompany firemen on a call.

12 | City Hall

To appreciate the complexity of covering the city hall beat, envision the legendary Greek labyrinth of seemingly endless tunnels and caves that twist, interconnect, and link into a confusing maze of passageways. To any reporter who has ever wandered down the hallways of a municipal building in search of a particularly elusive bureaucrat, the analogy is sound.

In previous chapters, the often precarious human relationships between officials and reporters that facilitate the acquisition of printable information has been carefully explored. The techniques of building and maintaining a system of informational sources are essentially the same on any beat, but the city hall beat offers an additional challenge: that of staying abreast of events in an organization that produces a huge flow of vitally significant, yet complex and varied news items.

The city hall labyrinth is lined with gold. Any competent reporter can wander through the corridors for an hour or two and emerge with a printable news item. Yet, effective and comprehensive coverage of this prestigious beat requires both a broad knowledge of each of the myriad functions performed there and the mental and physical stamina to cope with the news flow.

While there are many forms of city governments—ranging from the "strong-mayor" system of poiltical dominance of services to the technocratic "city-manager" system—a city hall commonly houses two powerful elements: an entrenched bureaucracy of career technicians who manage the day-to-day service functions of local government and a political enclave for successful local politicians. To illustrate city hall coverage, a city-manager form of local government will be examined. Most functions are easily transferable to other governmental forms.

For a setting, picture a Midwestern city of 250,000 people. Each citizen is crucially dependent on the ability of city hall to deliver basic services: safe water, sanitary sewerage and garbage disposal, police and fire service, an efficient transportation system, cultural and recreational outlets, animal control, and hundreds of other funtcions. Disruption of any single service, even for a brief period, causes civil chaos that can make life miserable. If garbage piles up during a strike by sanitation workers, if snow isn't removed from main streets during a storm, if a water shortage occurs, or if police are unable to provide reasonable safety, then city hall is besieged by angry citizens. Somewhere in the labyrinth exists an official in charge of that disrupted service. The reporter's job is to find him and obtain answers to those angry questions.

Let's take a look at a typical city manager-styled organization. In this governmental form, a professional city administrator manages the functions of government according to policies, laws, and limitations enacted by elected officials who comprise the city council. The mayor and council members are part-time officials who take care of city business in addition to their own career occupations. The mayor may be a practicing attorney, while the council may consist of a jeweler, a merchant, two attorneys, a banker, and a union president. They oversee this rambling domain:

1. *City Council.* Each week, council conducts a public meeting to openly consider any matters relating to the governing of the city. As a body, council can direct the actions of the city manager or dismiss him for failure to perform satisfactorily. All expenditures of public funds must be approved by council, usually in the form of an annual budget and a stipulation requiring approval for any single outlay of funds exceeding a minimum amount. This purse-string control serves to keep the city hall bureaucracy subservient. Legislative actions can either be city ordinances, informal resolutions, or formal resolutions:

(a.) A *city ordinance* is a law that entails punishment for violation. Council may enact an ordinance forbidding citzens from spitting on the sidewalk. Violators may be fined $50 in munipical court.

(b.) *Formal Resolutions* constitute official directives and legally binding declarations by city council. The annual budget may be approved by formal resolution. It can be changed only at a public hearing at which an amendment, also in the form of a formal resolution; is offered. Still another example may be a formal resolution to award a multi-million-dollar contract to a firm in return for specified services.

(c.) *Informal Resolutions* are non-binding declarations of sentiment or intent. A public declaration honoring a local astronaut would be made in the form of an informal resolution.

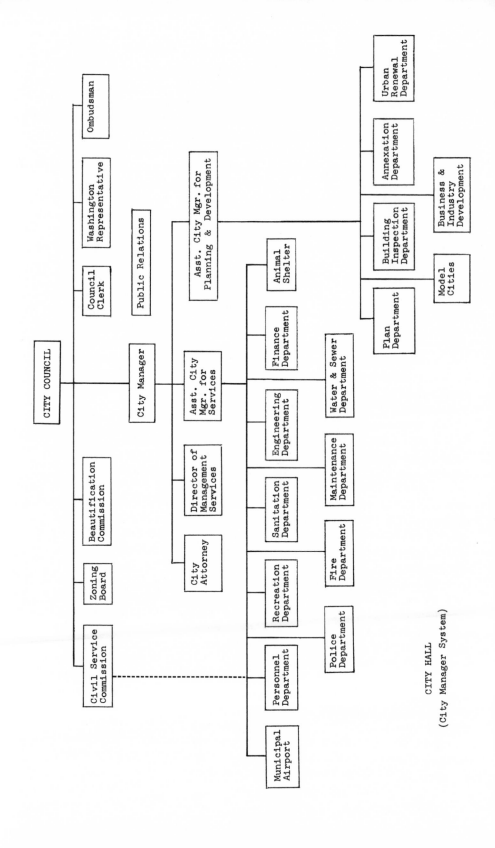

CITY HALL

(City Manager System)

With such authority and power invested in them, council members can exert direct influence even on the day-to-day conduct of city business. Perhaps a constituent complains to a council member about a pothole in the street in front of his house. The council member can quickly call the superintendent of street maintenance and facilitate the repair. If the official doesn't perform satisfactorily, the council member can escalate his pressure to the city manager.

Keep in mind that city council is a political body, often given to behind-the-scenes favor-swapping and politics. A city hall reporter, then, is obliged to not only accurately report the public activities of council, but to try to penetrate the public facade to discover and report the decision-making process behind public actions and its political implications.

2. *City Manager.* A professional public administrator, the manager's overriding responsibility is to make city government function to respond to the needs of citizens and to the directives of city council. No significant program, problem, or activity within city hall should occur without his knowledge, advice, or approval. For the city hall reporter, the manager is the ultimate informational source, the person who has the potential to answer or find the answer to any questions relating to city hall functions. The problem is that even the most cooperative city managers are so busy that their accessibility to reporters is limited. Cobwebs have formed on many reporters who sat in the manager's outer office, waiting for a few minutes of interview time, or simply hoping to catch the official as he hurried between meetings.

3. *Council Clerk.* This official's job description may seem deceptively minor: he is the administrative assistant to the council, facilitating the flow of official paper work and compiling the council's agenda for meetings. In fact, the council clerk should be one of the most knowledgeable and important news sources within city hall, bridging the gap between politics and service delivery. He is privy to most of the backroom politics that occur on any major council action and, to be effective in his job, he must be intimately familiar with the political state of the council at any given time and with the political ramifications of any action. Even his agenda-setting function offers a rich lode of information: in order to rationally plan a legislative agenda, the clerk must be fully informed of the importance and ramifications of each proposed item. The city hall reporter can gain invaluable information and insight from this source, assuming a relationship can be maintained. The clerk can also directly influence council actions by serving as a trusted advisor to all or several council members. He may schedule or delay an important item so that it falls on—or off of—a reporter's news cycle. And he may influence council members to confide to—or "close out"—a reporter.

4. *Washington Representative.* Many large cities employ special lobbyists to seek federal funds for city programs or to facilitate other forms of aid to their areas. While hardly a prolific source of news, a Washington representative can provide major stories on occasions when large grants have been obtained. The lobbyist works directly under city council.

5. *Ombudsman.* Some cities hire an official to serve as a bridge between the public and service components of city hall. Since council members are often inaccessible during the working day as they tend to their own vocations, an efficient ombudsmen relieves them of much public pressure by channeling and following up complaints and requests from citizens. Although major news stories rarely arise from this operation, the ombudsman can be a valuable source of story leads about persistent problem areas and about the general mood of the public.

6. *Beautification Commission.* This and other such special interest organizations occasionally provide stories when special projects, such as a large clean-up operation, are underway. Often, appointments to such bodies are made to honor political friends of council members.

7. *Zoning Board.* This important board determines the use of land within the city, according to guidelines established by city council. The zoning board's importance stems from the financial impact of its rulings, and from the direct effect that its actions may have on large numbers of citizens.

For example, a land-development firm may request that a large parcel of land be rezoned to accommodate the location of a multi-million-dollar industrial plant. Thousands of dollars of profit, and the potential of hundreds of jobs for citizens may be at stake as the zoning board deliberates. On the other side, nearby residents may strongly object to the change that could transform their quiet neighborhood into an industrial hub. Worse, if the plant will emit high levels of noise or noxious odors, property values could plummet. The zoning board, then, must weigh overriding public interest and act accordingly. A reporter must maintain close contact with the board for several reasons:

(a.) Major zoning issues are news. Contacts are needed to provide the often complicated interpretations necessary to translate technicalities into digestible news fodder.

(b.) A zoning change request is often the first clue to the arrival of a major new industry or business in the city. If a major automobile producer intends to build a plant in the city, it's page-one news, especially for the reporter who first learns of the plan.

(c.) The zoning board is especially susceptible to corruption and special interest favoritism. If a member can influence whether a firm will gain hundreds of thousands of dollars in commissions over a period of years, then the danger of bribery is constant. If the board routinely favors business interests whenever they conflict with those of the general public, then such favoritism is worthy of exposure. The reporter's watchdog function must be carefully maintained in this area.

8. *Civil Service Commission.* To guard against political favoritism, most cities establish a commission to impartially govern the hiring, firing, and promotion of city employees. The commission must be constantly apprised of any actions to increase or decrease the city payroll or to create or abolish even high-level career positions. Reporters must maintain contact, especially during present-day controversies surrounding policies that, perhaps unwittingly, discriminate against minority or female applicants.

Patterns of discrimination are especially noteworthy. If, for example, only 1 percent of female applicants are hired for city jobs compared with 47 percent of male applicants, then the pattern lends itself to scrutiny for clues or deliberate discrimination or the existence of unfair obstacles.

9. *Assistant City Manager for Services.* The city manager may have an assistant who oversees all day-to-day service functions performed by the municipal government. Organizationally, he serves as both a screen to relieve the city manager from routine or minor difficulties and as a troubleshooter who intervenes on behalf of the city manager to deal with major problems after informing his boss and discussing alternatives. Because of his direct relationship with all service situations, and because he may be far more accesssible than the city manager, this assistant is a valuable contact for the city hall reporter.

10. *Assistant City Manager for Planning and Development.* This assistant deals far more with tomorrow than with today, as he formulates then carries out plans to improve life in the city. He may oversee vast urban renewal projects, the planning and construction of a new civic center, negotiations to annex an abutting suburb, and the regulatory functions of city building inspectors, who ensure that structures are safely maintained. In addition, the assistant may serve as a "salesman" to convince businesses and industries to locate within city limits. Since almost any plan or project under this assistant's care is major news, he is another prime source for the city hall reporter.

11. *Director of Management Services.* Like many large industrial firms, city hall may provide an organization to furnish staff planning for the city manager. The director may suggest reorganization plans, provide budgetary analyses, and other special staff work for the manager. As a high-level staff member who is privy to planning and the inter-workings of city hall, the director may be a good news source.

12. *City Attorney.* This official provides legal services to all city employees, formulates contracts, and ensures that the city operates

within the limits of the law. Although his involvement in most projects doesn't occur until the final stages—after every reporter in town has published the details of the story—the city attorney may provide useful information when the city is involved in occasional court battles.

13. *Municipal Airport.* Often a financial asset to the city, the airport operation deserves an occasional glance by the city hall reporter, especially when major construction projects are underway or when problems, such as hijacking or a series of crashes, occur.

14. *Personnel Department.* During periods of negotiation with employee unions, the department is a major news source. A city may have to negotiate with a score of separate unions during the year, thus some reliable contact must be maintained by the reporter. The department maintains employee personnel records, assists employees in attaining benefits offered under contract, and constantly assesses jobs to determine the value of given positions.

15. *Police Department.* Although the police reporter covers the daily flood of crime and police news, some overlap often occurs between the city hall beat and the police beat. If, for example, the labor bargaining unit for policemen is negotiating with the city for a new contract, the city hall reporter has a legitimate involvement in the coverage. Edicts from city council and the city manager that affect police may also spur coverage by the city hall reporter.

17. *Fire Department.* Once again, an overlap may occur between the city hall and police beats during negotiations, council actions, and budgetary appropriations.

18. *Sanitation Department.* Although the daily function of garbage removal is hardly newsworthy, any disruption of that service is major news. Some interpretative coverage of ecology/environment-related issues to the disposal of waste is always a possibility.

19. *Maintenance Department.* Much like the sanitation department, the maintenance department is most often newsworthy only when something is amiss. Responsible for keeping city property, including machinery, streets, and buildings, in repair, even the most efficient department is usually deluged with complaints from citizens who can't understand why their streets were not promptly cleared during the last snowfall.

20. *Engineering Department.* Traffic control is the most newsworthy service of city engineers, who determine the timing of stop lights, plan for road-widening, and design bridges and overpasses.

21. *Water and Sewer Department.* Traditionally, this function is of public concern only during crises of water supply or the disruptive installation of new sewer lines. However, in recent years, some cities have used water and sewer service to "blackmail" unincorporated suburbs into annexation or to enforce an orderly growth pattern. By refusing to supply water and sewer service to areas outside the city,

or by charging outlandish rates, they add considerable enticement for annexation. A reporter should be constantly alert for such ploys as they may signal a new drive to expand city limits.

22. *Finance Department.* As the central disbursement center for all city cash outlays, including payrolls, the finance department is an important contact point for a reporter. Modern bookkeeping practices in efficient city government make it extremely difficult for any official to embezzle or misuse city funds without collusion with departmental officials. Among items that a reporter should routinely check are:

(a.) *Expense account records.* When officials travel out of town on city business, they must itemize their expenses to receive reimbursement. An occasional examination of such records may reveal excessive spending by top officials, or questionable judgment.

(b.) *The overall financial state of the city government.* Budgets are based on projected income from taxes, which may or may not materialize. If tax receipts are significantly lower than projected, the city can face a financial crisis that could result in curtailment of services.

(c.) *Investments.* Few cities simply stash receipts in an office safe. With careful financial management, most make short-term investments to gain additional revenue through interest, or they place the funds in a financial institution to safely draw a modest interest. While this practice is, of course, beneficial, a reporter should examine the list of investments for signs of favoritism to institutions with high-placed city hall connections. If a council member is also a banker, and if his bank benefits from city investments, then a conflict of interest may be present.

(d.) *Lucrative contracts and purchases.* Again, if a firm is tied to a high official and if it benefits from a disproportionately large amount of city business, the public has a right to know.

23. *Plan Department.* A staff of architects and city planners designs major urban-renewal and public-improvement projects. A new shopping mall, an industrial park, or a new civic center would first appear on their drawing boards. Such important changes require alert coverage.

24. *Model Cities.* Many major cities have a "model cities"-styled organization to improve the quality of life in troubled neighborhoods and to involve citizens directly in governing their neighborhoods. Administrative officials can provide insight to neighborhood problems and "grass roots" political sentiment. Also, a large amount of local and federal funding may be controlled by these semi-autonomous neighborhood organizations, thus the reporter should be alert for misuse or theft of these funds, since the financial accountability system is often less efficient.

25. *Building Inspection Department.* City building inspectors en-

force codes that are designed to ensure safe and sanitary buildings. Frequently, inspectors must joust with powerful "slumlords" and property owners to force them to make repairs in rental units. Because it's often cheaper to bribe a building inspector than to make repairs, the danger of corruption lingers in this department, thus necessitating close scrutiny by the reporter. Also, the identity of slumlords and others who risk the safety of tenants to increase their profits can be the basis for investigative stories, especially when a slumlord has high political or social standing. On occasion, frustrated inspectors may approach a reporter to offer information that will generate public pressure on a particularly stubborn slumlord.

26. *Business and Industrial Development.* An office may be established to solicit business and industrial relocation within city limits, or to work with existing enterprises to enable them to continue operating within the city. The role is important and newsworthy, since many jobs may be at stake.

27. *Annexation Department.* In recent years, many major cities have suffered from the migration of wealthy and middle-class citizens to outlying suburbs. Both the tax base and the leadership pool declines, and the physical expansion of the city is choked, since citizens who fled the city tend to vote against allowing annexation of their suburban homes. The annexation department attempts to chip away at the "iron ring" of stubborn suburbs that block expansion. Using persuasion and other enticements (such as the threat of denying water and sewer service), department officials seek to inch city boundaries ever outward. Any significant success by this function is major news.

28. *Urban Renewal Department.* Often dovetailing its efforts with the model cities operation, urban renewal seeks to replace or restore deteriorated neighborhoods. The implementation of a major urban-renewal project is major news, with the importance of the story relating directly to the size of the area to undergo change.

Obviously, the alignment and complexity of the city hall organization varies greatly with the size of a city and with the organizational philosophy of the administration. Yet, in almost any city, the major functions and services of government share this awesome collective tendency to produce news.

Even on the dullest news day, a city hall reporter should find himself pressed for time. If no news events are breaking, then he should pry beneath the surface of the city hall structure to examine situations that can become major news: finance department records, plan department activities, efforts by the annexation department, preparations for negotiations by the personnel department, and building inspection problems. If no newsworthy situations are developing, the reporter can use any free time to write feature stories on the people behind the services: a day with a garbage crew, a personal profile feature about a colorful department supervisor, a tour of city slum housing with a building inspector, or a day with a park supervisor. The story possibilities are virtually limitless.

As if all of this wasn't ample to keep the city hall reporter occupied, a vast additional responsibility must occupy much of his energy: political and legislative coverage of city hall.

As noted earlier, city hall is a bastion of local politics—the home of the successful office-seekers and the fortress from which they seek to defend or advance their political fortunes. Quite logically, then, the city hall reporter may also inherit the chore of covering all political activities within the city, including campaigns and organizational maneuvering. While this area is covered extensively in a separate chapter, politics often influences an important regular function: legislative actions by council.

COVERING A CITY COUNCIL MEETING

Coverage of the weekly city council meeting requires a thorough and methodical approach by a reporter. The legislative and policy-making actions that take place at the meeting are normally the weekly climax of beat activity, and they require coverage well in advance of the meeting. Let's examine that coverage, step by step:

1. Check the agenda a full day or two before the meeting to allow time for an advance story. The council clerk should have a tentative lineup of items to be considered well in advance. Consult the clerk and other sources to determine the significance and potential news value of each item. Also, consult city council sources to determine whether nonscheduled items may be introduced. If an item is especially important, obtain as much information as possible for an informative advance story.

2. Write an advance story for the final edition before the meeting. If a major issue is expected to come up for a vote, try to ascertain the likely outcome of the vote and provide the readers with a straightforward rendition of those factors. This is especially critical when the meeting occurs on a competitor's news cycle.

3. Before the meeting begins, obtain copies of any reports or documents to be presented at the meeting. If a new budget is proposed, a copy is critically important so that the margin of human error in reporting is reduced. With figures flying rapidly during deliberations, a reporter may easily fumble as he commits them to his notebook.

4. As council members arrive for the meeting, chat with them to gain insight about their sentiments and personal analyses of issues. If council conducts an informal, private discussion before the meeting

—an all-too-common occurrence—use sources on the council to find out the nature of the discussion. Often, a governmental body prefers to conduct its verbal bloodletting in private.

5. When the meeting begins, the reporter should:

(a.) Assess the audience. Is there a knot of angry citizens present to petition council for a grievance? Are political figures present, who may contest council actions or attempt to influence them? Are two normally hostile community leaders sitting together, thus indicating a strange political alliance against council, or for or against a given issue? Are any of the "regular troublemakers" on hand—people who faithfully attend each meeting to address council in a long-winded tirade on an inane issue? The audience composition may quickly inform the experienced reporter of any potential unscheduled battles or issues.

(b.) Be alert for unsual changes in parliamentary procedure. Council members are every bit as capable of "reading" an audience as a reporter is. The mayor may gavel a "troublemaker" to silence, or even call for a long recess in hopes that dissidents will drift away before the meeting resumes. Some mayors are masters of the "heavy gavel," and they can bully or browbeat a concerned citizen who raises unwelcome issues.

(c.) Concentrate on interplay between council members, especially if strong personal or political friction simmers behind the scenes. Perhaps Councilwoman Smith despises Councilman Jones, so she never misses an opportunity to embarrass him with cutting remarks that the public may not notice. A reporter is obliged to inform his readers of any such interplay, especially when it influences council action.

(d.) Watch out for changes in the agenda. If a major item is deleted at the last minute, the public should know why. It may signal an unreconcilable split among council members, or an effort to buy time for further consideration due to unusual developments.

(e.) Allot time and concentration carefully. If a long-winded "loony" is lambasting council about some nonsense, use the time to examine previously discussed issues and votes. Jot down questions to be asked after the meeting so that cloudy points can be clarified.

(f.) Be always alert for "railroading." If an item is approved quickly, without expected debate or dissention, then suspicions should be aroused. A behind-the-scenes deal may have occurred.

6. After the meeting, the reporter should take advantage of that rare moment when all top city officials are assembled in one room. Question council members about the reasons behind their votes, about the significance of the issues, and so on. Once satisfied that ample information has been gathered for the story about the meeting, the reporter can use this accessibility to seek comments and information

from normally elusive officials about other items. For example the director of personnel has been unavailable for comment on sensitive labor negotiations. The reporter is blessed with the opportunity to corner him after the meeting.

A Case Study

Now that the procedures for covering a council meeting have been outlined, let's illustrate the methods with an actual case.

As the day of a morning council meeting approached, a city hall reporter for an afternoon newspaper learned that council was very close to agreement on the appointment of a person to fill the unexpired term of a council member who had resigned. He obtained three names as the most likely candidates and wrote an advance story to explain the situation, and to provide other important items that were formally listed on the agenda. In the story, he explained that the council was bitterly split, with two warring members each proposing a favored candidate, and a third compromise choice being offered by the mayor. Using a neutral council member as his informational source, the reporter obtained a vivid account of the heated arguments.

Arriving early at the council's office suite in city hall, he watched the council members file into the mayor's office for a private discussion. Although the reporter was tempted by the keyhole, the mayor's secretary discouraged evesdropping. As minutes passed, the reporter used the time to read over reports and background material for items on the agenda.

When the council members finally emerged from the office the reporter knew immediately that the outcome had been decided: one combatant was grinning broadly, while his opponent was red-faced with anger. As the neutral source walked past, he whispered, "We will have an announcement during the meeting."

The reporter quickly called his city editor to alert him to the probable front-page story, then hurried to the council meeting room. As he assessed the audience, he was dismayed to note that several notoriously long-winded citizens were present to delay the meeting's outcome and add deadline pressure. This was especially critical, since the editor demanded a story for the early editions.

As the meeting droned on and on with few items of significant interest, the reporter pondered his problem and decided to file a story in which early-edition readers would learn of the pending decision and, based on the visual description of the emerging council members, they could draw their own conclusions about the identity of the new council member. When the first verbose citizen arose to rant on and on about his favorite unnewsworthy subject, the reporter slipped out of the room and walked to the council offices to borrow a telephone to transmit his hastily scribbled story.

On entering the outer office, he was amazed to behold the likely new appointee, sitting patiently as she awaited the announcement. After a quick interview, in which she confirmed that she was notified of her selection, the reporter called in his story, then rushed back to the council room just in time to hear the mayor gavel the rambling citizen to silence.

Shortly afterward, the victorious councilman moved for a vote on the appointment of the new councilwoman. The reporter, after considerable research in preparation for the meeting, had learned that by tradition such votes were unanimous, with the losers graciously joining the winners in a show of solidarity. In this case, the loser voted against the appointee, signaling a great political feud.

As soon as the meeting ended, reporters scrambled madly to an impromptu press conference held by the new appointee. Since he had already obtained the exclusive interview, the reporter ignored the rush and, instead, cornered the angry loser to obtain an explanation of his unprecedented vote. Then he talked with the equally angry winner, who chided his opponent for his "childish tantrum" in voting against his protégée. Further interviews with knowledgeable political experts who were present elaborated on the political significance of the action.

In summary, through alertness and good fortune, the reporter obtained *two* major stories, while his competitors concentrated on sharing the single story of the appointment. The political potential of the "no" vote—an exclusive story—was just as important as the appointment itself.

SUMMARY

Because of space limitations, the *techniques* of newsgathering in city hall have been largely passed over, in favor of a detailed overview of the news potential of the beat. A strong case can be made that the city hall beat is the most important and demanding local assignment. The reporter must carefully fill the watchdog function of constantly searching for governmental abuses, failures, and corruption, while struggling with a tidal wave of often complicated news.

EXERCISES

1. From a source in the plan department, you learn that a new civic center complex is being considered, to be located in a deteriorated neighborhood that is plagued by a high crime rate. Assuming that

you have reasonably reliable sources in each functional area, which officials would you contact for additional information (using the organizational chart on page 178)? What information would you seek from each of them?

2. Before a council meeting, you learn that the budget for next year will be proposed, and that dissention within council is expected over one item that reduces police department appropriations by 10 percent. List the steps you would take to gather material for the advance story.

3. Tipped just prior to a council meeting that, in collusion with the council, a private citizen would propose a 50 percent increase in the city income tax, you note with amusement that council members express admirably feigned surprise and spontaneous support for the measure. As a political ploy, involving both major political parties, community leaders decided to use the tactic to create the appearance of "grass-roots demand" for a tax increase. You recognize the "average" citizen as a precinct leader for a major party. As the meeting ends, how do you gather additional information?

13 | Politics

Hours before the first returns begin to trickle in, the crowd begins to grow at the county board of elections offices. Politicians and campaign workers nervously mill about, some confident, others vaguely hopeful, yet all tense as they await the public's verdict.

As soon as the polls close, the crowd becomes a high-strung mob, as political people, reporters, and curious citizens squeeze into the cramped confines while harassed clerks compile totals. An election official pushes through the crowd carrying a large, sealed canvas bag, filled with ballots from a nearby precinct.

At last, the chairman of the board of elections emerges from his office with the first tally, consisting of half a dozen precincts' votes. The din diminishes as he hands the tally to a clerk, who writes the initial count on the blackboard. Cheers and groans greet each listing.

The city hall reporter, who is handling local election coverage for his afternoon newspaper, quickly assesses the implications. With only 1 percent of the vote in, Mayor Greene holds a strong lead over his challenger, Robert Evans. However, the votes tabulated came from precincts that were expected to be heavily in favor of the incumbent mayor. Experts had confided that the mayor would need 65 percent of the vote in those precincts to win the election, since his opponent was expected to carry other areas. The early tally indicated that the mayor would win only 60 to 65 percent of the vote there.

The reporter inches over to a respected political expert, a former city councilman, who had earlier confirmed that the mayor had to carry these early precincts by a wide margin.

"It appears that the mayor may be in for a horserace," the reporter says.

"Maybe. He's not doing quite as well as he should be, but the vote is much heavier than expected on the East Side, so the big turnout could offset the smaller than necessary margin," the politician muses. "This one is going to be very hard to project for a while. If the turnout is as heavy as I've been told on the West Side, Evans' turf, then we could have a new mayor."

Election night is the climax of intensive reporting efforts for weeks leading up to that moment. Within a few hours, the politicians and their supporters will either be celebrating or mourning. Yet, after a work day that began at 6:30 A.M. when the first polls opened, the reporter's task will continue through most of the night, and on until the noon deadline the next day.

To examine the exhaustive chore of covering a local election campaign, let's first look at the political elements involved, and then scrutinize the steps of coverage. The campaign actually began two months before the election, on the final date of formal application for a place on the ballot.

As the 6 P.M. deadline for such applications approached, reporters at the board of elections offices frantically interviewed the candidates who arrived to file their applications. Most candidates were public figures who were old acquaintances of the journalists. Except for the acquisition of a few standard quotations to enliven stories, the interviews are superficial, since reporters know their qualifications or can obtain them from clippings. New faces on the political scene, however, require immediate definition: Who are you? What do you do? Why are you running? What are your qualifications? What are your views on major issues? From where do you expect to receive support?

As the deadline for filing passes, the reporter glances at the lineup:

Candidates for Mayor:

1. Incumbent Mayor Stanley Greene, fifty-two, an attorney who is seeking reelection after serving a four-year term. A colorful and controversial man, the mayor is a liberal Democrat, with a strong party organization behind him. His major support is in minority neighborhoods on the East Side, and in the upper-middle-class areas in the northern part of the city, which traditionally vote for moderate or liberal candidates. Although he enjoyed strong support from the heavily blue-collar West Side in his initial campaign, support for him has soured so much that even strong labor-union backing may not be enough to carry those areas.

2. Robert Evans, forty-one, owner of Evans Machine Shop on the West Side. A conservative Independent, Evans narrowly lost a bid for city council two years earlier. He has loudly and continuously attacked city hall for "wasteful, arrogant spending" and for "callously ignoring the wishes of the people." Evans finds strong support from

conservative organizations, small businessmen, and from disgruntled blue-collar workers.

3. Amos Brookes, thirty-seven, a radio talk-show moderator. Brookes is a gadfly who persists in waspish attacks on public figures of every political shading. His ideology is unclear, since he is maddeningly inconsistent, and his motive for running is suspect: He may be "ego-tripping" or simply trying to win publicity for his talk show.

Candidates for City Council (two seats will be filled at large):

1. Andrew Anderson, thirty-five, a labor-union president who attained a broad constituency as president of the board of education. Anderson is considered one of the up-and-coming young politicians who must be rated a strong favorite for one of the vacant seats.

2. Oscar Levi, sixty-one, a department-store owner, has been one of the most influential businessmen in the city for many years. A fiscal conservative, Levi has nevertheless supported even the most expensive programs to aid the city's poor. As chairman of the human rights commission, he quietly succeeded in attaining legislation to end many discriminatory practices and to ease racial tension during the tense years of the late 1960s. Generally identified with liberal politics, Levi has both strong support and strong opposition.

3. Theodore Brown, forty-five, a black attorney who is seeking reelection to city council. Brown, another liberal, is considered one of the city's most astute politicians, drawing support from the same groups as the mayor. Yet ill health may hamper his efforts, as he must convince voters that he has regained his strength after a serious heart attack three months ago.

4. Paul Miller, fifty-eight, a former police captain who has outspokenly criticized the city for "tolerating crime and refusing to support policemen." As a courageous and willful policeman, Miller led a special task force to purge police ranks of corrupt officers, arresting some of his closest friends in the process. He could have very strong support from conservatives.

5. Edwin Daley, thirty, a radio disc jockey. As one political wit observed, "Daley is ego-tripping. He doesn't have a chance, unless the voting age is lowered to thirteen."

6. Mark Manahan, sixty-two, a real estate developer, who had served sixteen years in the State Senate—ending ten years ago. "Mark's politics tend to be just to the right right of Attila the Hun," another politician observed. "He doesn't have a chance and he knows it. Yet he wants to enjoy a last campaign."

7. Larry Walters, fifty-seven, a bank executive and chairman of the county Republican Party. A highly respected, conservative businessman, Walters is seeking elected office for the first time, although he has long been a powerful, behind-the-scenes political influence. Although Republicans are generally weak in the city, Walters has such

a long and distinguished public service record that he may be a strong candidate.

With the noon deadline still eighteen hours away, the reporter has ample time to piece together an interpretative story for his first major effort of the campaign. By telephone and personal visit, he tracks down each candidate through the evening and obtains their views on major issues:

1. A proposed 50 percent increase in city income taxes.
2. Proposed construction of a $20 million civic center complex.
3. Scatteration of public housing construction, which would disperse pockets of impoverished citizens into all neighborhoods of the city.
4. The city's recent acquisition of a formerly privately owned bus company.
5. Establishment of neighborhood free health clinics, financed by public funds.

After obtaining the views of each candidate on these major issues, the reporter then contacts several politician experts for a preliminary assessment of the races.

The results: a page-one story that reveals the candidacies and summarized the political implications of the race, plus a sidebar offering "thumbnail sketches" of the credentials of each candidate and his issue positions. A second sidebar offers a political analysis based on interviews with local experts. Thus, from the outset, voters are given a comprehensive rendition of choices available to them and as much information as could be gathered for their intial step in selecting a candidate to support.

With the campaign officially underway, the reporter's coverage can be divided into four distinct stages:

1. *Early Campaign.* The major thrust of coverage is to discern and report the formation of blocks of support for each candidate and for and against major issues on the ballot. The reporter must also press for clearly defined positions on each issue by each candidate and for a clearer focus on the nature of the candidate.

2. *Late Campaign.* With the battle lines solidly formed, the emphasis is on public reception to each candidate and the candidate's reaction to public mood. This stage also lends itself to election handicapping, particularly in the last week, as political experts offer predictions on the possible outcome and on the factors that may affect that outcome.

3. *The Election.* Comprehensive coverage of the results, the reasons for the results, and the political significance of the outcome must be provided.

4. *Post Election.* Coverage of any suspected irregularities at the polling booths, recount demands, and financial accounting by each candidate should receive close scrutiny.

EARLY CAMPAIGN

Perhaps the most revealing indication of the nature of a given candidate at this stage is the company he keeps—and doesn't keep. By determining just who a candidate's supporters are (especially financial backers), the reporter and, in turn, the readers, can gain great insight as to what can be expected from the politician.

The task of sorting out supporters may be difficult, since key figures frequently prefer to remain in the background—especially major financial supporters.

However, special interest groups often announce their support with a fanfare and flourish. Perhaps city labor leaders agree to endorse candidates who have been sympathetic to labor interests. A major press conference would likely be called, with labor leaders standing arm in arm with the endorsed candidates.

Some more noteworthy support may lie behind the scenes. If a wealthy backer donates several thousand dollars to a candidate's campaign fund, neither the backer nor the candidate may be anxious to see a public disclosure. The candidate may fear that the public could rightly or wrongly conclude that he had been "bought" by the supporter. The supporter may fear that such heavy-handed involvement in politics could be detrimental to his reputation. Still another common form of behind-the-scenes support is that of a political "kingmaker," such as a political machine boss. While the kingmaker may publicly acknowledge his support of the candidate, he may not be as anxious to reveal the extent of his support and his power over the candidate. The reporter's task is to define that support for the readers.

Issues that are placed on the ballot for public referendum should receive similar treatment. For example, a tax increase issue would, of course, receive a full public endorsement from city hall, and perhaps political parties, labor, and even business interests. It may be loudly opposed by an ad hoc "taxpayer's lobby," anti-city hall politicians, and neighborhood councils. The nature of the support and the opposition may be far more significant than that indicated in public announcements.

For example, the city hall endorsement may go much further than a simple statement urging voters to approve the issue. The city hall establishment may flex its considerable resources to push the measure by physically coordinating the campaign, bargaining with opposition groups, and making dramatic maneuvers to herd voters into the "yes" column. The announcement of massive service cutbacks a week before the election may put voters in a sympathetic frame of mind. On any political issue, the behind-the-scenes battles are often far more interesting and enlightening to voters than mere public statements.

The second prime area of campaign coverage at the early stage is to somehow coax candidates into taking stands on issues. Quite naturally, some politicians are reluctant to take a stand on an issue until they can discern which stance is most acceptable to voters. In a related task, the reporter should also try to determine each candidate's depth of knowledge and ability to handle a given issue.

Perhaps the best means of eliciting clear stands on issues, and of gauging a candidate's knowledge and ability, is by conducting in-depth interviews. Before engaging in such an interview, the reporter must carefully and completely research each issue so that he can probe the candidate's position.

Let's say that the disc jockey, Edwin Daley, participates in such an interview. Daley's depth of knowledge about city problems and issues is already suspect, since he has either fuzzed over or fumbled initial questions. Sensing wide dissatisfaction with city hall, Daley has taken a strong but murkey "anti-city Hall" stand on each issue. After overcoming his initial nervousness in the interview, Daley becomes enraptured with his own tirade against "those wasteful, experimental problems designed to help special interest groups at the expense of the electorate at large. I intend to return to the basics, to force the bureaucracy to cut out the excesses and offer top-quality basic services that benefit all citizens."

Heartened by the increasingly cocky demeanor of the candidate, which seemingly subdues both prudence and caution, the reporter tosses out a key question in the manner of a fisherman presenting a dry fly to a trout:

"Can you give a couple of specific examples of excesses that you intend to curb?" the reporter asks in a matter-of-fact tone.

After a long moment of silence, during which Daley desperately squirms and searches for an example, he says, "Well, I'd certainly cut out the free neighborhood health clinics and shut down the food stamp and welfare programs."

With considerable restraint, the reporter subdues his glee behind a mask of puzzlement as he sets the hook: "But how are you going to shut down food stamp and welfare programs? They're both federal programs that are administered through the county. The city government has nothing to do with them."

While such an example is extreme (although based on a factual incident), the reporter is obliged to offer each candidate the privilege of demonstrating profound ignorance or ability to his readers. It should be emphasized that even in this example, the reporter didn't "get" the candidate. The candidate did himself in. By reporting the gaffe accurately, in a straightforward manner, the reporter allowed readers to determine Daley's qualifications.

Issues, of course, aren't the only factors that voters will consider as they cast their ballots. In fact, many voters may be more interested in the personal qualities of the candidate than in his stands and suggested solutions for all of society's ills. At some point in the campaign, the reporter may write a series of personal profile features to help readers discern a candidate's personal virtues and weaknesses. These feature stories can often be researched simultanously with the issues during in-depth interviews, and in the process of talking with sources, acquaintances, and even enemies in an attempt to focus on issues and sources of support.

LATE CAMPAIGN

The pace of coverage quickens as the election approaches. After establishing the nature of the candidacies involved, the alignment of support, and the positions of each candidate on an array of issues, the next major step is to observe and report the adjustments that each candidate makes in his struggle for votes. Frequently, a candidate's strength is accurately reflected by the degree of adjusting he makes during the latter part of a campaign. A candidate who is confident of election rarely makes major shifts, while an opponent who is "running scared" may desperately alter his stands and resort to a more strident tone of campaigning.

If a reporter notices a subtle but substantial shift on an issue, he should immediately make note of it. In the mayoral race, the incumbent mayor may sense that his opponent is rapidly gaining ground by appealing to moderate voters who are disturbed by the mayor's insistence on a tax increase. While the mayor can hardly abandon the measure that he helped introduce in the first place, he can shift slightly to blunt the edge of criticism. Perhaps he may say something along these lines:

"While I am convinced that the tax increase must be approved for the good of the city, I suggest that safeguards must be established to ensure that the additional revenues are spent wisely and effectively. If the tax increase is approved, I will form a blue-ribbon committee consisting of leaders from every segment of the community to study city hall efficiency and responsiveness, and to recommend to council ways to ensure that each dollar of public funds is well spent."

Although such a statement would seem hardly controversial, the mayor's shift from a previous campaign statement should be noted in the story:

"You know who I am, what I stand for, and what I intend to do if I'm reelected. My opponents have proposed to form special committees to advise council on urban redevelopment, city services, and a dozen other functions. I suggest that government by committee is a government of hesitancy, of indecision, and of weakness. You are voting for a decision-maker, not for the secretary-treasurer of your school's PTA."

The mayor's sudden willingness to accept committee guidance, when offered in the context of previous statements, may raise more doubts than votes.

Another form of issue shifting occurs when a candidate blithely tells any body of voters exactly what it wants to hear, even when it contradicts promises and remarks made to other groups. To put it indelicately, some candidates talk out of both sides of their mouths.

Perhaps candidate Anderson resorts to this technique in an effort to appease conflicting segments of his support. Speaking before a crowd in the city's poorest neighborhood, Anderson strongly endorses free neighborhood clinics. On the next evening, at a rally in a conservative West Side neighborhood, the candidate may promise to conduct an intensive investigation to determine the value of "that highly questionable program."

Still another adjustment is that of disassociating oneself from damaging ties or stigmas. In the early part of the campaign, the mayor and Anderson were closely and publicly associated together, endorsing each other and appearing at rallies together. As the mayor's strength wanes, the council candidate may suddenly find that he is committed to be elsewhere—anywhere else—if the mayor invites him to share a podium somewhere.

In the latter stages of the campaign, the reporter's task is made somewhat easier by the candidates themselves. They, like the reporter, have considerable interest in learning all that they can about each other, and in perceiving—and exposing—unscrupulous practices or gaffes by opponents. When a "foul" by an opponent comes to his attention, a candidate may publicly and loudly disclose the transgression, or he may secretly pass the tip to a reporter. In the latter case, the reporter should be prudent enough to carefully verify such a tip, for obvious reasons.

One of the best sources of campaign stories is the neighborhood "meet-the-candidates" event, which offers local citizens a chance to meet and query all vote-seekers. Such an event is essentially a command performance: A candidate who declines the invitation may very well write off that particular neighborhood. If local citizens aren't sufficiently slighted by the absence, they will be incensed by the rhetoric unleashed against him by opponents who may relish the chance for an uncontested slap. Because of the vast potential of such a meeting, let's take a detailed look at the coverage.

The West Side Citizen's Council is hosting a "Meet-the-Candidates" night. All ten candidates attend, with varying degrees of enthusiasm. Liberal candidates exhibit a gallows-style resignation, hoping only to salvage a respectable minority of votes. Conservative candidates happily anticipate a friendly audience.

Before the program begins, the reporter assesses the audience and notes that Anderson has infiltrated the crowd with campaign workers. An outspoken supporter from a distant neighborhood is sitting in the front row.

In chatting with the chairwoman of the hosting organization, the reporter learns that the moderator is a staunch supporter of mayoral candidate Evans. She also confides that "a fair number of strangers" are present, and that she noticed several such aliens chatting with Walters when they first arrived.

After making note of such intriguing tidbits, the reporter sketches the seating arrangement at the candidates' table, writes each candidate's name to indicate seating position, then numbers them from left to right. When accusations are hotly flying around the room, the reporter can save valuable time by keying numbers to statements, rather than having to scribble names or initials. Also, physical proximity between opponents can sometimes be significant.

As the program begins, the reporter notes that the moderator slips in sly partisan digs at Evans' opponents, then allows the incumbent mayor to speak first. Each candidate is given five minutes to offer his views. Brookes, who is Evans' other opponent, is allowed to speak after the mayor. Naturally, Brookes uses the opportunity to attack the mayor and to rebut the mayor's statement. The third candidate to speak is Evans, who uses the opportunity to rebut the statements of both opponents.

After each candidate has spoken, the moderator opens the floor for questions from the audience. Anderson's supporter ("plant") quickly gains recognition to ask the first question. In mock anger, the plant shouts abrasively:

"I came all the way from across town to track you down, Anderson. I hear that you said you'd investigate the free health clinics, the best thing that ever happened to my neighborhood. Now, I've heard of political snakes before, but you've got to be the worst. You tell me straight to my face if it's true."

The "hostile" outsider's abusive attack quickly wins sympathy for the candidate. Besides, among West Side people, the free clinics are highly unpopular and suspect. Some of the local citizens begin to shout angrily at the brazen intruder, until Anderson benevolently holds his hands up to request silence.

"First, let me say that I am offended by both your tone and your inappropriate choice of words. These people came to participate in a dignified and intelligent discussion of issues; they aren't interested in mud-throwing.

"To answer your question, I am clearly on record as favoring an intensive investigation into the free clinics program. Like most citizens in this city, I suspect that the program may be mismanaged, wasteful, and inefficient. Although I am not suggesting that the clinics should be closed, or that they have not been beneficial to many needy citizens, I firmly believe that any city function that involves $500,000 a year in expenditures should be carefully managed and brought to public accounting. I intend to do just that."

As the applause fills the room, the reporter appreciates the smooth ploy that the candidate used. When the trick is exposed in the next day's newspaper, the citizens may be less than amused to discover the deception.

Other questions are presented, answered, rebutted, and refuted among the candidates. The reporter notes that Walters' remarks are always greeted with suspiciously enthusiastic applause from the group of strangers present.

Finally, one citizen rises to ask Manahan about his supportive stand on the income tax-increase issue. Although generally liked and respected on the West Side, Manahan has lost support by adamantly backing the tax measure. Even so, the "old pol" has shown much stronger appeal than the initial analysis of his chances indicated. Moreover, his stands are far more moderate than political observers had anticipated.

Scowling angrily, Manahan eyes his questioner contemptuously, then says, "I've been sitting here for an hour, listening to you folks asking for more of everything. You want more policemen, more fire stations out here, better parks and streets, and even better dog catchers.

"All right, I'll give you all of that. I'll make this city a hell of a good place to live, to raise your children. But let me say something flat out. I don't think you are so damned stupid that you expect to get something for nothing. Of course I'm for the tax increase, because if I'm elected I'm going to deliver those things you ask for. Now look at that collection of mealymouthed polticians sitting around me. Them that's for the tax increase are trying to keep their mouths shut so you won't get mad at them. Them that's against it are promising you everything under the sun, for nothing. I know you aren't that stupid, so just sit down, shut up, and think about it."

Mark Manahan sits down amid loud applause. The reporter is aware that few minds were changed about the tax issue, but that many new Manahan supporters were won by such candor.

After the meeting, the reporter quickly samples reactions from citizens. As expected, Manahan has reaped a bonanza of support, at the expense of anti-tax candidates, even though few had changed their minds about the tax. Next, the reporter talks with Walters' imported supporters to obtain a sheepish verification that they had followed their candidate across town, and with the moderator who gladly offers his views supporting Evans.

With more caution, the reporter then stalks Anderson's "plant," following him to his car, which is parked next to his candidate's car. He is amused to note that Anderson and his "tormentor" are engaged in a seemingly friendly conversation. The amusement turns to satisfaction when he spots an "Anderson for Councilman" bumper sticker on the plant's car. Confronting the conspirators, he obtains a heated denial from both the candidate and the plant, who contends that after initially supporting Anderson, he became disenchanted. Miraculously, a reconciliation had just been reached because of the candidate's courageous answer.

The reporter will, of course, offer readers a straightforward account of the meeting, the apparent ploys and denials, and the political implications of the lively session.

As the campaign enters its last week, the reporter can focus his attention on providing readers with a solid wrap-up of information for their critical decision-making in the voting booths. The acquisition of information at this "home-stretch" juncture is relatively easy, since most of the material about the candidates, the issues, and the conduct of the campaign has been gathered previously. The problem, instead, is to assemble and present the information in a thorough but concise and readable form.

Let's say that it's a week before the Tuesday election, and the city editor informs the reporter that a full page has been opened for pre-election summaries in the Sunday issue. After groaning at the prospect of such a task, the reporter soon discovers that his notebooks already contain enough material for a half a dozen pages. After much thought, he suggests these elements to the city editor and news editor:

1. A table summary listing candidates and their positions on each issue.

2. A straight summary story of major issues, with arguments from both supporters and critics briefly rendered.

3. An in-depth look at the election, including an analysis of the support block alignment, financing/spending by candidates, the political intrigue that has occurred behind the scenes, and campaign oddities and trends.

4. An election forecast, including an analysis of factors that are expected to influence the outcome, and predictions by respected political observers.

While the first three items are perhaps obvious enough, the election forecast article may seem questionable. After all, with the election only two days away, why is it necessary to speculate on the outcome? Also, isn't there a danger that such predictions can be self-fulfilling by creating a bandwagon effect for likely winners?

The forecast story offers not only an interesting and entertaining bit of reading matter for subscribers, but it also gives them valuable insight into the murky world of politics. Just as football fans anxiously consume prediction stories before the Super Bowl spectacle, many citizens have an appetite for political projections. Since major national pollsters would hardly spend the effort to sample and predict the outcome of a local election, this appetite can be sated by knowledgeable local observers.

In any city, at least a handful of political experts should be available for consultation. Let's start with the unofficial campaign co-ordinator for the city income tax increase. A career city employee who is listed in organizational charts as a senior accountant, the official is actually city hall's best political analyst. His record in past election predictions is almost uncanny. In the last election, he correctly predicted winners in the order that they finished, and forecast the vote on a key referendum. In the latter situation, he predicted that the referendum would be defeated, drawing only 41 percent of voter support. The issue failed, drawing only 40.5 percent of the vote.

In interviewing the amazing forecaster, the reporter seeks these items:

1. His forecasts for the races and for the income tax referendum.
2. His analysis of trends.
3. Factors that will determine the outcome.

"I think we're in for a few surprises in the races. The mayor should win by a whisker if the turnout is heavy. If we have bad weather, Evans will win because his support is firmer and because his supporters are more likely to vote regardless of the weather. People on the West Side turn out in blizzards. That's where Evans' strength is. The other surprise is that Manahan is going to slip in. A lot of his supporters are going to vote against the tax increase, but for the man. He's a real pro.

"Right now, I'd have to say the mayor's race is too close to call. Anderson and Manahan should win the council seats, with Walters finishing a very close third. Anderson has lost ground lately, but he has a strong and broad base.

"As for the tax, that's another toss-up. With a very good turnout, I think it will squeeze by, with, say, 50.1 percent of the vote. With a moderate turnout, it will go down with only 49.8 percent. A low turnout would certainly kill the issue, as it would draw only 47 percent. The tax issue should very closely parallel the mayor's race. I expect 50 to 60 percent of the registered voters to vote."

In explaining factors on which the projections are based, the analyst listed several key items:

1. Labor unions can no longer deliver blocks of obedient voters. "Unless there's a clear-cut union issue at stake, union members here are only slightly influenced by their leadership."

2. An uncertain turnout in minority neighborhoods. "Until this generation, they have been excluded from voting. It takes time to establish a habit of going to the polls, of participating in the election process. Unless there's an issue that is vital to the minority community, it's hard to get a turnout."

3. The unpredictable senior citizens. "The aged tend to be extremely well informed. They have time to stay abreast of politics and they are very sensitive to trends that affect them. On the tax issue, older voters may support the measure, since they fear that the government might raise property taxes if the income tax fails. They can't afford higher property taxes. The problem is that bad weather can keep them away from the polls."

4. Effectiveness of organziations involved. "The Louis machine in the minority area is mobilized to turn out the vote for the tax issue and for the mayor. It's a very good organization, so it may be able to deliver an unexpectedly heavy turnout. However, I'm afraid that citizens' groups on the West Side may more than match us in organizing opposition."

5. The weather. "In any close election, the weather is a critical factor. In any race or issue, one side normally has hardier supporters than the other. In this race, the mayor and the tax issue essentially hinge on the weather."

Pulling out a thick folder of calculations, the analyst reveals a precinct by precinct projection on the two close races. "The first numbers are my projections in each precinct for each candidate and for the tax issue. The parenthetical numbers are my projections for the percentage of votes that the mayor and the tax must win in each precinct to win the election."

Finally, the analyst selected three "swing" precincts, where the election would probably be determined. "When the early returns come in, you can pretty well see the outcome as soon as these precincts report."

After leaving the city hall analyst, the reporter contacted a half dozen other respected observers, who generally confirmed the projections. Gaining additional insight from other sources, the reporter was prepared to write his forecast story, using the city hall analyst's figures as the story's backbone.

It should be noted that the projections would prove very valuable *after* the election, when the reporter undertook the task of explaining the "why" of the outcome.

ELECTION COVERAGE

As polls open on election morning, the reporter is already at work on his election day story for the noon deadline. Since polls don't close until that evening, returns cannot be obtained. The morning competition will break the news of election results because of its deadline cycle.

However, the reporter is obliged to offer his eager readers some election-day fodder, so he conducts a "straw poll" at the three key precincts listed by his source, the city hall political analyst. The reporter is acutely aware that his sampling is unscientific and highly unreliable. He should, in fact, carefully emphasize the flaws to his readers. Yet, the sampling does offer a glimpse at the rationale of voters who are interviewed, and it can substantiate the turnout trend at the key precincts.

Before the interviews begin, the reporter notes the mild and sunny weather, which should provide a slight edge to the mayor and the tax measure.

By law, the newsman cannot approach voters within a hundred feet of the polling facility, so he stands at the perimeter, next to campaign workers who offer sample ballots to voters—ballots conveniently marked to show them how to vote for the favored candidates.

As voters leave, the reporter introduces himself and asks how they voted and why. Many are hesitant to offer such personal information, some are flattered by the attention, and others simply tell the reporter to "mind your own business."

In one key precinct, deep in the heart of Evans' stronghold, the reporter is amazed to discover that most of the people he approaches claim that they cast their vote for Mayor Greene. His momentary puzzlement is finally lifted when he deduces the reasons: His newspaper had endorsed Greene. Many people were kindly lying so that the reporter's feelings would be spared or because they were afraid that the reporter would argue with them. When the returns from that precinct were later counted, the reporter was amused to note that although 55 percent of those interviewed said they voted for Greene, Evans carried the precinct by 68 percent of the vote.

After filing the story that contained straw poll results, comments from voters, and the indications of a large turnout, the reporter then checked with his best political sources to determine the outlook from the early trends.

"It's looking good for the mayor and the tax," the city hall analyst said. "Turnout on the East Side is heavy. However, I'm a little concerned that the West Side may be having a record turnout. If that develops, then everything may go down the drain."

From noon until 6 P.M., the reporter uses the lull before returns start trickling in to write segments of the story for the next day. He writes brief background sketches of the candidates. When results are known, he can select the winners and tag on a quote or two from them about their victory, their intentions, and such.

At 6 P.M., he arrives at the board of elections to join the throng awaiting the returns. Each time precinct results are posted, he jots down the vote breakdown, then glances at a sheet listing projections made by the analyst. Evans is doing slightly better than expected so far, and the tax vote is right on the forecast for early precincts.

At 7:15 P.M., the first key precinct vote is compiled, showing Mayor Greene breaking ahead of his minimum goal by several percentage points. The tax measure, surprisingly, falls below the "must vote" projection. The reporter approaches the city hall analyst with a puzzled expression.

"Don't ask," the analyst says. "The mayor just got reelected, but he won't have any money to run the city with."

"But why is the mayor running ahead of the tax?" the reporter asks.

"The senior citizen turnout was dwarfed by the record turnout. I never dreamed that we would hit a 75 percent turnout. It's unreal; 10 percent better than the record vote in a non-presidential election year. My calculations were based on a 65 percent maximum vote. Although both the mayor and the tax generally benefit from a heavy turnout, the tax issue has a point of diminishing returns. It is past that point," the analyst explained.

After interviewing the mayor on the assumption that he had won —the mayor was rejoicing, since he also had the analyst's projections —the reporter returned to the blackboard to jot down newly counted returns.

By 10 P.M., 90 percent of the vote was counted. The mayor, Anderson, and Manahan had won. The tax lost after receiving only 48.5 percent of the vote.

With interviews completed and press copies of all precinct returns in hand, the reporter returns to the newsroom for a night-long chore of writing and analyzing. A precinct by precinct tabulation is quickly compiled and analyzed. An interpretative story is written to explain the significance of the election outcome, and to answer the lingering question of "why?"

Early the next morning, after only two hours of sleep, the reporter staggers to city hall to talk with officials about the effect of the voters' rejection of the tax increase. The mayor, city manager, city council members, budget director, chamber of commerce president, and other tax proponents offered gloomy outlooks that were invariably coupled with a "but we'll manage somehow" that was missing during the campaign. Tax opponents happily predicted "a bright new day of government responsive to voters" as a result of the taxpayers' revolt. Lastly, the losers were contacted for comments on their future political plans, their reaction to defeat, and so on.

Since the election was decisive enough to make a recount unnecessary, the reporter's election coverage ended with the noon deadline. But the post-election coverage still lingered.

POST ELECTION

The final step in campaign coverage usually occurs within a week or so after the election, when financial reports must be submitted by each candidate. Although laws governing such reports vary from location to location, most specify that money received, expenditures, and the names of contributors who donated in excess of a minimum amount must be listed. The public is entitled to know about the financial income and outlay from each candidate.

Often, strange quirks of politics are uncovered in such accounting. Perhaps a losing candidate spent thousands of dollars, while a winner spent less than a hundred dollars. Names of major contributors are also interesting. Perhaps Manahan had received a thousand-dollar donation from the Democratic Party, while Anderson, supposedly a party favorite, only received five hundred dollars. Miller, the former police captain, may have received five hundred dollars from the Fraternal Order of Police. If the income/outlay figures are far apart, then the reporter may well ask the candidate about the disposition of the debts or surplus.

SUMMARY

Coverage of a local political campaign demands both astuteness and hard work on the reporter's part, but it is among the most fascinating of all assignments. By the time that the last post-election story is filed, the reporter will have interviewed scores of leading political figures, witnessed the rambunctious and often humorous events that spice any political campaign, and observed the interworkings of the American political system from an intimate vantage point. In the process, he will have established dozens of new informational source relationships that will, in time, enhance his ability to obtain news. In short, the rewards justify the rigors.

EXERCISES

1. Outline the steps in coverage of a local political campaign.

2. A losing candidate demands a recount. He lost by less than a thousand votes, and he contends that his supporters were turned away from the polls in eleven different polling facilities. You have two hours before deadline. Who would you contact? What information would you seek?

3. The mayor, who won reelection by a solid margin, has forgotten to file his financial report to the board of elections. Who would you contact? Why?

4. At a candidates' night rally, you note that a surprising number of Italian-Americans are present at the event, which is being held in an Irish-American neighborhood. What should you be alert for? Why?

14 | On-the-Scene Coverage

The newsroom din had long since subsided when, four hours after final deadline, the radio monitor picked up a fire captain's terse request for "all available equipment."

A major fire had erupted at the Juvenile Detention Center, and police were rushing to evacuate the young inmates. The facility is located six blocks from the newspaper offices, yet three panting reporters reached the scene on foot before firemen could lay down hoses. It was a three-alarm fire because of the threat to the dozens of young people inside the building.

The fire was in an underground electrical vault beneath the street, about thirty feet from the building. Great flames rose from the manhole and flickered across the building's brick front. Clouds of soot-black smoke billowed high into the air, filling the downtown area with the nose-crinkling odor of burning electrical insulation.

The reporters watched as firemen bathed the threatened building with a spray of water. As soon as electrical power was safely shut off, firemen approached as closely as they dared, then sprayed foam into the hole to smother the blaze. Meanwhile, police evacuated the youths through the rear exit.

"Chief, what's the situation?" the police reporter asked the fire chief, as soon as the official paused a moment after issuing a stream of commands.

"It's an electrical fire in a vault operated by the telephone company," the chief said. "I think we have contained it; I believe that the building will be saved. As you can see, though, we still have some work to do."

The chief's words were dramatically punctuated by a new gush of flames that forced firemen to scramble back. As the burning, super-heated gases rushed through the confined outlet of the manhole—

which had been enlarged considerably by the explosion—it emitted an eerie roaring whistle.

Except for the necessary observations of the fire and the efforts to contain it, the information-gathering process was relatively easy, with story essentials assembled quickly. The fire had erupted at 3:57 P.M., as the explosion lifted the manhole cover high into the air. It landed three hundred feet away, barely missing a pedestrian on the sidewalk. A guard at the detention center called the fire department at 3:58 P.M., and the first fire units arrived at 4:01 P.M. No one was seriously injured, although one fireman suffered from slight heat exhaustion. The 123 center inmates were evacuated by 4:12 P.M. The vault, which contained thousands of dollars worth of electrical equipment, was an access point for repairmen and technicians at the intersection of major underground cables.

One reporter sought additional details from the guard who had witnessed the explosion, as another interviewed a telephone company executive. As the police reporter observed firemen finally subduing the blaze, he was surprised to note that several firemen suddenly began loading equipment back on engines and trucks, though the fire was still shooting out of the vault.

"Aren't you leaving a little early," the reporter asked a fireman.

"We have another fire, a big one, over on the West Side," the fireman explained as he climbed onto engine, which had already started to creep forward. "Go to the corner and look west."

The reporter followed the suggestion and dashed to the corner. A massive cloud of black smoke hovered about four miles away. Running back to the remaining fire equipment, he caught the chief just as he was entering his car to go to the second blaze.

"We have a four-alarm fire at Acme Mattress Company on Evans Lane," the chief shouted as his driver pressed the accelerator.

Leaving this hectic, factually based episode for a moment, let's briefly focus on the challenge of on-the-scene reporting. When a disaster or dramatic event occurs within a city, it demands vivid and top-quality coverage, often under the most confusing and adverse circumstances imaginable.

A reporter doesn't actually have to be on the scene to provide the very basic coverage. By next day's noon deadline, detailed reports on both fires will amply answer all the whos, whats, and wheres that are required for a straight hard-news story. Whether the event is a fire, riot, homicide, or natural disaster, officials involved in coping with it will offer full documentation. Even under intense deadline pressure, much of the basic information can be gathered by telephone. If the fires had occurred at 11:30 A.M.—half an hour before deadline, the reporter may have been forced to assemble the facts from telephone calls to fire department officials, police, factory officials, and Juvenile Detention Center authorities.

Yet, even with this in mind, no self-respecting reporter would miss the opportunity to rush to the scene, often at the risk of bullets, tear gas, smoke-inhalation, falling walls, or frostbite. On-the-scene, eye-witness reporting can escalate a good news story into the lead story. Here's why:

Official reports allow little insight to the human tragedy, heroism, and folly that often occurs at such events. That human element is often far more interesting than the specifics of the event itself. For example, a story that simply states that three people died in a fire turns human lives into statistical data. A vivid account of vain efforts to save them, eyewitness interviews, and a description of the chaotic scene of men battling the awesome, destructive force of a major fire combine to translate the event into human terms that readers can digest.

Now, let's return to the reporters' unenviable task of choosing which major fire to cover—and of somehow performing that coverage.

Although the fire in front of the Juvenile Detention Center still roared out of control, the reporters quickly decided that the second fire deserved their attention. The danger to human life had subsided, although the center was still endangered by the intense heat. Ample material had already been gathered for an on-the-scene account— although that scene could change radically if the center actually caught fire. The deciding factor, however, was the action of the chief: The second fire was apparently so serious that he chose to rush to that scene, taking much equipment with him, even though the first fire was still raging.

Rushing back to the newspaper office, the reporters acquired a news car and hurried to the second fire. As they approached, they saw that flames engulfed the entire one-story building that occupied half a city block. Firemen hosed down nearby buildings, as flames and embers threatened the structures. Smoke and heat had driven onlookers back half a block from the fire, and police were firmly pushing them back even further.

Parking the car as close to the scene as possible, the reporters quickly pushed through the crowd, only to be confronted by a grim policeman.

"I'm sorry, gentlemen, but you're going the wrong way," he said. "Would you please step back?"

Recognizing the officer, the police reporter stepped forward.

"Joe, we have to cover this thing, and we have fire passes," he said.

"Oh, it's you," the officer said. "Yeah, you can go through, but I wouldn't advise it. The firemen are taking a real beating on this one. They carted off three of them a few minutes ago when the heat and smoke got to them. I don't know how much you get paid, but it's not enough to get killed for. Go ahead, but use your head and don't get underfoot."

Hesitating long enough to learn that the firemen weren't seriously injured and to thank the officer for his concern, the reporters trotted to the fire. They saw a photographer standing near the chief, busily snapping shots through a telephoto lens, as the chief conferred with his captains.

"What do we have, Lou?" the police reporter asked the photographer.

"It's the worst I've seen in ten years," the veteran photographer replied. "There are three guys missing, and they may be trapped inside. They stayed behind to try to fight the fire as other employees evacuated. One wall collapsed a few minutes ago, and two firemen barely got out of the way in time. I have a great shot of it."

The other two reporters fanned out to seek witnesses and plant officials, while the police reporter concentrated on the firefighters' battle. As the chief's conference with his captains ended, he stepped forward to interview him.

"Chief, can you give me a quick rundown?" he asked.

"You can see for yourself that the building is a total loss," the chief said. "The plant foreman and two subforemen are still in there. I don't think there's even the slightest hope for them. We tried to go in after them, but our guys were beaten back in a hurry. The plant manufactures highly combustible foam rubber products, like cushions and mattresses for camping and outdoor uses. The fire is unbelievably intense, steel girders inside have been twisted by it."

"How did it get out of control like this?" the reporter asked. "With all the workers inside, it would seem that someone would have noticed it and reported it in time for you to put it out before it got out of control."

"There was a delay in reporting," the chief said angrily. "The fire was discovered at 3:55, and no one called until 4:05. Our first units reached here at 4:08, and flames were already breaking through the roof.

"If we had been called right away, it would have been a minor fire. When you wait ten minutes, the heat produces gases that build up. As the heat continues to rise, it reaches the flash point, producing an inferno. Now, we have our hands full, with every piece of equipment I can summon. Half the city is essentially unprotected right now."

The reporter pressed for more detail. "How did the first start?"

"Witnesses say that someone flipped a cigarette butt onto a pile of foam rubber scrap. Once the rubber ignited, the fire spread very rapidly. Someone hit the fire alarm, and everyone scrambled out, except for the three who tried to fight it with extinguishers. In the confusion, no one thought to call us."

"Do you see any possible fire code violations?" the reporter asked.

"Dozens," the chief said bitterly. "The biggest one is that they didn't have a sprinkling system, which is required for any manufacturing plant that handles combustibles. We inspected them and cited them three months ago. We were, in fact, ready to file papers with the city attorney to shut them down until the violations were corrected. We couldn't move fast enough because the company had promised to comply immediately. Last week, we found that they hadn't done a thing. It takes a couple of weeks to get a court order to close them."

As the reporter was about to ask another question, the chief suddenly yelled to a captain, "Move those trucks back, we're about to lose them."

Two aerial ladder trucks were parked perilously close to the buildings so that firemen standing on the elevated platforms could effectively hose the roof. The wall facing the trucks had erupted in flame.

Leaving the chief to his task, the reporter cautiously circled the building, copiously jotting down descriptions and quotes from firemen who saw the fire from many varied perspectives. It was 5:15 P.M. before the chief pronounced the fire under control. Another hour passed before the firemen could enter the building to search for the missing men. They quickly found the bodies of two, who had apparently succumbed to the smoke and heat no more than fifty feet from a doorway.

"They almost made it," a fireman said sadly. "It looks like the gases got them. A lot of people are killed because they think that as long as they stay away from the heat, they're safe. Yet, the gases are as deadly as the flames."

After returning to the newsroom, the three reporters quickly assembled the information. Witnesses had described the panic of the evacuation and the bravery of the three victims who were trying to serve as a rear guard to control the flames long enough for co-workers to get out. Quotes from the fire chief, company officials, and others fleshed out the basic information about the fire itself and its consequences.

The next morning, after reading the competing newspaper's account to determine which angles were open to fresh pursuit, the police reporter returned to the scene where firemen still searched for the third victim. As he stood near a doorway after gingerly walking inside to view the hollow ruins, a man in a business suit approached.

"I'm looking for Acme Mattress Company, and I hope this isn't it," the man said with a note of horror.

"This is what's left of it," the reporter replied. "Are you a customer?"

"No, I'm a salesman for a fire sprinkling system firm. The company asked for an estimate on the costs of installing one of our systems, so I just arrived in town this morning. I can't believe this."

The salesman produced a work order to show that the plant had contacted his firm a week earlier. He agreed that a sprinkler system would have retarded the fire in its early stages.

As the deadline approached, the police reporter and his two colleagues obtained statements from the city attorney, the fire inspector who had initially cited the plant, company officials, and other sources. The result was massive and thorough coverage of a fire that had scandalous implications of criminal negligence.

Regardless of the nature of the event requiring on-the-scene coverage, confusion and danger are commonly present. A cornered criminal who is engaged in a shootout with police may not distinguish between a reporter and a detective. In a riot, there are no safe bystanders. Moreover, facilities for the press are rarely as convenient and cozy as a press box at a football stadium. Typewriters aren't available, and even if they were, the constantly changing situation hardly allows for the thoughtful composition of a story under deadline pressure. The nearest telephone may be half a mile away. Transportation to and from the scene may be snarled in confusion. Prime informational sources, such as ranking police and fire officers, may be far too preoccupied to grant interviews.

With these drawbacks in mind, let's look at some guidelines for on-the-scene coverage:

1. Do not expose yourself to unnecessary danger. Besides the obvious need for self-preservation, a reporter must be mindful that he cannot provide coverage for his newspaper from a hospital bed, or from the great beyond.

2. Do not impede officials who are trying to cope with the event. The duty of a policeman or fireman to protect the public is far more important to the immediate public interest than the duty of a reporter. Wait until the situation is under control, or until an official can spare a brief time, before approaching.

3. Remain calm. A reporter who becomes caught up in the frenzy of the event cannot effectively perform. While reporters are human enough to feel the anguish and the horror of a disaster, they must exercise self-discipine to remain coolly detached until their stories are filed. Then they can shakily indulge in human emotions.

4. Remember the deadline. Preoccupation with coverage has, on occasion, resulted in a peculiar professional disaster: Newsmen have failed to file their stories in time for deadline. A notebook filled with great information does little good unless a story is filed.

5. Quickly devise a plan for communicating the information. Even as a reporter approaches a scene, he should look for telephone booths or homes with telephone lines attached. Isolation is a frequent obstacle to coverage.

6. Stay close to prime information sources. If a reporter is so intrigued by the fire or police action that he wanders around, gazing like a fascinated child, he may miss vital information that pours into the official command center.

7. Organize your thoughts and actions to achieve efficiency. Intense concentration is needed at every stage so that each precious minute is well spent in acquiring information.

With these guidelines in mind, let's examine some other examples of on-the-scene coverage, all of which are based on actual experiences. The examples should provide an illustration of reporting techniques that are applied in the coverage of these varied situations.

PRACTICAL APPLICATION EXAMPLES

A Civil Disturbance

Tension between white and minority students at a high school had been building for several days, following a scuffle in the hall involving several students. As the end of the school day approached, a second fight erupted, forcing school officials to separate the youths by sending white students outside while detaining the outnumbered minority youths inside until police protection could arrive.

As the reporter reaches the scene, a violent mob of whites has formed across the street from the school. Entering the building, the reporter notes that a group of minority students is arguing with the principal, demanding to be allowed to leave.

"They have a score to settle with a gang of white kids," a teacher explains. "This is really sad because most of these kids get along fine. The trouble stems from a dispute between two small knots of racists on each side. They square off and others get caught in the middle. Now we have to keep them here for their own safety until buses arrive with police escorts to take them home."

Suddenly, the group of angry minority students pushes past the principal and bolts through the side door. As they emerge, the rival band of whites charges to engage them in a wild, fist-swinging, rock-throwing melee.

The reporter follows the students outside. Standing in the midst of the fighting, he ducks to avoid rocks. Police quickly plunge into the fray, tackling and grabbing offenders from both sides with indiscriminate firmness. The reporter sees two officers fall after being struck by large stones. Another officer firmly holds two youths apart, stoically ignoring their kicks and punches. After subduing the adversaries with the help of another officer, he mutters, "These stupid punks. If a grown-up had put up that kind of fight, I'd have broken my stick over his head. None of us can bring ourselves to use the sticks on them. They're just kids."

When the fight is under control, the reporter hurries back to the building, where he sees several school buses arrive. The mob grows more unruly. Standing on the steps, the reporter watches as the doors are opened and the students cautiously walk toward the buses. A rock bounces off the top of a bus. Then a shower of rocks pelts the buses and students, as the reporter takes cover on the protected side of the bus, praying that the frightened driver won't drive off.

A stream of police cars, filled with detectives, arrives. The reporter approaches the officer in charge, who is adjusting a riot helmet.

"We're going to be the heavies," the officer says, rubbing a two-foot baton. "Look at those grown-ups standing there, tossing rocks. They ought to be ashamed of themselves. We'll put a stop to this in a hurry."

The officers form a line, then move toward the mob as the chief orders the citizens to disperse or face arrest. The reporter follows a huge veteran officer, who is known for his persuasive ability. The officer approaches a broad-shouldered man who is holding a brickbat.

"If you throw that thing, you're gonna need a new head, 'cause I'm gonna play taps on it with my stick," the officer says gruffly. The man drops the brick and joins his fleeing cohorts.

With such firsthand observations, the reporter gathers the material necessary to provide a vivid account of the human tragedy of the disturbance. Interviews with the principal, teachers, students from both factions, parents, police, and other sources provide the factual backbone of the story.

In analyzing the performance, let's apply the guidelines to the coverage:

1. The reporter was remiss in exposing himself to unnecessary danger. It was good fortune, not good sense, that left him in physical condition to write a story after he blundered into the initial fray. He did, however, exercise prudence in seeking cover behind the school bus—and behind the largest available policeman.

2. He carefully stayed out of the way of policemen at each stage.

3. Although shaken and disgusted by the incident afterwards, he remained calm and detached throughout the action. In fact, his detachment contributed to his unthinking exposure to danger.

4. In this example, the deadline wasn't a factor, since the incident occurred two hours after final deadline. The need for communications was thus not a factor, since he could have walked back to the newsroom and written the story in the twenty-two hours remaining.

5. Although he strayed farther from prime information sources

than he would have under deadline pressure, he had ample time to interview them after the incident.

6. He organized his efforts well, since he remained very close to the action (sometimes too close) in each stage.

On-the-scene coverage of more common police actions, such as the investigation of major crimes, requires slightly different approaches to accommodate the particular situations. Let's turn to some of these "cops-and-robbers"-styled incidents.

A Homicide

The story began with a terse message from the police dispatcher, which was overheard by a reporter via a receiver in the pressroom: "We have a possible homicide at (address was given). Neighbors report that a small girl is screaming that her mother's been killed." Several police cruisers were sent to investigate, followed by the homicide squad, and, in turn, by reporters.

At the scene, the reporters wait for detectives to emerge from a wood-frame house. When the lieutenant in charge emerges, he tracks blood onto freshly fallen snow. Reporters press toward him to ask questions.

"We have a homicide," the lieutenant says. "A woman—(he names her)—has been stabbed to death. The body is lying in the kitchen."

"What about the kid?" a reporter asks, relating the dispatcher's message.

"There's a little confusion about that. We found a small baby inside, crying. The little girl was unharmed, but she seems to be weak from hunger. We're trying to find out if there was another child, or just what happened."

Further questions produced this information: The woman was fully clad, with no evidence of rape or robbery. The house was locked, and there were no indications of a break-in. The murder weapon had not been recovered. Police were still trying to piece together a likely version of the murder.

When the lieutenant returns inside the house, the police reporter begins questioning bystanders.

"Did you know the victim?" he asks. If the bystander says he or she did, then the reporter extracts as much information as he can. Was she married? What sort of a person was she? Was anyone angry with her? Where did she work?

Then the questions smoothly shift to a more delicate area: Did you call police? Did you hear or see anything last night that could have had something to do with this? Do you know who found the body? Do you have any idea why anyone would do this to her?

Many people refuse to talk with the reporter, but those who do provide useful information: The victim was legally separated from her husband. She retained custody of the baby, while her husband kept their eight-year-old daughter. No one had seen the husband in several weeks, though. The victim was described as being a quiet but friendly person. She was unemployed. Although she had no close friends among the neighbors, she had no known enemies.

Finally, one neighbor points to an elderly woman who stands silently at the rear of the crowd. "Ask her. She's the woman's aunt, and she's the one who heard the child."

The elderly woman tells her story: She had arrived early that morning to visit her niece. No one answered her knock, but she could hear the baby screaming weakly inside. Alarmed, she ran to the house next door and asked for help. The neighbor entered through an unlocked window, found the body, and quickly called the police. The baby's cries were misinterpreted in the telephone call.

When the lieutenant emerges again from the house, the police reporter tells him about the woman. The officer quickly sends a detective to interview her after thanking the reporter for his help.

The reporter then interviews the helpful neighbor to obtain detailed information about the scene inside and the circumstances of the discovery of the body.

The story was shaping up nicely, except for one small gap of information: the identity of the killer and the motive for the killing.

As the reporter is about to leave for the newsroom, as his deadline is approaching, the lieutenant approaches his car. After shooing other newsmen away, the officer repays the reporter's favor:

"We believe that this was a crime of passion," the lieutenant says. "She was stabbed dozens of times, probably in a frenzied attack. The body has been mutilated, but I won't say how. I can't tell you more right now, but we have a suspect in mind, and we may break this one soon."

The lieutenant refuses to be prodded into detail, other than the grim quotation: "Whoever killed her was really mad at her."

Elements of a major crime story had been neatly assembled: a gory murder, crime of passion, crying baby, exclusive quotation from the top investigative officer, the aunt, the neighbor, and bystanders. All that remained was to write it.

Bank Robbery

Hurrying to the scene of a bank robbery in a radio-equipped news car, a reporter and his photographer-partner picked up the basic information about the robbery from police radio dispatches:

Two armed men (physical descriptions given) held up a bank at (location given) at 10:30 A.M., after standing meekly in line with other customers. The robbers forced customers to lie on the floor as tellers filled large paper bags with money. The suspects had fled on foot and were thought to be escaping in a red convertible (which was described). Police cruisers were combing the area.

The newsmen's first stop, the bank, is unfruitful. Police and FBI agents have sealed it off and they refuse to answer questions or allow witnesses to answer questions. A friendly robbery squad detective, however, tells the reporter that a large sum was taken but no one was hurt.

The newsmen return to the car and, guided by radio traffic, rush to a church where the suspects are possibly "holed up." They watch gun-waving officers cautiously rush inside, only to find the church empty.

Meanwhile, other officers have stopped a car meeting the description of the getaway car. An alert detective had seen the car, then noticed that a male passenger matched one of the descriptions. The clincher came when he had recognized the woman driver as being the wife of a notorious, local robber who was then in prison.

The car was stopped and the man and woman were arrested. They claimed that she was driving the man home from a party—at midday. The man claimed to be the son of a prominent local businessman. Police and reporters had only smiled at such foolish denials.

The police reporter gathers information from the grinning detective who had alertly captured the suspects. No money had been recovered.

While at the scene, the reporter overhears a puzzling updated description of the robbery suspects: neither description matches that of the man in the car.

Returning to the newsroom, he makes a last-minute telephone call to a robbery detective, who warns him to be careful about the story of the capture. "Things just aren't fitting together," the detective said.

The officer then gives a strange account of the bank robbery:

The robbers were not disguised, even though a hidden camera—common in banks—clearly filmed the robbery. After filling their bags with money from tellers' positions, the two culprits fled—neglecting an open safe that contained hundreds of thousands of dollars. As they ran from the bank, the assistant manager followed, hoping to see the getaway car. The men turned, saw him in pursuit, then ran faster—until one of the paper bags split, releasing a pile of money. The thief stopped to scoop up some of the money, then ran as the assistant manager approached. The assistant manager stopped to pick up the rest of the money, letting the robbers flee. The assistant manager was unarmed.

Meanwhile, hysterical bank employees had called in inaccurate descriptions. "Those rogues could have waited at a bus stop, holding their money, and we wouldn't have recognized them," the detective says with a groan.

The reporter, faced with a critical deadline, writes his story, emphasizing the comedy of the robbery, and de-emphasizing the significance of the arrests. Forewarned, he omits the identities of the suspects and carefully explains that the arrests could have been honest mistakes.

Postscript: The original suspects were cleared after the deadline. Other news media, which had identified the hapless suspects and strongly implied guilt, were forced to carry quick retractions and apologies to head off legal suits. The robbers were soon apprehended in other states.

By going to the scene, the reporter could envision and describe the strange chain of events that was more interesting than the robbery itself.

GATHERING INFORMATION

With the preceding examples in mind, it may be apparent that the methods of coverage differ significantly—depending on the nature of the situation—because the sources of information differ. Here are key informational sources for various crimes and fires, along with lists of possible material that can be obtained from them:

Major Crimes

1. *The officer in charge* of the investigation/operation.
   (a.) The basic information about the nature of the crime, the people or property involved, and the general circumstances
   (b.) The progress of the investigation/operation, including arrests or promising leads, and the motive.
   (c.) The identities of witnesses who may be interviewed. (Note: Names may be omitted from the story.)
2. *Witnesses.*
   (a.) A personal account of what transpired.
   (b.) The names or descriptions of the suspects.
   (c.) In a homicide: information about the victim.
3. *Coroner's investigators* (homicide or suicide).
   (a.) The apparent cause of death.
   (b.) Weapons involved and injuries inflicted.
4. *Detectives.*
   (a.) Additional information, beyond what the officer in charge may be willing to offer, concerning the circumstances.
   (b.) Theories or insight to the crime.

5. *The scene.*
   (a.) A description of the setting of the crime.
   (b.) Relationship to other crimes (a dozen other robberies nearby?).
6. *Police radio monitor* (many news cars are equipped with them).
   (a.) Police broadcasts of names or descriptions of suspects, getaway vehicles, and other vital information.
   (b.) Indications that the scene of police action is shifting. Perhaps an officer is in pursuit of the getaway car, across town.
7. *Federal Bureau of Investigation agent in charge.* (bank robberies).
   (a.) Circumstances of the crime.
   (b.) Progress of the investigation.
   Note: FBI agents are often restricted from offering all but the most sketchy information to news media, until a formal press statement has been compiled and approved.

Fires

1. *The fire official in charge.*
   (a.) Full circumstances of the fire and of the problems confronting firemen.
   (b.) Description of the structure and its use.
   (c.) Owner's identity (if rented or leased, also obtain occupant's name).
   (d.) Names, ages, and addresses of casualties.
   (e.) Suspected cause of the fire.
   (f.) Contributing factors, such as late notification or fire code violations.
   (g.) A preliminary damage estimate.
   (h.) A list of equipment at the scene (Is the rest of the city vulnerable?).
2. *Witnesses.*
   (a.) An eyewitness account of the fire.
   (b.) Stories of heroism or tragedy.
   (c.) Information about the fire victims.
3. *Firemen.*
   (a.) Descriptions of the fire and their obstacles in dousing it.
   (b.) Comparisons with other fires (the worst they've seen?).
4. *Survivors..*
   (a.) A personal account of the experience.
   (b.) Human consequences ("I've lost everything I have").
5. *Heroes and heroines.*
   (Note: Often one person will be responsible for the rescue of

survivors. That person may be a parent, child, fireman, or neighbor. The hero/heroine element adds a bright note amid the tragedy.)

SUMMARY

The difference between on-the-scene coverage and behind-the-desk coverage is as striking as the contrast between a press box environment and a lineman's view of a football game.

The reporter who rushes to the scene of an event quickly becomes a part of the event, a participant in the drama that unfolds (though hopefully an objective and detached participant). Such participation is one of the most challenging and exciting facets of reporting, a source of great stories for the enlightenment of readers and, as time passes, of the reporter's grandchildren.

EXERCISES

1. You arrive at the scene of the aftermath of a fight between two street gangs. Two youths have been rushed to the hospital, but you don't know the nature or extent of their injuries. Police have picked up several participants, and cruisers are combing the neighborhood for others. A crowd of bystanders curses police angrily, as two officers struggle to control a prisoner. You recognize the police captain who is in charge of the scene. How do you proceed in providing coverage?

2. A bank has been robbed by three gunmen who had locked bank employees in the vault. Police and FBI agents refuse to allow reporters to enter the bank.. The FBI agent in charge promises to release a statement in an hour, but your deadline is half an hour away. Local police detectives are assisting, but they must officially defer to the FBI. How would you obtain essential information for a story? How would you provide on-the-scene coverage of the continuing drama (suspects are still at large)?

3. A major fire engulfs city hall. You arrive on the scene and discover that the mayor is trapped in his third-floor office. You watch as an aerial ladder slowly eases to his window to rescue him. How would you cover this event?

15 | Investigative and Interpretative Reporting

An aura of respectability hovered inside the restaurant, where several families partook of the excellent cooking. Two reporters, who sat at a table chatting with the owner, weren't especially impressed by the wholesome atmosphere. They knew that the owner was one of the city's most active "bookies," who served as a major figure in the area's largest gambling ring. The adjoining bar was the center of his bookmaking enterprise.

"Yeah, I know the police say that I make book here, but they're dead wrong," the man said bitterly. "We had a bartender here a year ago who was caught making book. I didn't know about it and I fired him after he was arrested. I'll admit that gamblers come into the bar, but I happen to own a few horses, so we do have a mutual interest. I enjoy talking with them, but I honestly don't know anything about illegal gambling."

"We're not accusing you of anything," the senior reporter assured him diplomatically. "We're just checking all angles, and we thought that you might be able to offer some information, especially about Silky Tavish."

"Tavish comes in here occasionally, but I don't really know him that well," the owner replied nervously. "I know he's a big gambler, but he loves horses and so do I, so we enjoy talking about them."

"You must know him fairly well, since you vacationed last month with him," the second reporter suggested.

The owner became flustered. "Well, yes, uh . . . Silky had a horse that was running down in Florida. My wife and I went down with him to see it run because we were considering buying it. It wasn't really a vacation . . ."

"Then it was a business trip?" the senior reporter asked.

"Now, don't put words in my mouth," the owner retorted. "You don't have to be a gambler to buy a horse from a gambler."

The interview continued for another half hour in which the owner adamantly insisted that he was a victim of guilt by association. With ostentatious politeness, the reporters and the owner shook hands and said goodbye. The newsmen walked briskly through the bar and left.

As soon as the door closed behind them, the owner sighed, gave the watchful bartender a worried glance, and hurriedly dialed a number on a telephone beside the bar.

"Silky? It's Charlie. Listen, those two reporters asked a lot of questions and I think they're working a leak somewhere. They knew about the Florida trip. Yeah. We could get a lot of heat. I'll keep in touch."

Neither Charlie nor his bartender paid attention to the intoxicated customer who teetered on the bar stool within earshoot of the telephone. Dressed in work clothes, he appeared to be just another factory worker who was intent on drowning his sorrows. He had slurred a long list of grievances about his wife to the bartender earlier. He was, in fact, the third member of the investigative reporting team.

INVESTIGATIVE REPORTING

The challenge and glory of investigative reporting have made it the most coveted assignment in journalism. Since Watergate, more and more newspapers are forming investigative teams to scour their cities in search of crimes and wrongdoing. Hundreds of reporters are intently looking under every rock in search of a Pulitzer Prize, for that special story that will catapult them to the pinnacle of journalistic fame and success.

While the rewards are certainly present and while such intensive reporting is overwhelmingly beneficial to the public, many would-be investigative reporters soon learn that not every journalist has the ability and the stamina for this specialized role.

It takes a special type of journalist to succeed in this often grueling job. Let's examine the characteristics of a good investigative reporter:

1. *A great capacity for work.* In the height of an investigation, a forty-hour work week may become an eighty-hour ordeal that would leave most mortals mentally, physically, and emotionally exhausted.

2. *Mental astuteness.* Investigative work demands both high intelligence and ingenuity. The ingenuity leads the reporter to the vital information and enables him to extract it. The intelligence allows him to piece together the often fragmentary tidbits of information into a meaningful and correct view of what's transpiring.

3. *Courage.* While physical courage is often needed in the face of

threats and danger, a moral courage is perhaps more important when the reporter repeatedly encounters dead ends or when he must confront people who may be devastated by the results of the investigation.

4. *Persistence. Washington Post* reporters continued to press their Watergate investigation in the face of, first, denials, then condemnation from the White House. Despite the daydreams born of hindsight that fill newsrooms across the country, it is doubtful that more than a handful of reporters would have persisted in the investigation after such an authoritative denial.

5. *Experience.* A successful investigative reporter must be tempered by a solid background of journalism. He must have a reputation and a relationship with potential news sources. A "Deep Throat" would be unlikely to confide in a new reporter or even a veteran with whom he had not established a prior relationship.

6. *An ability to deal with people.* Confidential sources comprise the ultimate weapon in investigative reporting.

To illustrate rigors of the specialty, let's examine an investigative reporting effort launched by *The Dayton Daily News* a few years ago.

Gambling is a large and lucrative criminal enterprise in almost any large city, and Dayton is no exception. A three-man investigative reporting team was formed to explore the city's gambling problem. The team was headed by Gene Goltz, who had won a Pulitzer Prize for his investigative reporting in Houston, Texas, and is now with the *Kentucky Post* (Kentucky edition of the *Cincinnati Post*). Dave All-baugh, a capable veteran, and a young police reporter (the author) rounded out the team.

The reporters divided their work to cover the city's three major forms of gambling: bookmaking, football betting cards, and numbers gambling. Within a few days, a flood of information began to accumulate in the team's small office, as the three men began to piece together the organizational structures of major gambling rings.

Goltz, a brazenly outgoing person who is blessed with the ability to quickly befriend an amazing diversity of people, somehow won the confidence of a tough, independent bookmaker, who served as an expert source of information on that specialty; he taught Goltz the intricacies of the trade and provided invaluable background on major bookmaking organizations.

Allbaugh methodically and doggedly accumulated material on football betting cards, discovering that cards were widely distributed in most of the city's industrial plants.

The police reporter used local and federal law enforcement sources that he had carefully groomed to gain access to reports and material on gambling that law enforcement agencies had already accumulated. He worked with friendly police investigators to piece together a view of the fascinating world of numbers gambling.

Perhaps the most interesting common characteristic of each of the three gambling forms is that individual bets are normally so small that, alone, they appear harmless. Yet, all totalled, the small bets swell into hundreds of thousands of dollars.

In bookmaking, most customers plunked down a few dollars to wager on a horse race, a football game, or some other sports event. Bartenders were frequently part-time bookies, who accepted the bets and funneled the money upward into the organization.

Football betting cards are even more deceptively cheap, costing as little as fifty cents to a dollar each. If the customer correctly selected the established number of winners from games listed, he could win a hundred dollars or so. The catch is that the odds against winning were so enormous that the organization's profits were astronomical.

Numbers gambling rings accepted wagers as low as a quarter. Gamblers would choose any number they wished, with the payoff ratio varying with the number of digets in that number. A winner could receive several hundred dollars. The winning number was derived with a complicated formula using closing New York Stock Exchange figures on the following day. Bets, normally placed by poor people who valued even the small amounts wagered, were collected by "numbers runners," then funneled through organizational layers to the "bank"—the central clearing house—which accumulated thousands of dollars on a given day.

While Goltz and Allbaugh spent countless hours plying their street sources for information, the police reporter accompanied a detective who was in the final stages of a surveillance that, he believed, would soon lead to a raid on a major organization's numbers "bank."

For hours each day, the reporter and the detective trailed a high-ranking member of an organization, watching him collect bets from "runners." One day, he stopped at an old house and remained there for an hour.

"This has to be the bank," the detective gleefully concluded.

The men then set up a stakeout in an abandoned building across the street from the suspected numbers bank, peering through binoculars and writing down auto license numbers belonging to people who entered. Business was so brisk that the detective and his partner told the reporter that "this has to be the biggest bank in the state."

In fact, business was too good. A numbers organization simply didn't allow that many people to know a bank's location. The detectives grew suspicious, then the second detective decided to brazenly stroll to the door, posing as a salesman.

To his partner's horror, the detective entered the building and remained inside as minutes passed.

"He's crazy," the policeman muttered. "If they find out he's a cop, they'll kill him. I'll give him five more minutes, then I'm going in. You can use the radio to call for backups."

Four minutes later, the partner emerged, munching on a hamburger. The "bank" wasn't a bank. It was the rear entrance to a small restaurant.

Such teeth-gnashing frustrations are common in investigative reporting. For every successful break, a dozen blind alleys must be explored and abandoned.

As the reporters convened for team meetings, they shared the information that they had acquired and posed problems from brainstorming. One problem was to figure out how to use the formula for determining the winning number for numbers gambling. The three supposedly intelligent, educated reporters spent hours trying to master the application of a formula that even the most slow-witted gambler could apply in one minute flat.

As the investigation progressed, working hours grew longer as the team worked well into the night to investigate a broad range of leads and activities. On several occasions, reporters were followed by suspicious gamblers, who wondered about the strangers who were asking questions.

Toward the end of the investigation, the time arrived for confrontations. Key figures, who were identified as active, high-level members of gambling organizations, were called or interviewed.

Typically, the conversation went along these lines:

Goltz: "We know that you are the head of the biggest bookmaking operation in the city, and we'd like to talk with you about that."

Gambler: "Where did you ever hear that? You been talking with the cops? Yeah, I used to be involved in gambling, but I'm retired now. I can't tell you anything, because I don't know anything."

Goltz: "Now, we're not trying to hurt anybody or cause trouble. We've just run across a few things that we'd like to ask you about."

Gambler: "I told you I'm retired, and I don't have anything to tell you."

Despite such reticence, the team carefully assembled and verified a volume of material, then pieced it together into a vivid and penetrating look at the city's gambling problem, its scope, impact, and the human tragedies that are frequently involved, as compulsive gamblers lose pay checks routinely, leaving their families destitute; and as violence constantly looms to threaten those who fall in debt to the gamblers.

During the investigation, the three reporters had severely limited time to spend with their families—to even sleep. Their efforts constantly exposed them to the risk of danger, as they visited rough bars where gambling occurred and openly assembled information that, when published, could create severe problems for gamblers. Although the work was frequently fascinating and adventurous, more often it was sheer drudgery. Hours and hours were spent digesting the bits and pieces of information compiled, pouring over public records that might or might not yield a slender thread of material, or following leads that simply proved fruitless.

Guidelines for Investigative Reporting

In the perspective of the case study, Gene Goltz's insights to investigative reporting vividly illustrate the challenge and frustration that the job demands.

Goltz composed the following guidelines in an informal letter to a journalism teacher. Although the form is far from indicative of his polished writing, the casual, pondering style offers a lode of perspective. Goltz's guidelines are:

1. *Never go to your target source until the last possible moment.* By target, I mean that if you are investigating the mayor, for instance, do not start out by interviewing him and asking him whether it's true he is embezzling the city funds. And do not go to him in the middle of your investigation, even when you have doubts about what you are doing, that is, if the investigative probe is valid or not. *Never.* Always save the target (mayor) for last. The reason is that you will have collected, we hope, a bushel of evidence, documents, interviews, and such, so that when you finally do interview the mayor, he will not be able to lie to the reporter in his customary fashion. Every time he opens his mouth and tells a lie, you will be able to say, "yes, but . . .," then pull out a piece of paper to refute him.

2. *It is absolutely necessary to be one's own devil's advocate.* By that I mean when you are investigating something, every little piece of material you dig up tends to get you very excited. You say to yourself, I've really got a strong case against this guy. At that point, you must sit down quietly and think about it from the other guy's point of view (or the other guy's *lawyer's* point of view, for you may end up in libel court). You must say to yourself, wait a minute, maybe there were good and valid and necessary reasons for these apparently suspicious acts. You must, in effect, try your best to shoot down your own story. I really mean this, because if you don't try, when it does come out in the paper, the target of your probe might shoot down the story with a blast that gets you fired.

3. *You must sniff the scent and follow where it leads you, not where the editor thinks it ought to lead.* By that I mean this: A hundred times I have been sent out to do what looked like a promising investigative story and have, almost invariably, come back with a different one. The good editors accept this: the bad editors are always

miffed and hurt because they think that somehow you have betrayed them and circumvented their brilliant ideas.

4. *Don't give in to discouragement.* Always, without fail, halfway through a tedious, drudgery-ridden investigative story, I get discouraged. I think that the story is never going to jell, that I am wasting my time and the company's money, that my reputation will suffer and my editor will be mad and I will be fired. My advice on this one is:

Keep plugging away—at least 90 percent of the time. Because the next day, or the next week, the breakthrough will come, a missing piece of the puzzle will turn up, and you'll be back on the track. I say 90 percent, because on rare occasions it just isn't there. And I say, very strongly, never be afraid to tell the editor that the story doesn't seem to be there. It's his job at that point either to tell the reporter to keep plugging or to give it up. And never be afraid to tell the editor that the story *may* be there but you can't find it. It is his job then to sit down and think of something you might have missed, of some new direction in which you might go.

5. While I'm on the subject of thinking, it is my absolutely firm opinion that *an investigative reporter is better off if he investigates one hour, then thinks for two.* Most of the time when I'm in a hard, tough, investigative story, I spend a lot of time just sitting around, trying to sort it all out. Bad editors—at this moment—entertain the idea that I am not working; the good editors know that this is the time I am working hardest, that this is the time that will produce the results they are hoping for. You can collect a lot of facts in a hard investigative story, but trying to figure out what they mean, trying to put them together, to synthesize them, is the trick that separates the men from the boys in this business.

6. *Listen to your instinct.* I almost hesitate to mention this one. I can't define it. Sometimes it has been referred to as having a "nose for news." At any rate, on nearly every investigative story I've been on in the last fifteen years, when all the facts and all the logic tells me I am on the wrong track, that there is nothing there, that I should cash in the chips and quit the trail—when all this stares me in the face, but some inner inclination, some very strong unexplainable urge tells me, "Keep going, it's there, you just haven't found it yet"—I always listen to that voice, that instinct, and although I can't explain it, it's invariably right. So, for what it's worth to young reporters, if you have such an inner signal, listen to it with all your heart, for it is more correct than all the visible logical signals you can possibly invent.

After listing his guidelines for successful investigative reporting, Goltz pondered the meaning of it all, then summarized his hard-nosed view of the calling in a manner that conveys both his deep love for the job and his gritty approach. A strong dash of lingering, quixotic idealism still lingers in one of America's best reporters:

> By this time, I suppose you figure I am missing the boat altogether. The question is, how do you go about investigative reporting?
>
> Well, I don't even know the answer. I have read a lot of wisdom about it in books written by eloquent people, but in truth they (don't come close). I don't have a system; all I do is get a subject or an assignment or an idea and begin plugging away at it. Every one I do turns out to be a little different; every story demands a slightly different technique. I suppose it is not too much to say that brains, persistence, ingenuity, and half a dozen other attributes help when you start plugging away at an investigation. And sometimes, courage. Not every reporter can do it. Not everyone wants to. But for those who do, and who can, the rewards are great such as the knowledge that you are helping to straighten out the rotten so and sos who are always trying to corrupt the populace, and that you are helping make this a better world.

Goltz's lesson on investigative reporting must stand without comment. His message comes from the heart and soul of American journalism. It captures the essence.

INTERPRETATIVE REPORTING

Investigative reporting generally overlaps into a closely related area: interpretative reporting. Essentially, the same skills are often needed for the acquisition of material for an interpretative story. The difference between the two forms is often subtle:

> Investigative reporting is aimed at producing an exposé of wrongdoing, based on the actions or inactions of people. The exposé, itself, is the news.

> Interpretative reporting produces an account of a situation that affects the public, and in a manner that offers readers a full insight to that situation. Interpretative stories illuminate a known event or situation by emphasizing the elements that contribute to an event, and by explaining the possible consequences.

Perhaps a war between two street gangs has erupted, resulting in several shootings and murders. Each bloody incident is, by itself, a significant news story. Yet, the public cannot fully understand the tragic situation until an interpretative story pieces it together.

The interview was easily arranged because gang members knew and respected one of the two reporters assigned to write the interpretative story. The two journalists sat nervously in the living room of an old house, surrounded by the notoriously unpredictable gang members, listening to the leader boast of violent victories and accuse the other gang of starting the war by ambushing and killing a member of his gang.

"They're as good as dead now," he says, caressing a revolver.

"How do you know for sure that they killed Louie?" a reporter asks.

"It's like this," he says impatiently. "Louie and Snake, their leader, got in a fight over this girl. Louie almost wasted him in the fight. The man said he would get Louie, and Louie was wasted that night. I'm not stupid, man. I can put two and two together. Besides, I checked it out. Donnally, the head man of the Eagles, told me he heard Snake bragging about it. Snake is gonna be very dead."

Suddenly, a skinny youth rushes inside from his lookout post on the porch.

"They're coming down the street, and they got pieces (guns)," he yells. The hosts scramble to produce an arsenal of weapons, as the two reporters look at each other in shock. They realize that they have walked into the middle of a "rumble."

"Well, since you gentlemen are going to be otherwise occupied for a while, we will leave now," a reporter says, smiling. "Thanks for talking with us, you've been most helpful."

The reporters walk shakily down the street and encounter the invaders.

"Hey man, what's happening?" a reporter asks the leader of the attackers, eyeing the shiny revolver in his hand and noting the lumps and cuts on his head.

"We're gonna kill those (explitives deleted). They jumped me and three of them worked me over. They are gonna bleed for that. Stick around, you'll get a real story," he suggests.

"Well, I don't want to butt into your business, but those guys are armed to the teeth, and you're outnumbered. Besides, I've got a funny feeling that somebody is playing a game on you both. If you go up there and waste each other, the guy who really started this is going to be awfully happy."

Despite the effort to persuade the attackers to reconsider, they are too angry to withdraw. So the reporters sit down on a street curb half a block away and watch the two gangs approach each other on the street.

"Most of it's just talk," a reporter observes. "But if only one of them gets trigger-happy, we could have a battle."

As the gangs face off, cursing and threatening, a police cruiser suddenly rounds the corner. A veteran officer sees the two reporters, slows for a few seconds, and shouts:

"What are you idiots doing here? I'll deal with you later."

The officer is a tough but friendly acquaintance, who holds a reputation of competence that had won respect from both street gangs and reporters.

When the gang members recognize the officer, guns miraculously disappear, as two youths from each gang collect them and flee. The others suddenly smile at their would-be foes and walk arm in arm with them to the cruiser.

"What are you supposed to be up to?" the officer demands gruffly.

"Oh, we're just having a friendly talk, that's all," a gang leader assures him. "Nothing's happening, man."

"Nothing better happen, either," the officer grumbles. "If you want to kill each other, do it on somebody else's beat. I'm going to stay around here for a while, just to make sure you remain friendly."

The officer then backs up to the reporters.

"Nothing's going to happen, so you can leave if you like," he says. "If you stick around here, I'm not going to feel responsible for what might happen to you idiots. You got to be out of your minds."

The interviews continue for several days, as the reporters talk with members of both gangs, police, and detectives who specialize in dealing with youth gangs. As homicide detectives piece together information about the initial killing, it becomes increasingly apparent that a third party has committed the murder. The reporters time their story to coincide with the arrest of a third gang leader, who had sparked the gang war in hopes that the two rival gangs would kill each other off, thus elevating his gang to supremacy.

In addition to the major news story about the arrest, the interpretative story traced the violent saga of the war that ensued and, through quotes and factual explanation, gave readers a clear insight to the code of the streets that made the war inevitable after the initial killing, the philosophy and lifestyle of the gang members that made violence acceptable, and the tragic human consequences that touched not only the gang members and their families, but spawned an aura of terror in the community where they lived.

Interpretative stories can be written on subjects far less dramatic. Beat reporters often write such articles to offer readers insight to issues and controversies on their beats:

1. The city hall beat reporter may do an extensive analysis of a controversial piece of legislation considered by city council, offering both sides and all options and consequences that can be foreseen.

2. The courts beat reporter may offer readers an interpretative article about the judicial logjam of cases that results in plea-bargaining and delayed justice, examining alternatives and consequences.

3. The police beat reporter may write an article on burglary, offering readers a detailed look at the incidence of this crime, the

manner in which burglars operate, police problems in combating burglary, and expert advice on means of protecting one's home from burglars.

4. A general assignment reporter may write an article examining pollution problems affecting the river that flows through town, the sources of the pollution, its consequences, and the means of correcting the problem.

5. The health beat reporter may write an extensive article on the rising costs of hospitalization, explaining the causes and consequences.

6. The education beat reporter may write a probing article examining the quality of education in city schools, comparing it with other school systems and explaining problems that the educational system is facing.

7. The county beat reporter may write an article that looks ahead ten years to the anticipated growth of the area, its facilities, and the problems that are entailed by such growth.

The list is, of course, endless. Yet, each diverse topic shares the commonality of lending itself to meaningful, interpretative reporting that will enable readers to digest a situation in a broad perspective.

Interpretative reporting does not offer the journalist the license to become an editorial writer by drawing conclusions or by expounding any particular viewpoint. Material must be assembled from every viewpoint, and presented fairly and in context, without arbitrary judgment.

Guidelines for Interpretative Reporting

Regardless of the topic of the story, the reporter is well advised to heed these general guidelines:

1. At the outset, make a list of all conceivable sources of information that may have a bearing on the situation.

2. Approach each source, even those who are considered capricious or unreliable. The reader, not the reporter, must judge the merits of any particular viewpoint.

3. After initial interviews and research have been completed, make a second listing of additional sources who weren't included on the initial list. Very often, secondary sources become apparent as research progresses.

4. If sources offer contradictory information, confront them and try to determine the truth. If one particular source offered provably erroneous information, offer that proof after quoting the assertion.

5. Be as fair and objective as humanly possible. Reporters invariably have opinions—perhaps unshakable convictions—supporting a particular viewpoint on a given controversy. A well-written story will leave readers uncertain about where the reporter stands, or, perhaps,

both sides will determine that the reporter is either for or against them.

Let's take an interpretative story and follow it through the process:

A controversy between a citizens' group and mobile home parks in the city appears to be approaching a climax, as city council considers an ordinance that would add restrictive zoning requirements to halt the expansion of such parks. The ordinance would also greatly increase the property taxes of each mobile home park operator.

The citizen's group contends that not only do mobile home parks detract from property values in the surrounding neighborhoods, but park owners do not assume a fair share of their tax burden because the assessment process does not take into account the impact of the mobile home communities on requirements for city services and schools.

Mobile home park operators deny both allegations, claiming that their parks are clean and attractive additions to the city, that they offer good housing to low-income families that would otherwise be crammed into shoddy tenements, and that they do indeed pay a fair share of taxes.

In compiling a list of sources, the reporter decided to contact:

1. The president of the Mobile Home Owners' Association.
2. The chairman of the citizens' group.
3. The city planning department—about zoning restrictions.
4. The city finance department, which controls assessments.
5. The school superintendents—to determine school impact of the parks.
6. The police chief—to determine whether the parks spawned crime problems.
7. The councilman who submitted the ordinance.
8. Several mobile home park operators—to discuss their operations.
9. Residents and businessmen in areas around the parks.
10. Mobile home park residents.

The initial interviews produced a wealth of information, some of which was contradictory. The reporter's personal inclination was to agree with the citizens' group that park operators weren't sharing a reasonable part of the tax burden that they generated. Yet, he personally agreed with park operators that most parks were well kept and that they provided safe and adequate homes for many who otherwise couldn't afford good housing.

From police, he learned that the incidence of crime in areas around and within mobile home parks was not any higher than in other parts of the community that provided housing for low-income people. Businessmen in the areas near such parks generally considered them an asset. Reaction among homeowners nearby was mixed. Many were concerned about a possible adverse effect on property values, yet most admitted that they had no personal complaints about the operations, nor the residents there.

In visiting the parks, he found that the operators were generally irate about the proposed ordinance. "I've run this park for fifteen years, and I can't recall a single complaint from anyone in the surrounding neighborhood," one said. "My customers are good people, but too many people equate mobile homes with caravans of vagabonds. I'd say half of our people have been here for at least five years. They aren't transients, they're permanent residents. We pay a fair property tax assessment, and our rentors contribute directly through their rent. In addition, they all pay city sales taxes, and most pay payroll taxes—those that aren't retired. What's more, many are very involved in the community. We have many PTA members, active church workers, charity volunteers, and even a few policemen and firemen." Others presented similar viewpoints.

Mobile home residents were also upset by the proposed ordinance. Most of them praised their park community and expressed satisfaction with the operators' management. Several emphasized that mobile homes offered them the best possible housing that they could afford.

After completing these and other interviews noted on the initial list, the reporter pondered additional sources. He added these to his list:

1. City building inspectors, who were familiar with both mobile homes and comparatively priced housing in apartments.

2. Realtors, who could add insight to the effect of mobile home parks on surrounding neighborhoods.

The building inspectors agreed that, for their investments and rent payments for park lots, mobile home residents fared comparatively well. "They may get somewhat less floor space, but the mobile homes are generally kept in good repair, since most residents also own them. Also, keep in mind that they build some equity. After ten years, they can sell their homes and recoup much or all of their investment if they keep them in good shape."

Realtors were less enthusiastic about the virtues of mobile homes, since would-be customers were investing in them instead of housing or rentals. Yet, most realtors agreed that the presence of the mobile home park had little or no adverse affect on property values, since the parks were also located near lower-income housing.

Contradictory information came from the two major adversaries: the citizens' group and the mobile home operators. The citizens' group offered figures that seemed to back up their allegation that mobile home operators were paying relatively low taxes. When confronted with the figures, the operators countered with their own estimate of taxes paid, which was almost double the amount suggested by the citizens' group. The reporter then visited the tax assessor, who provided actual documentation of taxes paid. In writing his story, the reporter listed the adversaries' estimates, then followed with the amount that the tax assessor had collected.

The story offered all viewpoints in detail, along with relevant information that the reporter had ascertained to be valid. After the edition that carried the story appeared, the reporter awaited the telltale reaction.

The first call was from the president of the Mobile Home Operators' Association: "I just wanted to call to say how much we appreciate your article," he said. "You really gave both sides, but I don't see how any sane person could support that ordinance after reading your account."

Moments later, the chairman of the citizens' group called: "That was a good story; we are delighted to see it. I feel sure that it will help push through the ordinance."

The reporter, a five-year veteran, chuckled as he hung up the telephone. Each side had been so intent on reading the story from its respective viewpoint that each had happily concluded that the reporter had leaned its way.

EXERCISES

1. Discuss the differences between investigative reporting and interpretative reporting. Give three examples of each.

2. List and discuss Goltz's six guidelines for investigative reporting. Compare the set of guidelines with your image of investigative reporting.

3. List the six characteristics of a successful investigative reporter. Candidly compare your own strengths and weaknesses against that list. Discuss why you do or do not want to enter investigative reporting.

4. List five topics for an interpretative story that can be done on campus. Choose the best topic, then research and write the story.

5. You are an investigative reporter, assigned to explore persistent rumors that the county sheriff is accepting bribes to allow a large gambling organization to function without interference. An honest deputy is willing to be a source of information. Outline your plans for the investigation. (Use your imagination, within the bounds of reasonable possibilities.)

16 | General Assignment Reporting

Perhaps one of the most striking oddities in the job of the general assignment reporter is that as often as not, he hasn't the faintest idea of the nature of work awaiting him when he arrives for work on a given day.

The unpredictable nature of the assignment is both exciting and unnerving. While most beat reporters toss restlessly in their sleep, besieged by nightmares stemming from the hellish horror of losing major stories to their competition, the general assignment reporter may happily leave the pressures behind as he leaves the office. Instead, his nightmare begins when he reports for work and the city editor yells . . .

"An automobile just went into the river near the Twentieth-Street Bridge. Get a photographer, and try to pull something together for the first edition. There are two women inside, and police are trying to rescue them."

Minutes later, the general assignment reporter stands on the river bank, assessing the hectic situation. The police beat reporter has also arrived at the scene to share coverage. The reporters interview witnesses and police to learn that the car had suddenly swerved from the road and gone down a gradual, fifty-foot embankment, without any apparent effort to stop.

"They were only going about thirty miles an hour," a witness says. "The bank is dry and firm, so they could have stopped easily, unless the brakes failed. They didn't even slow down. Police rescued an older woman, but the other woman got out of the car and started swimming downstream in the middle of the river. She didn't even try to make it to land. A policeman jumped in and tried to swim to her, but the current was too strong, so he had to turn back."

As the police reporter interviews the shivering, soaked policeman, the general assignment reporter runs to a waiting ambulance, where the survivor is receiving emergency treatment.

The reporter sees that the woman is hysterical, so he turns to a police sergeant who is scribbling down notes for his report.

"It looks like an attempted suicide at this stage," the sergeant says. "That's all I can say right now. Her (the survivor's) daughter was driving. She's missing now, and witnesses saw her go under. The fire department is bringing up rescue boats to try to find the body."

"Can you give me their names?" the reporter asks.

"I'm sorry, but you'll have to wait until the next of kin has been notified," the officer says.

As the ambulance drives away, the general assignment reporter hurriedly confers with the police reporter.

"You cover the scene and try to get more information from police," he says. "I'll head for the hospital and try to get identification there."

At the hospital, the general assignment reporter persuades a nurse to disclose the woman's name, after promising not to publish the name until the family has been notified. He also learns that she is listed in good condition, although she is being kept for observation.

Returning to the newsroom, the general assignment reporter grabs the city directory, locates the victims' address, and scribbles down the telephone numbers of immediate neighbors.

Pausing only for a moment to compose an approach, he dials a neighbor's telephone number. When a woman answers, he identifies himself and says:

"I have been trying to reach Mrs. Moore, but she doesn't answer. Would you happen to know where I could reach her?"

"Well, Mrs. Moore is a legal secretary at Evans, Shaw, and Johnson. I recall seeing her and her daughter leave for work at around 7:30. Why, is there something wrong?"

"I'm not really sure, at this point, that I have the right Mrs. Moore," the reporter says smoothly. "Can you tell me which church she attends?"

"All Saints Episcopal on Cherry Street," the puzzled neighbor replies. "Why on earth do you need that?"

"It may help me determine whether I have the right person," the reporter replies truthfully. "I have to rush now; thank you very much for your help."

A minute later, the reporter calls the Reverend Norman Blackwell. After identifying himself, he says, "Father Blackwell, it appears that Mrs. Moore and her daughter were involved in a serious accident. Are you aware of the situation?"

"Yes, I am," the priest confirms. "Mrs. Moore's son, Louis, called a few minutes ago, and I am about to leave for the hospital."

"I hope you understand that I don't want to add to the family's grief, but my job demands that I gather some additional information so that our account will be accurate. Could I ask you a few brief questions?"

The brief questions yield valuable information: The daughter had suffered a nervous breakdown after her husband had died in an accident. She had attempted suicide on three occasions. Although her family had tried to have her placed in a state mental hospital, officials had refused to admit her on the grounds that space was very limited. As the interview ends, the reporter asks for the name of a family member who would most likely be capable of speaking for the grief-stricken family. The son, Louis, is nominated.

After contacting and interviewing Louis, officials at the state mental hospital, and the family physician, the general assignment reporter gathers material for a story depicting the human tragedy behind the suicide, which appears next to the police reporter's account of the drowning.

From the example, several general characteristics about the general assignment reporter can be drawn:

1. He is a highly capable professional, well versed in the techniques of reporting.

2. He is extremely versatile, capable of accepting a major assignment in any given field without advance preparation.

3. He is knowledgeable of all major informational sources needed to piece together material on almost any general subject.

This depiction of a general assignment reporter is contrary to the traditional image of a young, inexperienced "legman" who does "odds-and-ends" reporting chores while learning the trade.

Before this image is carried too far, however, it may be worth noting that the young reporter who is unhappily writing obituaries and weather reports from the vantages point of the least-desirable desk in the city room is also a general assignment reporter.

In his three-months of employment, the young reporter has covered such exciting events as chamber of commerce luncheons, speeches by low-ranking state politicians, garden shows, and sales conventions. When the obituary writer is on vacation, he inherits that grim duty. If the farm writer submits a column on soybean production in the state, the city editor may toss it to him with the terse instruction: "Chop it in half and translate it into English." An assistant city editor, holding a fist full of public relations news releases, may stalk him for the unpleasant chore of reducing hundreds of words of puffery into two paragraphs of filler material.

That strange dichotomy of general assignment reporters into subclasses of inexperienced newcomers and able, jack-of-all-trades veterans offers the city editor the ultimate fail-safe net to use in catching news that would otherwise fall through the cracks of the beat system, or the gaps that occur when a beat reporter is either absent or overburdened with too many major stories to handle simultaneously. Moreover, in the case of the newcomers, it offers a great training ground of exposure to almost every type of news and news source.

VETERAN GENERAL ASSIGNMENT REPORTERS

In examining these two divisons, let's take a close look at the veteran general assignment reporter first.

After several years of experience, during which she has worked as police, courts, and labor reporter, his newswoman has news contacts in almost every beat area. If a beat reporter is absent, she can take over that assignment with ease.

She is also capable of covering major events that fall outside the normal beat structure. If the United States Secretary of Health, Education and Welfare is speaking at a convention of state mayors in town, she can provide lucid and professional coverage of the range of urban problems that the secretary may discuss. An hour later, after filing a story, she may fill in for the education beat reporter at a board of education meeting.

Let's take a typical morning with the general assignment reporter. Checking with the city editor upon arriving, she is given several tasks, pending further developments as the morning progresses:

1. Assist the police beat reporter in gathering information about the fire that destroyed the foam rubber products plant yesterday. Specifically, she is to obtain statements from company officials and from the city prosecutor about alleged criminal negligence that contributed to the disaster.

2. Try to verify a tip that a major hotel chain plans to build a large hotel downtown.

3. Take dictation from reporters who call in stories.

The first task requires a hard-nosed, straightforward approach. Calling the company president, she coolly ticks off several alleged fire-code violations, quotes the fire chief's accusation that "the company officials did not keep their promise to take immediate corrective action after they were initially notified of these violations," then offers the president the opportunity to respond. As he desperately offers that "we were taking action just as we promised, but we simply didn't have enough time to complete the repairs and installations," she penetrates through his hastily contrived defense by asking:

"If you were taking immediate action after being notified of the code violations, can you explain why you waited three months before even asking for an estimate on the installation of a sprinkler system?"

The subsequent response of refusing further comment until the firm's attorney could be consulted detracted considerably from the official's credibility in denying negligence.

The second task, that of investigating the rumor of a new hotel, requires a different approach.

The reporter telephones the assistant city manager for planning and development on the assumption that city hall would have actively worked to entice such a beneficial business to the city. The official is a long-standing acquaintance, so she takes a warm, personal approach.

"Eddie? This is Helen from the News. How would you like to be a highly placed city hall source this morning?"

"The last time I played that role, it almost cost me my job," the official says, chuckling. "What can I do for you, Helen?"

"Well, it seems that the Star Hotel chain is going to build a huge new hotel downtown," she says with confidence and enthusiasm. "I'm trying to pull together some details. How long did it take you to lure them here?"

"Now, where did you hear that?" the official says, surprised. "You're going to blow a perfectly elaborate press conference that we had planned for next week. After three months of hard work, I think we're entitled to break the news in grand style."

(Note: At this point, the conversation becomes coded. The official, taking the reporter's cue, is confirming the story and offering information. Yet, he is maintaining a protective innocence that will allow him to deny purposefully leaking the information, should higher officials trace the leak to him.)

As the conversation continues, the reporter learns the size, cost, scope, and planned completion date for the project.

Thanking the official, the reporter then calls the firm's corporate headquarters in a distant city. She asks to speak with the president of the corporation and, as expected, finds herself transferred to the director of public relations.

"I hate to spoil your press conference, but I have most of the details about your plans to build a hotel here," she tells him. "Since this is an exclusive, you will get page-one play today, so I hope that you can help me verify my information."

With a sigh of frustration over the loss of the grand announcement, the public relations man reluctantly provides additional information and confirms the details that she has already gathered.

As the deadline nears, she writes the hotel story, then clears her typewriter to take dictation from reporters. The first call comes from the police beat reporter, who is covering a bank robbery.

"What do you have?" she asks.

"Slug it bank robbery," the police reporter says. "I'll have to dictate from raw notes, so touch it up if you have time."

"Go ahead," she says.

"A pair of bungling bank robbers held up the Westview Bank at 10:30 A.M. today, taking several hundred dollars from tellers' drawers while overlooking an open vault containing half a million dollars.

"As if this costly oversight wasn't blunder enough, a paper sack containing part of the loot split as the thieves fled, spilling a trail of dollars on the sidewalk.

"Despite the robbers' blunders, confusion and ineptness on the part of police enabled them to elude a massive manhunt . . ."

"Whoa!" the general assignment reporter says. "You're slipping into an editorial. Take a deep breath and just give me the facts."

"Yeah, I guess I am," the police reporter agrees. "Try this: Despite their blunders, the robbers managed to elude a massive police manhunt after officers were hampered by a bizarre chain of events.

"Initial descriptions of the suspects, which were broadcast to cruisers that were rushing to the scene, were so flawed that police were looking for the wrong men.

"In another strange twist, the assistant bank manager chased the thieves on foot in hopes of sighting the getaway car. When the robbers saw him pursuing, they ran faster. When the sack split, spilling the loot, one robber stopped to pick up part of it, then ran as the assistant manager neared. The would-be hero then gave up pursuit as he stopped to gather the remaining money . . ."

"Just a minute," the general assignment reporter said. "Can I change 'would-be hero' to 'bank employee'?"

With astute guidance, the veteran general assignment reporter enabled the police reporter to dictate a good account of the robbery. After taking the story, she quickly checked clippings in the reference library to determine that the same bank had been robbed three times in the past four years. A telephone call to a bank vice president netted additional details, which she added to the story. A quick check in the telephone directory revealed that the police reporter had given the wrong address for the bank. Although the story appeared under the police reporter's by-line, the skilled contributions of the general assignment reporter enhanced both its accuracy and substance.

INEXPERIENCED GENERAL ASSIGNMENT REPORTERS

As might be expected, the morning tasks of the inexperienced newcomer are somewhat less glamorous than those of assembling a page-one story on a new hotel or of grilling a hard-pressed company president.

The reporter may begin with the tedious and unpleasant task of handling the obituaries. The job is deceptively difficult, and responsible. Even the slightest error in an obituary can ignite a storm of angry calls from relatives who were dismayed to note that the obituary listed Uncle Charlie's age as sixty-seven instead of the accurate seventy-seven. Although the error may seem nitpicking to the reporter, the obituary will be a treasured family keepsake that will be part of the scrapbook lore for future generations to see. Naturally, the family wants a perfect item to clip.

The job begins with the assembling of obituary notices to run in the first edition. By policy, the newspaper may carry a given obituary in each edition for a full cycle. If the notice first appeared in yesterday's second edition, it must run through today's first edition.

After clipping the obituary section from yesterday's final edition, the reporter crosses out those that appeared for the full cycle, instructing the compositors to continue running those remaining. Then, using the morning newspaper's obituary column as a source of new items, the reporter may contact each funeral home to verify information, and to gather new items. (The system varies from city to city. In some cities, the funeral homes each call the newspaper. Some newspapers accept only paid advertisements for death notices—thus transferring responsibility to the advertising department—except when a highly prominent citizen dies.)

The process is repeated with each edition; obituaries that have run for a full cycle are deleted and new ones are added.

During lulls in the obituary task, the reporter may be asked to take dictation, rewrite news releases, or perform research for other reporters.

As noted earlier, such new reporters also inherit the task of covering low-level meetings and speeches—events that the city editor may deem too unproductive for the assignment of an accomplished reporter, yet worthy of at least some mention.

For example, one new reporter was dismayed to find that the city editor routinely spoiled his lunch hour by assigning him to cover luncheons of various civic and business organizations. His presence was actually more for public relations value than for news value.

Bored to tears by the regular ordeal, the reporter grumpily attended a chamber of commerce luncheon. Assuming that nothing newsworthy was at hand, he had neglected to obtain an advance agenda of the meeting. Entranced by the strange pattern formed by his alphabet soup, the young newsman tuned out the introduction of the guest speaker—whoever he was. Yet, the serenity of his boredom was abruptly shattered when a familiar and dreaded voice wafted through his fog of inattention: his editor's voice. The boss was the guest speaker.

POST-DEADLINE ACTIVITY

After a deadline has passed, life becomes more interesting for both the veteran and the inexperienced general assginment reporter. It is time to pursue feature stories and investigative assignments.

Feature stories provide a common ground in which the enthusiasm and fresh view of an inexperienced reporter can evenly match the skill and experience of the veteran. Such assignments give reporters the opportunity to display both imagination and pure writing skill.

For the newcomer, feature writing is an opportunity to "shine."

Even the most boring feature assignment can be transformed into a sparkling story by a talented writer. In one instance, a new reporter was told to provide feature coverage of a 4-H Club cattle show at the state fair. The reporter, a lifelong urbanite, didn't know one end of a cow from the other. Yet, he was blessed with a fresh view and lively imagination.

The parade of carefully groomed cows, bedecked with ribbons, and led by nervous yet hopeful youngsters became a bovine beauty contest, in which the reporter artfully sprinkled standard beauty contest cliches into the story with hilarious effect. Yet, he tempered the humor with a warm and sensitive view of the hard-working, ever-hopeful youngsters.

The veteran general assignment reporter may divide his time between feature writing and freewheeling reporting. With a diverse and abundant supply of news sources, the reporter may pursue tips of stories that somehow escaped the net of other reporters. A police sergeant may complain that private security guards are generally poorly trained and even dangerous to the general public.

To investigate this situation, the reporter decides to become a private security guard. He dons old clothes and strolls into the office of a security guard firm to apply for employment.

To determine whether the firm made any serious attempt to screen applicants, the reporter truthfully fills out the application form, except for the blank that requests the name of his employer. Instead of writing in the name of his newspaper, he lists his occupation as city sanitation worker. Even a cursory check by the firm would expose his real occupation.

A week later, the reporter happily reports for duty wearing a uniform that the newspaper purchased for him and sporting a revolver that the police sergeant loaned to him. In the story that followed, the reporter carefully notes that he had no firearms training. In fact, if he had been forced to use his weapon, there would have been a substantial risk that he would have shot himself in the foot.

This investigative piece, researched and written during non-deadline hours, resulted in an enforcement crackdown on security guard operations.

Meanwhile, his less-experienced colleague was busy piecing together an interpretative story on changing consumer purchasing habits in the wake of sharp retail food price increases.

Interviews with supermarket managers, shoppers, and food-chain executives offered a detailed look at both sides of the food price inflation question. Supermarket officials carefully explained why their prices were increasing, pointing to rising labor costs, rapidly soaring wholesale costs, rising income to farmers, and the vast increases in production costs that fueled higher farm income needs. Consumers, especially consumer activists, bitterly complained that the food industry was bilking the public of millions of dollars.

Regardless of who or what was to blame, the reporter found that consumers were drastically reducing purchases of meats and luxury items, while increasing purchases of cheese and other dairy products, fish, and poultry.

While the targets and difficulty of researching these two articles differed greatly, the value of flexibility in general assignment reporting becomes evident. While the veteran's story could have fallen into the police reporter's domain, his freedom to pursue stories on any beat enabled his newspaper to print a story that had been lingering unnoticed for several years. During the next week, the veteran may dig up a story on city hall graft, violence in a labor union, or school teachers who are forced to moonlight because of low pay—all of which would fall within established newsbeats. In most cases, the beat reporter may be far too preoccupied with daily coverage to obtain these stories.

It should also be noted that, at times, a beat reporter may ask for assistance from a general assginment reporter. If, for example, the police reporter learns that many officers are illegally accepting gifts from merchants, he may well fear that by disclosing the scandal, he could face the retaliation of losing many good news sources. If the illegality is of a purely technical nature in that officers do not provide favorable treatment in return for the normally small gifts, then he may decide that the value of the disclosure to the public is not as great as the cost of his effectiveness as a beat reporter.

The general assignment reporter then enters the picture as the "bad guy" who can callously expose the "freebies" situation without worrying about the loss of vital sources. The police reporter can, meanwhile, loudly agree with the officers that the stories constitute a "cheap shot."

SUMMARY

Whether he is a new, inexperienced reporter or a seasoned "vet," the general assignment reporter fills the vital role of plugging the gap in news coverage and, frequently, supporting the beat reporters throughout the coverage system.

The assignment entails an atmosphere of freedom not found on established beats, yet that freedom carries with it a constant uncertainty that can be unnerving to those who cherish a stable routine.

EXERCISES

1. Discuss the dichotomy of roles within the ranks of general assignment reporters. How are the functions similar? How are they dissimilar?

2. What opportunities are offered to new, inexperienced reporters by general assignment? How can this assignment be used as a springboard to more prestigious beats?

INDEX